MAKING ROOM

# MAKING ROOM

*Recovering Hospitality as a
Christian Tradition*

Christine D. Pohl

WILLIAM B. EERDMANS PUBLISHING COMPANY
GRAND RAPIDS, MICHIGAN / CAMBRIDGE, U.K.

© 1999 Wm. B. Eerdmans Publishing Co.
255 Jefferson Ave. S.E., Grand Rapids, Michigan 49503 /
P.O. Box 163, Cambridge CB3 9PU U.K.

Printed in the United States of America

04 03 02 01          7 6 5 4 3


**Library of Congress Cataloging-in-Publication Data**

Pohl, Christine D.
    Making room: recovering hospitality as a Christian tradition /
written by Christine D. Pohl.
        p.      cm.
    Includes bibliographical references.
    ISBN 0-8028-4431-6 (paper: alk. paper)
    1. Hospitality — Religious aspects — Christianity.
2. Christian life.   I. Title.
BV4647.H67P64   1999
241'.671 — dc21                                     99-31765
                                                      CIP

*In memory*
*of my grandparents*
*whose door was always open to family, friends, and strangers*

# CONTENTS

## III. RECOVERING THE PRACTICE

# PREFACE

IN MANY WAYS, THIS BOOK EMERGED FROM A CONVERSA-
tion that transcended centuries. Scripture texts, ancient Christian writers,
and contemporary practitioners of hospitality joined together to share
from their wisdom about hospitality. Sometimes I imagine that I hosted
the conversation because I arranged the details for our meetings, asked
the questions, and interpreted the responses. But for much of the time, I
knew I was a privileged guest, welcomed to an abundant table and fed by
the conversation itself.

My journey into hospitality began twenty years ago as I worked with
refugees and poor people in my local church. Even before then, however,
I had felt specially drawn to people with disabilities and to those troubled
folks who simply needed a friend. I noticed how they were frequently
overlooked in the busyness of everyday life and sensed that their invisibility was a loss to everyone. Often, as my life intertwined with theirs, I
found myself enriched and changed. During those years I did not have
access to the vocabulary of hospitality, but I knew intuitively that I had
touched on something very important.

While the energy for this book came out of my experience with people on the margins of society, my hope is that attention to their gifts and needs will also precipitate a deeper sensitivity to people closer to us. Family and friends, coworkers and classmates, neighbors and church members flourish in the context of hospitality. Welcoming those most in need of human connection is crucial, but hospitality also enriches the life of every human being. Attention to some of the difficulties and complexities of hospitality will, I trust, help us to undertake regular expressions of welcome with more confidence and less hesitation.

Hospitality is a way of life fundamental to Christian identity. Its mysteries, riches, and difficulties are revealed most fully as it is practiced. When I remember some of my difficult experiences with hospitality, I am deeply grateful for those times when I was forced to work through the failures. They reshaped my naive romanticism into something more hardy. I am equally thankful for faithful coworkers who refused to grow cynical or cold in the midst of hard work.

Lengthy sojourns in two churches taught me much of what I know about church-based hospitality. Community Bible Church in metropolitan New York had a heart so big that it welcomed hundreds of refugees, local poor people, and troubled souls. It was multiethnic before that was popular, and it introduced ordinary New Yorkers to the joy of hearing a hymn sung in four or five languages simultaneously. It was there I learned to cherish potluck dinners where you were never entirely sure what you were eating but it usually tasted good, and the fellowship tasted a bit like the Kingdom. At CBC I discovered that hospitality to strangers required a sense of humor — especially the capacity to laugh at ourselves, to trust God to rescue us and others from the unintended consequences of our good efforts, and to continue on when we realized we'd been used.

With the people of Community Bible Church, I experienced the bone weariness that came with responding to unrelenting need and learned the necessity of sustaining a spiritual life in the midst of ongoing work. I discovered just how heavy large pots of soup could be and just how precious it was to share a meal with a lonely person. At CBC we learned together about hospitality, and we were forever changed.

At Brick by Brick United Methodist Church in Lexington, Kentucky, we are learning to welcome one another across racial and socioeconomic differences. With a profound commitment to racial reconciliation as an expression of the power of the gospel, we have pushed past the superficial layers of friendliness to the deeper strata of respect, care, and honesty. It has not always been easy, but it has been an excellent context in which to think hard about hospitality to strangers as well as to sisters and brothers.

The rich diversity at Brick by Brick has allowed a very unusual assortment of people to find welcome. The church hosted one of my first efforts to introduce this material to a lay audience in a nine-week class on hospitality to strangers, a class that was as diverse as the congregation. We began each session by eating together, and we quickly experienced the unexpected blessing of shared meals when our Wednesday night dinners provided a setting into which we could invite neighborhood children who had begun spending time outside the church building. They shared dinner with us and gradually became part of the congregation.

Years ago, another Christian community helped to shape my early understandings of hospitality. Along with thirty other students and seekers, I lived with the families of L'Abri Fellowship in England. It was there that I first saw how much more powerfully the gospel spoke when those who were teaching opened their homes and their lives to strangers — with no pretense, no perfection, but extraordinary faithfulness and generosity. Their hospitality made the Christian life both credible and inviting to many who stayed with them.

The experience of generous and gracious hospitality often draws us into the practice. As I researched this tradition and wrote this book, I was nourished by a host of gracious strangers, wonderful friends, and treasured family members. The wisdom they shared with me illumined my study; their kindness fed my life.

I was a grateful guest in eight communities of hospitality that opened their lives to me and my questions. They allowed me to probe their practices, explore their failings, and celebrate their strengths. I interviewed over fifty practitioners for many hours and spoke with a significant number of guests as well. Special and sincerest thanks to the people — too numerous to identify by name — at L'Abri Fellowship (Massachusetts), Annunciation House (Texas), L'Arche (Washington, D.C.), The Catholic Worker (New York), Good Works, Inc. (Ohio), Jubilee Partners (Georgia), The Open Door (Georgia), and St. John's and St. Benedict's Monasteries (Minnesota).[1] Beyond these communities, a number of prac-

---

1. See the Appendix for a brief description of each community.

titioners and academics shared their experiences and studies; I am grateful to Riggins R. Earl, Jr., Joyce Hollyday, Rosetta Ross, and Edith Schaeffer. This book and I are wiser because of the hundreds of stories, experiences, and insights these many people graciously shared with me.

I am very grateful to the Louisville Institute/Lilly Endowment for the resources to visit and interview the various communities. Through their generous sabbatical grant program, I was able to take the additional time away from my teaching responsibilities at Asbury Theological Seminary to do more comprehensive study. During my sabbatical year, I was enriched by a semester at the Institute for Ecumenical and Cultural Research in Collegeville, Minnesota. The community of scholars at the Ecumenical Institute and at St. John's and St. Benedict's Monasteries provided a wonderful setting within which to think and write about hospitality. My connections with the Louisville Institute spawned a crucial relationship with Dorothy Bass and the Valparaiso Project on the Education and Formation of People in Faith/Lilly Endowment. Dorothy Bass and Craig Dykstra opened the door for me into a fascinating community of scholars and practitioners working on recovering Christian practices.

For institutional and personal support, I am deeply grateful to Asbury Theological Seminary. I have been blessed with the privilege of working in a community that takes seriously the practices of the Christian life. Many of my colleagues offered the kind of encouragement one comes to depend on in a close-knit community. James Thobaben and Joel Green carefully and critically interacted with each of the chapters. Asbury students provided crucial feedback in a course on the "Ethics of Hospitality." My secretary and friend, Jeanne Sullivan, spent countless hours transcribing the interview transcripts. In addition to an exceptional job in interpreting some difficult recordings, she encouraged me continually by describing the transformation she experienced by listening to the interviews.

My research into hospitality as a central dimension of the Christian moral life is greatly indebted to several of my former teachers, but especially to the exceptional academic mentoring of Stephen C. Mott and Jon P. Gunnemann. Ongoing conversation with my close friend, Nicola Hoggard Creegan, helped me refine my thinking and make my arguments more precise.

I am thankful for a number of opportunities to present early versions of the chapters of the book. In particular, my time with the students and faculty of Associated Mennonite Biblical Seminary was very helpful. Their responses to the material and their sensitivities to Christian community and social justice enriched my reflections considerably.

I offer special thanks to Jon Pott, editor-in-chief at Wm. B. Eerdmans Publishing Company, for his interest in the project and for his expertise in helping a novice book writer find her way amid the stops and starts of chapters.

For my dear friends and family who sheltered me with love and hospitality while I tried to write about it, I am profoundly thankful. I am especially grateful to my brother and sister-in-law, who embody the "naturalness" of hospitality. They and their five children often and easily make room for unexpected guests. Insights from their practice, from our long conversations about the topic, and from their careful readings of the manuscript have strengthened the book and blessed my life. I offer my most heartfelt thanks to my mother for her careful editing work on the manuscript, her prayers for the project, and her unfailing enthusiasm for its significance.

A mystery of hospitality is how often one senses God's presence in the midst of very ordinary activities. Even in writing on the topic, I frequently found myself walking on holy ground. Over and over again, I've come to see that in God's remarkable economy, as we make room for hospitality, more room becomes available to us for life, hope, and grace.

# I. REMEMBERING OUR HERITAGE

# 1. INTRODUCTION: A NEW LOOK AT AN OLD TRADITION

*"If there is any concept worth restoring to its
original depth and evocative potential, it is
the concept of hospitality."*

HENRI NOUWEN[1]

"WOULD YOU DESCRIBE YOUR MINISTRY AS OFFERING
hospitality to strangers?" I asked the founder of a community for rural
homeless people.

"No, not really," he responded.

Surprised, I pressed him further, "Well, then, how would you describe what you are doing?"

"We welcome needy strangers into a home environment; we give
them a safe place. I think of hospitality as entertaining family and friends;
that's not what we're doing." His response echoed Henri Nouwen's observation that, for most of us, hospitality conjures up images of "tea parties, bland conversation, and a general atmosphere of coziness."[2]

1. Henri Nouwen, *Reaching Out: The Three Movements of the Spiritual Life* (New
York: Image Books, 1975), 66. Nouwen, a Roman Catholic priest, made a significant
contribution to the recovery of hospitality through his writings. His chapters on hospitality in *Reaching Out* stand behind many contemporary discussions. Nouwen spent the
last years of his life as pastor of the L'Arche Daybreak community in Toronto, practicing
hospitality with people with severe disabilities.

2. Ibid.

In past centuries, hospitality certainly would have been the right term to describe my friend's ministry. Welcoming strangers into a home and offering them food, shelter, and protection were the key components in the practice of hospitality. That my friend did not describe his work as hospitality reflects how much the use of the word has changed over the last three hundred years. For the most part, the term "hospitality" has lost its moral dimension and, in the process, most Christians have lost touch with the amazingly rich and complex tradition of hospitality.

Today when we think of hospitality, we don't think first of welcoming strangers. We picture having family and friends over for a pleasant meal. Or we think of the "hospitality industry," of hotels and restaurants which are open to strangers as long as they have money or credit cards. Perhaps large churches come to mind, with their "hospitality committees" that coordinate the coffee hour, greet visitors, or help with the parking. In any case, today most understandings of hospitality have a minimal moral component — hospitality is a nice extra if we have the time or the resources, but we rarely view it as a spiritual obligation or as a dynamic expression of vibrant Christianity.

Those of us with resources can usually avoid depending on the personal hospitality of strangers for food, shelter, and safety. Away from home, we buy our meals and book comfortable hotel rooms. Unless we travel in a foreign country, live through the devastation of a storm or an earthquake, or run into car trouble on the road, we're unlikely to know what it is to be a vulnerable stranger needing someone else's help. In a highly individualistic and commercial society, depending on the generosity of others is difficult and sometimes feels degrading. Whereas in ancient times all strangers depended on someone else's hospitality, today, it is those without resources who depend most on the free provision of food, shelter, and protection that characterizes hospitality.

In many other societies — and in a few distinct communities in our own society — hospitality to strangers remains a highly valued moral practice, an important expression of kindness, mutual aid, neighborliness, and response to the life of faith. But even those of us who do not depend on hospitality for basic needs know something of the joy of being welcomed warmly. We also know the pain of being excluded. Although hospitality has lost much of its earlier significance, memories and feelings associated with it can still be very powerful.

In a number of ancient civilizations, hospitality was viewed as a pillar on which all morality rested; it encompassed "the good."[3] For the people of ancient Israel, understanding themselves as strangers and sojourners, with responsibility to care for vulnerable strangers in their midst, was part of what it meant to be the people of God. Jesus, who was dependent on the hospitality of others during much of his earthly sojourn, also served as the gracious host in his words and in his actions. Those who turned to him found welcome and rest and the promise of reception into the Kingdom. Jesus urged his human hosts to open their banquets and dinner tables to more than family and friends who could return the favor, to give generous welcome to the poor and sick who had little to offer in return. Jesus promised that welcoming the stranger, feeding the hungry person, and visiting the sick were acts of personal kindness to the Son of man himself.

Paul urged fellow Christians to welcome one another as Christ had welcomed them. He challenged the early believers to "pursue" hospitality; in fact, hospitality was a qualification for leadership in the early Christian communities. The writer of Hebrews reminded readers to offer hospitality to strangers for, like Abraham and Sarah, they might be entertaining angels. Indeed, Christian believers were to regard hospitality to strangers as a fundamental expression of the gospel.

The richness of the story of hospitality continues beyond the many biblical texts. Early Christian writers claimed that transcending social and ethnic differences by sharing meals, homes, and worship with persons of different backgrounds was a proof of the truth of the Christian faith. In the fourth century, church leaders warned clergy — who might be tempted to use hospitality to gain favor with the powerful — to welcome instead the poorest people to their tables. In doing so, they would have Christ as their guest. Wealthy female converts to Christianity became exemplary providers of Christian hospitality, using their family fortunes to offer food and shelter to the poor, sick, and pilgrims. They did not, however, use their wealth to exempt themselves from providing the care with their own hands.

---

3. Shepherd of Hermas, *Mandate* 8:8-10, translated in *The Apostolic Fathers,* by Kirsopp Lake, Loeb Classical Library (Cambridge, Mass.: Harvard University Press; London: William Heinemann, 1914; hereafter cited as LCL), vol. 2. See also John Koenig, *New Testament Hospitality* (Philadelphia: Fortress, 1985), 2.

John Chrysostom, both eloquent and persistent in advocating Christian hospitality, insisted that such hospitality should be face-to-face, gracious, unassuming, nearly indiscriminate, and always enthusiastic. He and other leaders of the fourth- and fifth-century church founded various institutions of care for pilgrims and the poor to supplement home and church-based hospitality. Monasticism, which held the demands of hospitality in tension with the ideal of separation from the world, carried the Christian tradition of hospitality through the Middle Ages.

In the Reformation period, Martin Luther wrote that when persecuted believers were received hospitably, "God Himself is in our home, is being fed at our house, is lying down and resting."[4] "No duty can be more pleasing or acceptable to God" than hospitality to religious refugees, promised John Calvin, who viewed such practice as a "sacred" form of hospitality.[5] Calvin encouraged believers to see in the stranger the image of God and our common flesh.

For most of the history of the church, hospitality was understood to encompass physical, social, and spiritual dimensions of human existence and relationships. It meant response to the physical needs of strangers for food, shelter, and protection, but also a recognition of their worth and common humanity. In almost every case, hospitality involved shared meals; historically, table fellowship was an important way of recognizing the equal value and dignity of persons.

Hospitality, because it was such a fundamental human practice, always included family, friends, and influential contacts. The distinctive Christian contribution was the emphasis on including the poor and neediest, the ones who could not return the favor. This focus did not diminish the value of hospitality to family and friends; rather, it broadened the practice so that the close relations formed by table fellowship and conversation could be extended to the most vulnerable.

Even a superficial review of the first seventeen centuries of church history reveals the importance of hospitality to the spread and credibility of the gospel, to transcending national and ethnic distinctions in the

4. Martin Luther, *Luther's Works,* vol. 3: *Lectures on Genesis, Chapters 15–20* (St. Louis: Concordia, 1961), 189.

5. John Calvin, *Commentary on the Prophet Isaiah,* vol. 1 (Grand Rapids: Wm. B. Eerdmans, 1948), 484; and *Commentary on the Harmony of the Evangelists, Matthew, Mark, and Luke,* 3 vols. (Grand Rapids: Wm. B. Eerdmans, 1949), 1:xxxi.

church, and to Christian care for the sick, strangers, and pilgrims. Granting that the practice was rarely as good as the rhetoric, still, we pause to wonder, if hospitality to strangers was such an important part of Christian faith and life, how did it virtually disappear?

The answers are multiple, fascinating, and often ironic. Concerns about hospitality to needy strangers gave rise to the development of hospitals, hospices, and hostels, and eventually these more anonymous and distanced ways of responding to strangers became the norm. Hospitality as personal, face-to-face, gracious welcome became primarily associated with attempts to gain power and influence, especially in the Middle Ages where it was increasingly detached from connections with needy persons and was reserved for those of equal or higher rank. The nature of the household itself changed over the centuries, from a setting which included extended family, work, and religious practices to the highly insulated, individualized, small household of today. The structure of the church and its relation to the state and to social welfare also changed over the centuries. Each of these major institutional shifts had an impact on hospitality, on its practice and its meanings. By the eighteenth century, hospitality was viewed by many as an antiquated practice, out of step with busy commercial society, a relic from an earlier time.

And so, over the years, important, older understandings and stories of hospitality have nearly disappeared. Because of this, we know little of how earlier generations of Christians struggled with issues of recognition and dignity, transcending social differences, building community, distributing limited resources, and negotiating the tensions between maintaining identity boundaries and welcoming strangers. But their experiences, their shining successes and abysmal failures, can assist us as we try to respond to some of the most serious problems in contemporary American churches and society. We struggle to find better ways to respond to homeless people, people with disabilities, immigrants and refugees. Questions about diversity and inclusion, boundaries and community challenge us daily. We search for more personal ways to respond to youth who are detached and alienated from family, school, and church. In many cases, we feel as if we are strangers ourselves, even in our own families and churches, and we long for bonds that give life and meaning.

Even among Christians, many of the current discussions about poverty and welfare, inclusion and diversity, scarcity and distribution, are conducted without the benefit of any coherent theological framework. Often, the result is that our stands on complex social and public policy concerns are little affected by our deepest Christian values and commitments. Hospitality as a framework provides a bridge which connects our theology with daily life and concerns.

Is it possible that by looking back we can find resources for moving forward? Recovering the tradition of hospitality suggests the ironic possibility that in revitalizing an ancient practice, we may discover some radical and fresh responses to contemporary difficulties. Discussions about whether there are "deserving vs. undeserving" poor, whether people will take advantage of generous hospitality, and whether it is too risky to respond to strangers are as ancient as early Christian texts and as current as today's talk shows. Practitioners of hospitality from centuries past can teach us from their wisdom and their struggles.

Recovering hospitality is important for another set of reasons as well. Hospitality is central to the meaning of the gospel. The New Testament theologian Krister Stendahl writes that "wherever, whenever, however the kingdom manifests itself, it is welcome."[6] A fuller awareness of the richness of the hospitality tradition and the extraordinary experiences associated with hospitality enriches Christian faith and brings Christian practice into closer alignment with the basic values of the Kingdom. Hospitality is a lens through which we can read and understand much of the gospel, and a practice by which we can welcome Jesus himself.

Recovering hospitality as a vital aspect of Christian life will be more complex than simply resurrecting an old-fashioned practice. In addition to learning the richness of the ancient understandings of hospitality, we will also have to discern how those meanings fit with the institutions of family, church, work, and polity. Recognizing the significance of the changes in those institutions over the centuries, and in the values associated with them, is essential for recovering hospitality into our own particular institutional settings and cultural values.[7]

6. Krister Stendahl, " 'When you pray, pray in this manner . . .' a Bible Study," in *The Kingdom on Its Way: Meditations and Music for Mission,* RISK Book Series (Geneva: World Council of Churches, 1980), 40-41, quoted in Letty Russell, *Household of Freedom* (Philadelphia: Westminster, 1987), 76.

7. The history and practices of hospitality are complex, varied, and rooted in many cultures and traditions. In this book, we can only explore part of the rich story of

A wholesale, indiscriminate recovery of any ancient practice is neither possible nor desirable. Certain aspects of the Christian tradition of hospitality are deeply disturbing. Only honest and serious attention to the failures, omissions, and tragedies in the story will allow us to make use of its strengths.

We become proficient in a skill by performing it regularly, and by learning from persons who are masters of it. Hospitality is a skill and a gift, but it is also a practice which flourishes as multiple skills are developed, as particular commitments and values are nurtured, and as certain settings are cultivated. In addition to theological and historical discussions of the practice of hospitality, we need contemporary models from whom we can learn what hospitality to strangers might look like today.

Fortunately, there are a number of Christian communities for whom hospitality is an organizing practice. For several reasons, these communities have recognized that hospitality has an important, even essential, place in our fractured, individualistic, results-oriented society. During the course of my research, I visited eight of these communities and spent several days living within each of them, interviewing persons about their understandings and experiences of hospitality, strangers, guest/host roles, and resources. Insights from these visits and interviews provide crucial contemporary material which supplements the historical research.

I had originally intended to visit both church congregations and intentional Christian communities involved in substantial amounts of hospitality. As the project developed, it became evident that although some congregations offer hospitality to strangers as a dimension of their ministry, few do it in a sufficiently intense and regular way to surface the issues as effectively as do those communities which provide hospitality full time. Because of this, I chose to study communities that have substantial and long-term experience with hospitality to different kinds of strangers. To gain as rich an insight into contemporary Christian hospitality as possible, I chose communities from the Roman Catholic, mainline Protestant,

---

hospitality and focus only on some of the biblical and historical sources which have significantly affected churches in the United States. There are cultural and religious traditions that deserve much fuller study and development than can be covered in a single book.

and evangelical traditions. Recognizing the importance of hospitality to African-American and Hispanic Christian identity, I sought wisdom from various racial/ethnic traditions as well. Anticipating that hospitality might vary with the kinds of strangers welcomed, I chose communities whose focus included refugees, homeless people, students and seekers, and persons with disabilities.[8]

The contemporary church hungers for models of a more authentic Christian life in which glimpses of the Kingdom can be seen and the promise of the Kingdom is embodied. More than words and ideas, the world needs living pictures of what a life of hospitality could look like. Over sixty years ago, Peter Maurin wrote that "we need Houses of Hospitality to show what idealism looks like when it is practiced."[9] Communities of hospitality combine in daily experience the rigor and sacrifice, joy and empowerment, of faithful living. Many of those interviewed commented that living in a community of hospitality was the hardest and the best thing they had ever done.

A community which embodies hospitality to strangers is "a sign of contradiction, a place where joy and pain, crises and peace are closely interwoven."[10] Friendships forged in hospitality contradict contemporary messages about who is valuable and "good to be with,"[11] who can "give life to others."[12] Such communities are also signs of hope "that love is possible, that the world is not condemned to a struggle between oppressors and oppressed, that class and racial warfare is not inevita-

8. See the Appendix for a brief description of each community. In selecting the communities for study, I worked with several additional criteria. I looked for communities that (1) consistently use hospitality language in their literature — welcome, shelter, making room, refuge, home, open door, strangers; and (2) explicitly identify their life and work with biblical texts important in the hospitality tradition. I identified communities in which guests and hosts eat together regularly at the same table. In each community significant social boundaries are continually transcended and "hosts" share life, home, and ordinary routines with people who in some way had been strangers. Every community has stood the test of time — some are very old; all have been offering hospitality to strangers for at least fifteen or twenty years. All of the communities incorporate additional teaching and/or advocacy ministries.

9. Peter Maurin, *Easy Essays* (New York: Sheed & Ward, 1936), 46.

10. Jean Vanier, *An Ark for the Poor* (New York: Crossroad, 1995), 110.

11. Ken Weinkauf, "Contradictions," *The Good Newsletter,* 17/ 2 (Summer 1997): 3.

12. Vanier, *An Ark for the Poor,* 57.

ble."[13] The gift of hope embedded in these communities of hospitality nourishes, challenges, and transforms guests, hosts, and, sometimes, the larger community.

Not every church member would choose the substantial life-style changes that community living requires. However, there is much to be learned about hospitality from these intentional and intense community settings that can be applied to more conventionally structured households and churches. These communities have found ways to cope with the awkwardness, risk, and high demands associated with hospitality to strangers. They have developed structures that allow an ancient practice to thrive in the postmodern world. None set out to be an exemplar of Christian hospitality, but, because of their long-term viability and vitality, a number of them do offer a model to which others are drawn.

Thus, practitioners of hospitality also become teachers of hospitality. In addition to welcoming strangers in need, most of these communities also welcome visitors/strangers who want to learn from their ministry and life together. Internships, short-term volunteer opportunities, and brief visits both enrich and complicate the practice of hospitality. Guest and host roles merge and reconfigure when a person with serious mental disabilities welcomes the new intern, or when a formerly homeless young adult prepares the evening meal for the volunteer group.

Almost all of the communities I visited had simple, inauspicious beginnings in which individuals, families, or small groups of friends opened their homes and their lives to the needy strangers around them. Hospitality grew from that context, and people learned hospitality by doing it. Often they turned to biblical texts for motivation and direction; some communities also depended on insights from the monastic tradition of hospitality. Many practitioners could point to the example of a grandmother who fed hoboes on her porch or a family that always found enough food or room to welcome a lonely child or a traveling preacher.

Contemporary communities with the longest unbroken tradition of hospitality are those associated with Benedictine monasteries. The *Rule of Benedict,* which has guided Benedictine life for fifteen hundred years, makes hospitality to strangers a basic part of monastic identity and practice.

13. Jean Vanier, *Community and Growth,* rev. ed. (New York: Paulist Press, 1989), 312.

For a surprising number of communities, the most formative understandings of hospitality were shaped by Dorothy Day, Peter Maurin, and the Catholic Worker movement. In the 1930s, Catholic Worker understandings of hospitality were developed through Maurin's recovery of hospitality from the Irish monastic tradition and his conviction that a personal approach to care and responsibility was essential to the Christian life and to human well-being. The story of the Catholic Worker demonstrates how significantly one effort can touch the lives of multiple communities. Jean Vanier and the L'Arche communities have been influenced strongly by the monastic tradition and by the Catholic Worker. Subsequently, Vanier's insights from L'Arche have become an important resource for others in the recovery of hospitality. Several other communities tie their hospitality commitments more exclusively to the biblical tradition.

Philip Hallie, an ethicist who spent years studying the human capacity for evil and good, concluded that "the opposite of cruelty is not simply freedom from the cruel relationship, it is hospitality."[14] The communities I studied offer hospitality in the context of larger environments that are often inhospitable to certain kinds of strangers and indifferent to their needs. Rather than being overwhelmed by the heartlessness and by the need, these communities understand their welcome to strangers as "little moves against destructiveness."[15] Practitioners of hospitality are rarely romantics or cynics; they are often startlingly honest about their own frailties and failures, about the difficulties as well as the joys of hospitality.

A close look at these contemporary communities and at their ancient counterparts reveals important commonalities. The practice of hospitality almost always includes eating meals together. Sustained hospitality requires a light hold on material possessions and a commitment to a simplified life-style. The most potent setting for hospitality is in the overlap of private and public space; hospitality flourishes at the intersection of the personal, intimate characteristics of the home and the transforming expectations of the church. Practitioners view hospitality as a sacred practice and find God is specially present in guest/host relationships. There is

14. Philip Hallie, "From Cruelty to Goodness," *The Hastings Center Report* 11 (1981): 26-27.

15. Philip Hallie, *Lest Innocent Blood Be Shed* (New York: Harper & Row, 1979), 85.

a mutual blessing in hospitality; practitioners consistently comment that they receive more than they give. Almost all insist that the demands of hospitality can only be met by persons sustained by a strong life of prayer and times of solitude.

When most of us practice hospitality, we typically welcome those with whom we already have some established bonds and significant common ground. Hospitality builds and reinforces relationships among family, friends, and acquaintances. It is one of the pleasures of ordinary life. Yet even this most basic form of hospitality is threatened by contemporary values, life-styles, and institutional arrangements which have helped to foster the sense that we are all strangers, even to those to whom we are related.

Strangers, in the strict sense, are those who are disconnected from basic relationships that give persons a secure place in the world. The most vulnerable strangers are detached from family, community, church, work, and polity. This condition is most clearly seen in the state of homeless people and refugees. Others experience detachment and exclusion to lesser degrees.

When we offer hospitality to strangers, we welcome them into a place to which we are somehow connected — a space that has meaning and value to us. This is often our home, but it also includes church, community, nation, and various other institutions. In hospitality, the stranger is welcomed into a safe, personal, and comfortable place, a place of respect and acceptance and friendship. Even if only briefly, the stranger is included in a life-giving and life-sustaining network of relations. Such welcome involves attentive listening and a mutual sharing of lives and life stories. It requires an openness of heart, a willingness to make one's life visible to others, and a generosity of time and resources.

For most who offer hospitality the experience is deeply enriching as well as quite demanding. Strangers rarely bring only their needs; within the hospitality relationship, hosts often experience profound blessing. Acts of hospitality participate in and reflect God's greater hospitality and therefore hold some connection to the divine, to holy ground.

In joining physical, spiritual, and social nourishment, hospitality is a life-giving practice. It is both fruitful and fertile.[16] Rooted in practical

16. Ibid., 72.

acts of care, shaped by a tradition that gives it rich meaning, Christian hospitality is also an important theological concept. Its vibrancy as a concept is inextricably tied to its practical expression.

Abstract theological reflections on hospitality and welcoming the "other" are presently popular in some academic and pastoral circles. It is crucial that these discussions include making a physical place in our lives, families, churches, and communities for people who might appear to have little to offer. Hospitable attitudes, even a principled commitment to hospitality, do not challenge us or transform our loyalties in the way that actual hospitality to particular strangers does. Hospitality in the abstract lacks the mundane, troublesome, yet rich dimensions of a profound human practice.

Practicing hospitality always involves risk and the possibility of failure, but there is greater risk and loss in neglecting hospitality. Dorothy Day, reflecting on years of work at the Catholic Worker houses of hospitality, commented, "Mistakes there were, there are, there will be. . . . The biggest mistake, sometimes, is to play things very safe in this life and end up being moral failures."[17] Philip Hallie, after studying a French Protestant community that offered hospitality to thousands of Jewish refugees during World War II, concluded, "Deeds speak the language of the great virtues far better than words do. . . . Words limp outside the gates of the mystery of compassion for strangers."[18]

Recovering a rich and life-giving practice requires attention to good stories, wise mentors, and hard questions. In the following chapters we will hear from ancient and contemporary practitioners of hospitality, explore the history, and dwell in the story. Key questions emerge as we attempt to remember, reconsider, and recover hospitality.

Where does hospitality fit in the biblical story and in our identity as children of God? Why does Jesus, both as needy guest and gracious host, make hospitality compelling for us? What does the ancient church teach about a distinctive form of Christian hospitality? What did hospitality mean in the first centuries of the church; whom did it include?

17. Dorothy Day, quoted in Robert Coles, *Dorothy Day: A Radical Devotion* (Reading, Mass.: Addison-Wesley Publishing Co., 1987), 40.
18. Philip Hallie, *Tales of Good and Evil, Help and Harm* (New York: Harper-Collins, 1997), 42.

If hospitality was so important in the ancient church, why and how did it get lost in later centuries? When hospitality was vibrant, where did it happen? What settings and social changes undermined hospitality as a personal and a church practice? What happened when concerns about hospitality led to specialized institutions separate from the church?

What makes hospitality potentially subversive and countercultural? How is hospitality related to human dignity and respect for persons? What does it mean to see Jesus in every guest? Can some forms of hospitality humiliate persons in need? Why is eating together so important? What about failures in hospitality — what are the consequences when persons are excluded or denied welcome?

Does every stranger need hospitality? What makes someone a stranger? Aren't we all strangers at some level? If welcoming strangers is important, how do we reduce the possible risks; how can we get beyond some of the strangeness? Was it easier to offer hospitality in the past? Who needs welcome today?

Why is the experience of being a stranger crucial to being a good and gracious host? What is the relation between hospitality, seeing ourselves as aliens and sojourners, and our attitudes toward property and possessions? How are hospitality and power related?

Why is hospitality so easily distorted — what makes it a fragile practice? Why does using hospitality instrumentally or for advantage undermine it? Are there always enough resources for hospitality? Do we say yes to everyone who comes to us? Are there appropriate limits or boundaries in the context of generous welcome?

How can we make a place for hospitality in our lives, homes, churches, organizations and agencies, and communities? What are the characteristics of hospitable space? In our present circumstances, can we find creative ways to recover an ancient practice?

What are the challenges and difficulties of recovering hospitality today? What practices constitute welcome; what gestures express hospitality? What makes a good host? How do we learn the practices of hospitality? How can we sustain and nurture hospitality so that it becomes a vibrant and life-giving practice?

# 2. ANCIENT AND
# BIBLICAL SOURCES

---

*"When you give a feast, invite the poor, the
maimed, the lame, the blind, and you will
be blessed because they cannot repay you."*

LUKE 14:13-14

GOD'S GUEST LIST INCLUDES A DISCONCERTING NUMBER
of poor and broken people, those who appear to bring little to any gathering except their need. The distinctive quality of Christian hospitality is
that it offers a generous welcome to the "least,"[1] without concern for advantage or benefit to the host. Such hospitality reflects God's greater hospitality that welcomes the undeserving, provides the lonely with a home,
and sets a banquet table for the hungry.

Images of God as gracious and generous host pervade the biblical
materials. God provides manna and quail daily in the wilderness for a
hungry and often ungrateful people. God offers shelter in a hot and dry
land, and refreshment through living water. Israel's covenant identity includes being a stranger, an alien, a tenant in God's land — both dependent on God for welcome and provision and answerable to God for its
own treatment of aliens and strangers.

Writers in the New Testament portray Jesus as a gracious host, welcoming children and prostitutes, tax collectors and sinners into his pres-

---

1. Matt. 25:40, 45.

ence. Such welcome startled and annoyed those who generally viewed themselves as the preferred guests at gatherings. But Jesus, God incarnate, is also portrayed as a vulnerable guest and needy stranger, one who "came to his own home" and often received no welcome (John 1:11). In his life on earth, Jesus experienced the vulnerability of the homeless infant, the child refugee, the adult with no place to lay his head, the despised convict.

This intermingling of guest and host roles in the person of Jesus is part of what makes the story of hospitality so compelling for Christians. Jesus welcomes and needs welcome; Jesus requires that followers depend on and provide hospitality. The practice of Christian hospitality is always located within the larger picture of Jesus' sacrificial welcome to all who come to him.

## Defining Christian Hospitality:
## The Early Writers

Most of the ancient world regarded hospitality as a fundamental moral practice. It was necessary to human well-being and essential to the protection of vulnerable strangers. Hospitality assured strangers at least a minimum of provision, protection, and connection with the larger community. It also sustained the normal network of relationships on which a community depended, enriching moral and social bonds among family, friends, and neighbors.

A distinctively Christian understanding of hospitality developed in the early centuries of the church. Partly in continuity with Hebrew understandings of hospitality that associated it with God, covenant, and blessing, and partly in contrast to Hellenistic practices which associated it with benefit and reciprocity, Christian commitments pressed hospitality outward toward the weakest, those least likely to be able to reciprocate. In the fourth century, writers articulated a clear statement of the scope of Christian hospitality.

Lactantius, the tutor to the son of Constantine, explicitly contrasted Christian hospitality with classical practices. Recognizing hospitality as a "principal virtue" for philosophers and Christians alike, Lactantius criticized those philosophers who tied it to advantage. He noted that Cicero and others urged that the "houses of illustrious men should be open to illustrious guests." Rejecting the argument that we must bestow "our bounty on 'suitable' persons," Lactantius argued instead that "the house of a just man ought not to be open to the illustrious, but to the lowly and abject. For those illustrious and powerful men cannot be in want of anything."[2]

Greek and Roman views of benevolence and hospitality stressed formal reciprocal obligations between benefactor and recipient.[3] Because a grateful response from the beneficiary was key to the ongoing relationship, the tradition emphasized the worthiness and goodness of recipients rather than their need. Relations were often calculated to benefit the benefactor. In Lactantius' words, such hospitality was "ambitious" and was offered for "advantage."[4]

For John Chrysostom, as for Lactantius, Christian hospitality was to be different. Chrysostom recognized the earthly benefits Christians could gain from entertaining persons of high status but he criticized such a practice:

> Whereas if thou entertain some great and distinguished man, it is not such pure mercy, what thou doest, but some portion many times is assigned to thyself also, both by vain-glory, and by the return of the favor, and by the rising in many men's estimation on account of thy guest.[5]

Rather than entertaining persons who had something to offer, and thereby gaining advantage from their hospitality, Christians were deliberately to welcome those who seemingly brought little to the encounter.

For Chrysostom, Lactantius, Jerome, and other leaders of the an-

---

2. Lactantius, *The Divine Institutes,* bk. 6, ch. 12, The Ante-Nicene Fathers, ed. Alexander Roberts and James Donaldson (Edinburgh: T. & T. Clark, 1867-72; hereafter cited as ANF), vol. 7, p. 176.

3. See Stephen C. Mott, "The Power of Giving and Receiving: Reciprocity in Hellenistic Benevolence," in *Current Issues in Biblical and Patristic Interpretation,* ed. Gerald F. Hawthorne (Grand Rapids: Wm. B. Eerdmans, 1975), 60-72.

4. Lactantius, *Divine Institutes,* 176.

5. John Chrysostom, Homily 20 on 1 Corinthians, A Select Library of the Nicene and Post-Nicene Fathers of the Christian Church, First Series, ed. Philip Schaff (Buffalo and New York: Christian Literature Company, 1886-90; hereafter cited as NPNF1), vol. 12, p. 117.

cient church, hospitality was a significant context for transcending status boundaries and for working through issues of respect and recognition. Christian hospitality was to be remedial, counteracting the social stratification of the larger society by providing a modest and equal welcome to everyone. High social status was not to be honored with special recognition by Christians; in fact, to entertain persons who had few needs was not really hospitality at all.

Jerome challenged clergy to "let poor men and strangers be acquainted with your modest table, and with them Christ shall be your guest." He warned Christian leaders who might be tempted to entertain the powerful with grand hospitality, even in the effort to gain benefits for the poor, to remember that they were servants of a crucified Lord, one who had lived in poverty and on the bread of strangers. It would be better, Jerome insisted, to depend directly on Christ for provision than to compromise holiness with ambitious entertainment.[6]

Hospitality meant extending to strangers a quality of kindness usually reserved for friends and family. The focus, however, was on strangers in need, the "lowly and abject," those who, on first appearance, seemed to have little to offer. Ministry to them differed categorically from "ambitious" hospitality to illustrious guests who could further the host's position in the world. Nature and human relations required that persons do good to a relative, neighbor, or friend, "but he who does it to a stranger and an unknown person, he truly is worthy of praise, because he was led to do it by kindness only." For Lactantius, hospitality to strangers was ultimately equated with justice: "But in what does the nature of justice consist than in our affording to strangers through kindness, that which we render to our own relatives through affection."[7]

The emphasis on needy strangers as the recipients of hospitality did not rule out hospitality to family and friends, Lactantius was careful to explain. Such hospitality was taken for granted in this life, but to welcome those who could not give anything in return is "our true and just work," the work that relates to God.[8]

Offering hospitality without concern for gaining advantage could

---

6. Jerome, Letter 52: "To Nepotian," in *Select Letters of Jerome,* LCL, pp. 217-19.
7. Lactantius, *Divine Institutes,* 176-77.
8. Ibid.

seem quite costly to those accustomed to a calculating approach. But according to these fourth- and fifth-century writers, hospitality made sense in the economy of God. Generous hosts, though not seeking gain, would find themselves blessed in the hospitality relationship. By offering hospitality to a person in need, one ministered to Christ, and in this context the discrepancy between small human acts of care and the extravagance of divine hospitality was underscored.

> "Thou receivest Me," He saith, "into thy lodging, I will receive thee into the kingdom of My Father; thou tookest away My hunger, I take away thy sins; . . . thou sawest Me a stranger, I make thee a citizen of heaven; thou gavest Me bread, I give thee an entire kingdom, that thou mayest inherit and possess it."[9]

Augustine similarly argued that such acts of kindness fit into a network of need. Both giver and recipient were in need before God and although God needed none of a person's goods, God had "vouchsafed to be hungry in His poor. 'I was hungry,' saith He, 'and ye gave Me meat.' "[10]

## The Teachings of Jesus

For the Christian tradition, two New Testament texts — Luke 14 and Matthew 25 — shaped the distinction between conventional and Christian hospitality. Jesus' instructions in Luke 14:12-14 are explicit about invitations:

> When you give a dinner or a banquet, do not invite your friends or your brothers or your kinsmen or rich neighbors, lest they also invite you in return, and you be repaid. But when you give a feast, invite the poor, the maimed, the lame, the blind, and you will be blessed, because they cannot repay you. You will be repaid at the resurrection of the just.[11]

9. Chrysostom, Homily 45 on Acts, NPNF1, vol. 11, p. 276.

10. Augustine, Sermon 10, NPNF1, vol. 6, p. 294; see also Sermon 210, "For the Lenten Season," in *Sermons on the Liturgical Seasons,* trans. Sr. Mary Sarah Muldowney, The Fathers of the Church, vol. 17 (New York: Fathers of the Church, 1959), 107.

11. Unless otherwise noted, all biblical quotations are taken from *The Holy Bible: Revised Standard Version*.

Ordinary hosts invited friends, relatives, and rich neighbors to their banquets. In so doing, they solidified relationships, reinforced social boundaries, and anticipated repayment from their guests. By contrast, hosts who anticipated the hospitality of God's Kingdom welcomed the poor, lame, crippled, and blind, those who were more dependent and lived on the margins of the community. While such hosts expected no immediate benefit, they would ultimately experience God's repayment at the resurrection.

The parable in Luke 14:15-24 provides the larger context for Jesus' instructions to his earthly host (vv. 12-14). In the great banquet in the Kingdom of God, the same four groups — the poor, maimed, blind, and lame — are drawn into the celebration. When the expected guests turn down the invitation, God's universal welcome is displayed. No one would be excluded except those who rejected the host's invitation because they were too busy to recognize its significance. Just as God would welcome all to the feast in the Kingdom of God, so earthly hosts ought to open their tables to those in need and without ability to repay the kindness. In God's economy, all would then experience blessing. The character of God's hospitality frames appropriate earthly behavior.

Jesus challenges narrow definitions and dimensions of hospitality and presses them outward to include those with whom one least desires to have connections. The poor and infirm come with their inconvenient needs and condition, with their incapacity to reciprocate. But in welcoming them one anticipates and reflects the welcome of God.

Jesus intensifies the implications of hospitality when he tells the story of the great judgment in Matthew 25:31-46. The Son of man will separate the nations as a shepherd separates sheep and goats. To the sheep on his right hand, the King will say:

> "Come, O blessed of my Father, inherit the Kingdom prepared for you from the foundation of the world; for I was hungry and you gave me food, I was thirsty and you gave me drink, I was a stranger and you welcomed me. . . ." Then the righteous will answer him, "Lord, when did we see thee hungry and feed thee, or thirsty and give thee drink? And when did we see thee a stranger and welcome thee? . . ." And the King will answer them, "Truly I say to you, as you did it to one of the least of these my brethren, you did it to me."

Those who have welcomed strangers and have met the needs of persons in distress have welcomed Jesus himself, and are themselves welcomed into the Kingdom. God's invitation into the Kingdom is tied to Christian hospitality in this life. This passage sets up a fundamental identification of Jesus with "the least of these" and personally and powerfully connects hospitality toward human beings with care for Jesus.

This has been the most important passage for the entire tradition on Christian hospitality. "I was a stranger and you welcomed me" resounds throughout the ancient texts, and contemporary practitioners of hospitality refer to this text more often than to any other passage.[12] Acts of welcoming the stranger, or leaving someone outside cold and hungry, take on intensely heightened significance when it is Jesus himself who experiences the consequences of our ministry or the lack of it. Dorothy Day explained the ongoing significance of this passage in her life of hospitality to destitute people.

> There He was, homeless. Would a church take Him in today — feed Him, clothe Him, offer Him a bed? I hope I ask myself that question on the last day of my life. I once prayed and prayed to God that He never, ever let me forget to ask that question.[13]

Practitioners often speak of seeing Jesus in the people in the soup line, seeing Jesus through their dirty clothes and broken spirits, seeing Jesus "in a distressing disguise."[14] The sight of Jesus does not eclipse the particular human being who stands there in need, but it challenges Christians to offer the most gracious welcome possible.

The biblical passage itself is not entirely clear concerning who is being judged and who the persons are who have been cared for or neglected. Whether in Matthew's text, "the least of these" refers to any person in need, to Christian missionaries and apostles, or to any Christian who is suffering,

---

12. This passage provides the basis for the corporal works of mercy: feeding the hungry, giving drink to the thirsty, clothing the naked, sheltering the homeless, visiting the sick, ransoming the prisoners, and burying the dead. In the Christian tradition, these works were often encompassed in the practice of hospitality.

13. Robert Coles, *Dorothy Day: A Radical Devotion* (Reading, Mass.: Addison-Wesley Publishing Co., 1987), 69.

14. Mother Teresa, quoted in Eileen Egan, "Dorothy Day, Pilgrim of Peace," in *A Revolution of the Heart: Essays on the Catholic Worker,* ed. Patrick G. Coy (Philadelphia: Temple University Press, 1988), 105.

the passage has often been interpreted and applied in ways that are broader than its immediate context. It converges with other biblical passages to produce a more particular statement of responsibility for responding to needy persons and a more universal statement of Jesus' identification with those in need. The parable of the Good Samaritan (Luke 10:29-37), which widens understandings of responsibility to the neighbor, and Jesus' teaching on including one's enemies in the circle of love (e.g., Matt. 5:39-44, Luke 6:27-31), have tended to broaden interpretations of "the least of these" in Christian practice. Responsibility may begin with the "household of faith" but it extends to all who need help (Gal. 6:10). Whoever "the least of these" are, they are persons in need of human care.

John Wesley recognized the ambiguities of Matthew 25:31-46 but did not allow them to deter him from reponding to persons in need. To those who wondered "what does it avail to feed or clothe men's bodies, if they are just dropping into everlasting fire?" Wesley responded, "whether they will finally be lost or saved, you are expressly commanded to feed the hungry, and clothe the naked. If you can, and do not, whatever becomes of them, you shall go away into everlasting fire."[15] He strongly resisted any attempts to narrow the scope of responsibility or to dull the intensity of the passage.

Throughout the entire tradition, the words of Matthew 25:31-46 and Luke 14:12-14 are recalled in extending the definition and the reach of hospitality. By suggesting not only that God welcomes the needy and disadvantaged, but that God is actually welcomed in these people, the passages press Christians to include those most likely to be overlooked.

## Stories of Hospitality

Alongside these important teachings of Jesus, certain biblical narratives have powerfully shaped understandings of and commitments to hospitality. Many stories of hospitality contain elements of mystery and surprise because God is so often present in unexpected ways. Needy strangers turn out to be angels, beggars are somehow Jesus in disguise. Resources are in short supply yet miraculously sufficient; sometimes there is even abundance

---

15. John Wesley, *The Works of John Wesley,* vol. 1: *Sermons 1:1-33* (Nashville: Abingdon, 1984), Sermon 24: "Sermon on the Mount 4," pp. 545-46.

when what is available is shared. Many stories have their roots in Scripture, but they are frequently contextualized and retold through the generations. Contemporary practitioners collect their own sets of hospitality stories — stories of food that stretched miraculously or appeared just when needed, people who came unexpectedly and brought exactly the skills required that day, situations of risk that turned out to be filled with blessings.

Several Old Testament narratives are foundational to the tradition of hospitality; they contain crucial themes and tensions which recur throughout history. The story of Abraham, Sarah, and the three guests in Genesis 18 is the most significant of these, having a persistent formative role in the instruction and motivation of the people of God. The writer of Hebrews gives this story special status by referring to it in chapter 13: "Do not neglect to show hospitality to strangers, for thereby some have entertained angels unawares" (v. 2).

In the Genesis account, Abraham graciously welcomed three visitors who mysteriously appeared as he sat outside his tent in the heat of the day. He addressed these unexpected guests with honor and deference, offered them water to wash their feet and an opportunity to rest. With his wife Sarah and their servant, Abraham quickly prepared a lavish meal for them.

Abraham welcomed his guests as any Near Eastern host would. While the reader is told in Genesis 18:1 that the Lord appeared to Abraham in this interaction, it seems that Abraham only gradually came to understand this as a divine encounter. These three guests, in whom God was somehow present, brought to Abraham and Sarah a confirmation that they would have a son in their old age. During the visit, moreover, they warned Abraham of the impending destruction of Sodom and Gomorrah. Both messages, as well as the identity of the visitors, were revealed only in the context of a hospitable welcome to strangers.

This first formative story of the biblical tradition on hospitality is unambiguously positive about welcoming strangers. It connects hospitality with the presence of God, with promise, and with blessing. The story that immediately follows it, however, is more ambiguous. On the same day that Abraham received his guests, two of them continued on to Sodom and there encountered Lot at the city gate (Gen. 19). Lot greeted the strangers graciously and invited them home for the night. Initially the strangers resisted Lot's invitation but then they agreed to go with him and share in a feast he prepared. Before everyone retired for the evening, the men of Sodom surrounded Lot's house and demanded that he give up his guests to them for sexual exploitation. Lot left his house to reason with the mob, pleading with them to "do nothing to these men, for they have come under the shelter of my roof" (Gen. 19:8).

In ancient times hospitality included protection of the guest and, when extended by a particular household, the entire community was also bound to protect that guest. However, Lot's appeal to conventional moral practice was ignored by the men of Sodom who dismissed him as an alien without authority. It was the two strangers/angels who rescued Lot from his failed attempt to protect them. They not only rescued him immediately but, then on the following morning, saved Lot and his family from the total destruction of Sodom.

Lot attempted to fulfill his obligation to vulnerable strangers but in the context of an utterly sinful city was unable to provide for their protection. His suggestion to the mob that instead of his guests they take his virgin daughters and do what they like with them (Gen. 19:8) was an appalling attempt to bargain for his guests' safety. Lot seems to show no regard for the enormous potential costs to the more vulnerable members of his own household.

Lot's story demonstrates that when hospitality is contrary to the intentions of the larger group, it can be dangerous — an act of defiance, a challenge to the unity and expectations of the community. In the context of a supportive environment, hospitality is often a taken-for-granted act of mutual aid. Lot's treatment of the strangers distinguished him from his social context, and for this he is commended in the later tradition (2 Pet. 2:7-8, 1 Clement 11:1).[16]

Two other Old Testament stories describe the hospitality of women to traveling prophets. (Later writers on hospitality frequently refer to them to encourage women to provide hospitality from within their own households.) In the midst of doing battle with foreign gods, the prophet Elijah went to a foreign town and foreign widow to ask for hospitality (1 Kings 17–18).[17] Anticipating death by starvation for herself and her son, the widow of

16. See T. Desmond Alexander, "Lot's Hospitality: A Clue to His Righteousness," *Journal of Biblical Literature* 104/2 (1985): 289-91.

17. The importance of Elijah's sojourn and miracles in the household of a *foreign* widow is noted by Jesus in Luke 4:25-26.

Zarephath responded helplessly to Elijah's request for drink and food. Elijah, however, assured her that if she would share her last meager resources with him, the God of Israel would provide for her needs; her supplies of flour and oil would not run out until the drought ended. The woman took him in as her guest and supplied him with food and shelter for a lengthy time. But, in fact, it was Elijah, through God, who supplied her and her household with food during that period. In the midst of his sojourn with her, Elijah restored life to her dead son. The prophet, in need, turned to a woman in need and together they received God's provision.

Elisha, too, experienced such hospitality. Acknowledging Elisha to be a "holy man of God" (2 Kings 4:9), a wealthy Shunammite woman arranged to build a special guest chamber for Elisha so that he could stay in her household whenever he passed near Shunem. The story provides details of the furnishings of the special room: a bed, table, chair, and lamp (4:10). Elisha, grateful for her kind hospitality, sought to repay her. As in the story of Abraham and Sarah, the woman and her husband experienced the reward of the promise of a son. As in the story of Elijah and the widow, the son later died, and was brought back to life by the guest/prophet.

In most of these stories, guests brought their hosts into special connection with God. But this connection frequently resulted in more mundane forms of blessing as well. Almost every host experienced some benefit following his or her hospitality. In the stories of women who provided hospitality to men of God, there is an especially strong sense of reward. But the most important story for the hospitality tradition — that of Abraham's hospitality — is also strongly connected to wonderful blessing.

Acts of hospitality and inhospitality in the biblical narratives tended to reveal and reflect the underlying good or evil of a person or community. Frequently these acts demonstrated covenantal loyalty to the God of Israel or to God's chosen representatives.[18] Deliberate acts of inhospitality, such as are seen in the stories of the men of Sodom (Gen. 19) and Gibeah (Judg. 19), as well as the account of Nabal's encounter with David (1 Samuel 25), exposed foolish, evil, or corrupted character. Rather than blessing, these men experienced destruction subsequent to their inhospitality. The contrast between hospitality and inhospitality in Genesis 19 and Judges 19 highlights the utter lawlessness and degradation of the communities.

18. See the story of Rahab's hospitality to the Israelite spies in Joshua 2.

All of these stories provide glimpses into hospitality at the personal level. Hospitality was based in the household although the interaction often began outside the household in a more public space (e.g., at the city gate). Most hospitality involved brief welcome. The guests were brought into the household, were refreshed or protected, and then went on their way. The expenditure of resources was limited because the numbers of guests were few and their stay was brief. Only in the story of Elijah and the widow did the guest stay at length and in this case God miraculously supplied the necessary resources.

## The Overarching Story:
## Strangers Welcoming Strangers

In addition to particular Old Testament stories which helped to shape the hospitality tradition, the overarching "grand narrative" of Israel's history is crucial. Embedded within the covenant between God and Israel was Israel's identity as an alien and its related responsibility to sojourners and strangers. God had called Abraham away from family and familiar land to be a stranger in a foreign land. There Abraham received God's promises that he would have offspring as innumerable as the stars and the land for his descendants to inhabit. In the midst of these promises, however, Abraham was warned, "Know of a surety that your descendants will be sojourners in a land that is not theirs, and will be slaves there, and they will be oppressed for four hundred years" (Gen. 15:5-21).

When Israel finally inherited the promised land after its sojourn in Egypt, God reminded the people that the land belonged to the Lord and that "you are strangers and sojourners with me" (Lev. 25:23). They were to view themselves as aliens in their own land, for God owned the land and they were to be its stewards and caretakers, living in it by God's permission and grace. They were the chosen people — chosen, yet still aliens.[19]

Israel lived by God's grace, and its self-proclaimed identity as cho-

---

19. See Walter Brueggemann, *The Land: Place as Gift, Promise, and Challenge in Biblical Faith* (Philadelphia: Fortress, 1977), for an extensive discussion of the significance of Israel's relation to the land.

sen-yet-alien was a continual reminder of this relationship of dependence and faithfulness, gratitude and obedience. But this alien identity also provided an experiential basis from which Israelites could know the feelings and needs of sojourners and powerless people living in their midst. This connection is most explicit in Exodus 23:9: "You shall not oppress a stranger; you know the heart of a stranger, for you were strangers in the land of Egypt." Israel's experience of vulnerability and dependence was expected to yield a sympathetic and gracious treatment of the vulnerable aliens in its own land.[20]

Sojourners or aliens (Hebrew: *gerim*) were often landless in an agrarian society where land was usually distributed by inheritance and where access to land was essential to life. Without special attention, resident aliens would be marginal to most Israelite institutions — to extended families, as well as to legal, economic, political, and religious institutions. Their status was precarious and their well-being depended on the willingness of the community to welcome them into its life. Often powerless and vulnerable to injustice and exploitation, sojourners were frequently grouped with the poor, the widow, and the fatherless in the biblical text.[21]

Israel's neighbors in the Near East were also typically bound to provide hospitality to the strangers at their door. Occasional strangers were fed, sheltered, and protected, usually for brief periods of time. Such hospitality, given in an attitude of honor and respect, was recognized as a sacred duty throughout the ancient eastern world. What was distinctive to Israelite society was the explicit legislation regarding the protection of and provision for the resident alien. The parallel commands in Leviticus 19 to "love your neighbor as yourself" (v. 18) and to love the alien as yourself (v. 34) appear to have been unique to Israel.[22]

The covenantal structure of their faith framed Israelite responses to the alien. Just as God "executes justice for the fatherless and the widow, and loves the sojourner," so Israel was to act with justice that could not be bought and with love that welcomed and provided. As God's love for

---

20. See also Deut. 26:1-15.

21. See Deut. 24:14-22; 27:19; Job 31:13-32; Pss. 94:5-7; 146:9.

22. Hans Walther Wolff, *Anthropology of the Old Testament* (Philadelphia: Fortress, 1975), 188.

aliens provided them with food and clothing, so Israel was to express its love in practical, active ways. Specific laws required that Israel avoid mistreating and oppressing sojourners but instead actively seek their well-being.[23] The protected sojourner owed the God of Israel certain acknowledgment, and with increased loyalty to the God of Israel, the sojourner was increasingly included in the religious life of the society.[24]

In summary, the theological and moral foundations for Old Testament hospitality were tied closely to Israel's special relationship of dependence on and gratitude to God. Israel's obligation to care was nurtured by an emphasis on its own experience as an alien and by reflection on God's gracious character. The teachings of the Law, the warnings of punishment for disobedience, and the promise of blessing on obedience reinforced Israelite hospitality toward strangers,[25] as did the individual hospitality stories: guests might be angels, messengers from God, bringing divine promise or provision.

## Kingdom Hospitality:
## The New Community

New Testament discussions of hospitality continue and extend, but also transform basic Old Testament understandings. In Romans 15:7, Paul urges believers to "welcome one another" as Christ has welcomed them. Jesus' gracious and sacrificial hospitality — expressed in his life, ministry, and death — undergirds the hospitality of his followers. Jesus gave his life so that persons could be welcomed into the Kingdom and in doing so linked hospitality, grace, and sacrifice in the deepest and most personal way imaginable.

In the church, the household of God, hospitality is a fitting, requisite, and meaning-filled practice. Hospitality is important symbolically in its reflection and reenactment of God's hospitality and important practi-

23. Deut. 10:17-20; 24:14-15; Exod. 22:21-27.
24. See Deut. 29:10-14; Num. 9:14; 15:14-16; Exod. 12:43-49. The covenantal structure of Israelite life also required the exclusion of certain strangers — those who could threaten Israel's identity or unity. This will be discussed in Chapter 7: "The Fragility of Hospitality."
25. See Deut. 27:19; 14:28-29; 24:19.

cally in meeting human needs and in forging human relations. Though part of everyday life, hospitality is never far removed from its divine connections.

Especially in the context of shared meals, the presence of God's Kingdom is prefigured, revealed, and reflected. Jesus as gracious host feeds over five thousand people on a hillside, and later explains to the crowd that he is the bread of life, living bread for them from heaven. He offers living water to any who are thirsty (John 6–7). He is himself both host and meal — the very source of life.

In the Last Supper with his disciples, Jesus fills the basic elements of a meal with richest symbolic meaning — the bread is his body, the wine, his blood.[26] Eating together, ritualized in the Lord's Supper, continually reenacts the center of the gospel. As we remember the cost of our welcome, Christ's broken body and shed blood, we also celebrate the reconciliation and relationship available to us because of his sacrifice and through his hospitality. The Eucharist most fundamentally connects hospitality with God because it anticipates and reveals the "heavenly table of the Lord." In that sacrament, we are nourished on our journey towards God's banquet table, even as we experience the present joy and welcome associated with sharing in that table.[27] A shared meal is the activity most closely tied to the reality of God's Kingdom, just as it is the most basic expression of hospitality.

The theological importance of eating together helps explain why practitioners of hospitality so often report that they feel closest to God in times of shared meals. A sacred element infuses the shared meal of the Eucharist as well as ordinary communal meals. A practitioner explains, "Everyone wants to be at supper because if you miss that, you've missed everything. It is here that we recognize Jesus in the breaking of the bread."[28] A woman, recalling her childhood experience of revivals in the black church tradition, remembers the meal times as the most powerful and holy part of the week. In many communities of hospitality, meals and worship are regularly intertwined.

26. Matt. 26:26-29; Mark 14:22-25; Luke 22:19-20.
27. Eugene LaVerdiere, *Dining in the Kingdom of God* (Chicago: Liturgy Training Publications, 1994), viii, 9.
28. Sheila Durkin Dierks and Patricia Powers Ladley, *Catholic Worker Houses: Ordinary Miracles* (Kansas City, Mo.: Sheed & Ward, 1988), 56.

The story of Jesus' post-resurrection encounter with two disciples on the road to Emmaus reinforces the promise of Jesus' presence in shared meals (Luke 24:13-35). Jesus comes to them as a stranger (they do not recognize him), but they welcome him as a guest, and in breaking bread together, Jesus becomes their host. In this moment of table fellowship they recognize him as their risen Lord. Jesus is known to them in the breaking of the bread — an anticipation of the Eucharist and a foretaste of the final Kingdom banquet.

The epistles provide strong evidence for the practical importance of hospitality in early Christian life. Paul instructs believers to practice or pursue hospitality (Rom. 12:13), the writer of Hebrews reminds believers not to neglect hospitality (Heb. 13:2), the author of 1 Peter challenges the community to offer hospitality ungrudgingly (1 Pet. 4:9). Hospitality, in each of these passages, is a concrete expression of love — love for sisters and brothers, love extended outward to strangers, prisoners, and exiles, love that attends to physical and social needs. Within acts of hospitality, needs are met, but hospitality is truncated if it does not go beyond physical needs. Part of hospitality includes recognizing and valuing the stranger or guest.

Hospitality is not optional for Christians, nor is it limited to those who are specially gifted for it. It is, instead, a necessary practice in the community of faith. One of the key Greek words for hospitality, *philoxenia,* combines the general word for love or affection for people who are connected by kinship or faith *(phileo),* and the word for stranger *(xenos).* Thus, etymologically and practically, in the New Testament, hospitality is closely connected to love. Because *philoxenia* includes the word for stranger, hospitality's orientation toward strangers is also more apparent in Greek than in English.

In the New Testament texts, hospitality primarily refers to care for strangers, though often these strangers appear to have been other Christians in need of assistance. Care for them, however, did not diminish concern for needy persons in the larger community. In fact, it is not clear that hospitality to these two groups was distinguished at all. The believer's responsibility moved outward from fellow Christians to the world (Gal. 6:10; 1 Thess. 3:12).

Several aspects of early Christian life combined to make hospitality central to Christian practice. First, shared meals were a significant setting for struggling with cultural boundaries in the early church, especially in working through the incorporation of Gentiles into the early communities. At meals together, tensions surfaced between rich and poor believers; meals provided the context for instructions on equal recognition and respect. Hospitality practices in the Christian community were to portray a clear message — that of equality, transformed relations, and a common life.[29]

Second, the gospel initially spread through the ministry of believers who traveled widely and depended on the hospitality of others. Hospitality to those first missionaries and the reception of their message were very closely connected. From a hospitable household base in a city, the message spread.[30] Hospitality was the practice within which early Christians met the needs of traveling missionaries and leaders, religious exiles, and the local poor.

Third, the early church regularly met for worship in the households of believers. In such a location, hospitality was a natural and necessary practice. It helped to foster family-like ties among believers and provided a setting in which to shape and to reinforce a new identity.[31]

Important to the entire community of believers, hospitality was also a special mark of fitness for leadership within the household of God (1 Tim. 3:2; Titus 1:8). Traveling Christians and the local poor depended on hospitable church leaders to oversee the distribution of resources. The important role of Christian women in providing hospitality is clear from 1 Timothy 5:9-10, where offering hospitality is said to be evidence of a woman's life of good deeds.

As the first Christians brought the good news to the world and welcomed the stranger into their communities, they, like the ancient Israelites, also emphasized their own alien status. As members of God's household, Christians were to live as aliens in the world — aliens who practiced hospitality to strangers.[32] Alien status suggested a framework

29. See Acts 10–11; Gal. 2:11-14; 1 Cor. 11:17-34; James 2:1-13.

30. Acts 16:14-15, 29-34; 18:1-3, 11; 28:30. See Donald Wayne Riddle, "Early Christian Hospitality: A Factor in the Gospel Transmission," *Journal of Biblical Literature* 57 (1938): 141-54.

31. See Wayne A. Meeks, *The First Urban Christians* (New Haven: Yale University Press, 1983), 75-77, and Abraham J. Malherbe, "Hospitality and Inhospitality in the Church," in *Social Aspects of Early Christianity* (Philadelphia: Fortress, 1983), 96-101.

32. These images are condensed in 1 Peter. See John Elliott, *A Home for the Homeless* (Philadelphia: Fortress, 1981, 1990), 127, 145-48.

for transformed loyalties and relationships, and a distinctive life-style for citizens of heaven who were simultaneously residents on earth.

For the early church, then, hospitality both participated in and anticipated God's hospitality.[33] Christians offered hospitality in grateful response to God's generosity and as an expression of welcome to Christ "who for your sake was a stranger."[34] For them, hospitality was connected to the promises of God and to the presence of Christ. It condensed attention to spiritual, social, and physical dimensions of life into one potent practice which was fitting conduct within the household of God.

Hospitality to needy strangers distinguished the early church from its surrounding environment. Noted as exceptional by Christians and non-Christians alike, offering care to strangers became one of the distinguishing marks of the authenticity of the Christian gospel and of the church.[35] Writings from the first five centuries demonstrate the importance of hospitality in defining the church as a universal community, in denying the significance of the status boundaries and distinctions of the larger society, in recognizing the value of every person, and in providing practical care for the poor, stranger, and sick.

Our contemporary situation is surprisingly similar to the early Christian context in which the normative understandings and practices of hospitality were developed. We, like the early church, find ourselves in a fragmented and multicultural society that yearns for relationships, identity, and meaning. Our mobile and self-oriented society is characterized by disturbing levels of loneliness, alienation, and estrangement. In a culture that appears at times to be overtly hostile to life itself, those who reject violence and embrace life bear powerful witness.

People are hungry for welcome but most Christians have lost track of the heritage of hospitality. The riches of the first centuries have been obscured from view and from memory, and even today's practitioners of hospitality have only a limited sense of the larger story within which they

33. Rowan A. Greer, *Broken Lights and Mended Lives* (University Park: Pennsylvania State University Press, 1986), 140. See Greer's entire chapter on hospitality in the early church, 119-40.

34. Gregory Nazianzen, "Oration on Holy Baptism," NPNF2, vol. 7, p. 371.

35. See "1 Apology of Justin," ch. 14, p. 167 and ch. 67, p. 186, ANF, vol. 1. Also Aristedes, "Apology," ch. 15, ANF, vol. 9, p. 277. Also, Tertullian, "The Prescription Against Heretics," ch. 20, ANF, vol. 3, p. 252.

might locate their ministry. Without romanticizing the tradition, we can affirm that there are biblical and historical resources from which to draw that will help us live more fully and more faithfully.

Reconnecting with the ancient tradition of Christian hospitality is enriching for both Protestants and Catholics because it takes us back to our shared history. As contemporary practitioners draw on these early sources, they enrich the conversations across traditions and provide one another with additional insights into this important practice. In several communities of hospitality, this is resulting in a very rich spirituality that transcends some traditional denominational practices and theological divisions.

Living in and with the biblical stories while practicing hospitality brings texts alive in remarkable ways. One seminary-educated practitioner observed that while he had struggled with the complexity of certain passages for years, "the scriptures make more sense" as hospitality is lived out. The texts take on intensely personal meaning when they are embodied in a community's life.

As the biblical texts on hospitality are lived out, and as the Scriptures illumine and interpret present practices, Christians find their lives infused with the presence of Christ. "Hospitality becomes for the Christian community a way of being the sacrament of God's love in the world,"[36] a role which certainly fits the image in Romans 12 of hospitality as an expression of our lives offered up as "living sacrifices." While we might imagine sacrifice in terms of one moment of heroic martyrdom, faithful hospitality usually involves laying our lives down in little pieces, in small acts of sacrificial love and service. Part of the mystery is that while such concrete acts of love are costly, they nourish and heal both giver and recipient.

After the first centuries, several historical factors helped to undermine the dynamic and transformative understandings and practices of ancient Christian hospitality. In the Middle Ages, grand hospitality became an important means for extending power and influence in the church, monastery, and lay society. Hospitality was often deliberately connected to the host's ambition and advantage. Partly in reaction, Protestant reformers emphasized offering modest hospitality without ex-

36. David Kirk, "Hospitality: Essence of Eastern Christian Lifestyle," *Diakonia* 16/2 (1981): 112.

pectation of reward or benefit. While recovering some of the ancient understandings of hospitality, however, early Protestant writers tended to de-emphasize its sacred elements, especially the expectation of God's special presence and blessing, which was so much a part of the early Christian understanding of hospitality. With major socioeconomic changes, hospitality became less effective as a primary means for caring for the poor and strangers. Later, hospitality became highly commercialized as travelers increasingly depended on inns to meet their needs for shelter and food. Hospitality to the needy became bureaucratized in social services provided by benevolence organizations and the state. And in the churches, hospitality had little moral, spiritual, and physical significance.

Critics within Christianity, however, continued to turn to ancient church understandings and practices to challenge contemporary excesses and neglect of hospitality. The Christian tradition never rejected the focus of hospitality forged in the early centuries. Hospitality to the least, without expectation of benefit or repayment, remained the normative commitment by which each generation measured its practice — until, that is, the term itself became emptied of moral meaning in the last several centuries.

# 3. A SHORT HISTORY OF
## CHRISTIAN HOSPITALITY

*"In a commercial country, a busy country,
time becomes precious, and . . . hospitality
is not so much valued."*

SAMUEL JOHNSON
(18TH CENTURY)

FOR MANY PARTS OF THE WESTERN CHURCH, HOSPITAL-
ity got lost in the eighteenth century. People were having trouble finding it
for several centuries before then, but it disappeared as a significant moral
practice in the 1700s. Strangers were still cared for, but responses to their
needs were less frequently called hospitality. People worried about equality
and respect but they did not discuss those concerns in the language of hospitality. Churches provided for orphans and widows but rarely regarded
hospitality as a category of ministry. Over the past few centuries, the scope
of hospitality as a term has diminished; it now chiefly refers to the entertainment of one's acquaintances at home and to the hospitality industry's
provision of service through hotels and restaurants.

Surprisingly, as early as the mid-sixteenth century, John Calvin
mourned the demise of ancient hospitality. "This office of humanity has
. . . nearly ceased to be properly observed among men; for the ancient hospitality celebrated in histories, is unknown to us, and inns now supply the
place of accommodations for strangers."[1] He warned that the increasing

---

1. John Calvin, *Commentaries on the Epistle of Paul the Apostle to the Hebrews*
(Grand Rapids: Wm. B. Eerdmans, 1948), 340.

dependence on inns rather than on personal hospitality was an expression of human depravity.

In early seventeenth-century England, social critics also mourned the loss of hospitality. The authors of a pamphlet entitled "Greevous Grones for the Poore" protested that no hospitality was being provided even as the numbers of poor people were increasing. They wrote, "And how may I complaine . . . of the decay of Hospitality in our Land, whereby many poore soules are deprived of that reliefe which they have had heeretofore. The time hath bene, that men have hunted after Worshippe and Credite by good House-keeping and therein spent great part of their Revenuewes."[2] Times had changed: hospitality was no longer a primary route to honor and credit for the wealthy; nor was it a satisfactory response to the needs of poor people.

Later in the same century, John Owen, a Puritan theologian and pastor, commented on the significant changes in the meaning of hospitality. He wrote that in "the younger days of the world," hospitality was offered to needy strangers, "but with us it is applied unto a bountiful, and it may be, profuse entertainment of friends, relations, neighbours, acquaintances, and the like."[3]

Samuel Johnson, the eighteenth-century English writer, expressed the changes in both the perceptions and practices of hospitality most clearly, explicitly connecting them with his society's new social and economic conditions. In answer to James Boswell's question about "how far he thought wealth should be employed in hospitality," Johnson responded:

> You are to consider that ancient hospitality, of which we hear so much, was in an uncommercial country, when men being idle, were glad to be entertained at rich men's tables. But in a commercial country, a busy country, time becomes precious, and therefore hospitality is not so much valued. No doubt there is still room for a certain degree of it; and a man has a satisfaction in seeing his friends eating and drinking

2. "Greevous Grones for the Poore," attributed to Thomas Dekker and to Michael Sparke (London, 1621; Ann Arbor, Mich.: University Microfilms), 14.

3. John Owen, *The Works of John Owen,* ed. William H. Goold and Charles W. Quick (Philadelphia: Leighton Publications, 1869), "An Exposition of the Epistle to the Hebrews," vol. 7, pp. 386-87.

around him. But promiscuous hospitality is not the way to gain real influence. You must help some people at table before others; you must
ask some people how they like their wine oftener than others. You
therefore offend more people than you please. . . . Besides, Sir, being
entertained ever so well at a man's table, impresses no lasting regard or
esteem.[4]

For Johnson, all that remained of a historically rich moral concept and
practice was its dubious usefulness in garnering power and influence. Antiquated in its deference to rank, and out of step with busy commercial
life, hospitality was reduced to the satisfaction of sharing food and drink
with friends. The traditional practice of hospitality had come to seem
awkward in a somewhat more egalitarian world.

John Wesley, Johnson's contemporary, must have shared in this general assessment. Wesley rarely employed the term even though he frequently worked with the biblical and patristic texts central to all prior discussions of hospitality. Wesley recovered many of the practices of early
Christian hospitality, recognized their connection with the vitality of the
ancient church, but did not call them "hospitality." In one of his few references to hospitality, Wesley identified it with self-indulgence, luxury, and
neglect of the poor. He wrote in his sermon on "Dives and Lazarus":

I know how plausibly the prophets of smooth things can talk in favour
of hospitality, of making our friends welcome, of keeping an handsome
table, to do honour to religion, of promoting trade and the like. But
God is not mocked: he will not be put off with such pretenses as these.[5]

By the eighteenth century, the term "hospitality" had been emptied
of its central moral meaning and left only with its late-medieval trappings
of luxury and indulgence. With the major economic and social changes of
the period, the practice of hospitality was a less adequate means of responding to the needs of the poor and strangers. Hospitality seemed to be
dying along with the old social order, that of the great household with its

4. James Boswell, *The Life of Samuel Johnson, L.L.D.* (New York: The Modern
Library, 1931), 408. A portion of this quotation appears in Christopher Hill, *Society and
Puritanism in Pre-Revolutionary England* (New York: Schocken Books, 1964), 273.
5. Wesley, *Works of John Wesley*, vol. 4: *Sermons 4:115-151* (Nashville: Abingdon,
1987), Sermon 115: "Dives and Lazarus," p. 12.

many dependents and complicated interdependencies. The new day celebrated industry, manufacturing, and independence.[6]

As a result of these socioeconomic changes, and also changes in polity, church, and cultural values, hospitality faded as a significant and coherent moral practice. Hospitality did not entirely disappear, but the practices became more hidden as they were diffused over multiple specialized institutions. They were, for the most part, detached from both the language of Christian hospitality and its sources. The eclipse of hospitality was almost complete, and later generations of Christians were left with little sense of the theological and practical richness of the hospitality tradition.

## The Locations of Hospitality:
## A Key to Its History

The location of hospitality has always strongly influenced its meaning and practices. Changes in the household, church, economy, and political life have had a major impact on the practice of hospitality, but hospitality and its commitments have also helped to shape those institutions. By taking a closer look at the settings in which hospitality flourished, and at the social arrangements during which hospitality nearly disappeared, we can gain a better idea of what might be necessary for the recovery of hospitality in our time.

By definition, hospitality involves some space into which people are welcomed, a place where unless the invitation is given, the stranger would not feel free to enter. When we think about locations of hospitality, we usually think first of the home. Hospitality has always been most closely tied to the home or household, though never exclusively. For Christians, the other site most commonly associated with hospitality is the church and the institutions which have derived from the church, such as monasteries, hospitals, and hospices. In addition to these primary locations, certain aspects of hospitality to strangers have also been located in the economic and political spheres.

6. See Hill, *Society and Puritanism,* 273.

## The Old Testament Settings

In Old Testament stories about Abraham, Lot, and the angels, Rahab and the spies, Abigail and David, the widow of Zarephath and Elijah, and the Shunammite woman and Elisha, the practice of hospitality occurred within the household.[7] Strangers were welcomed into family settings, individual households within which they could usually expect several days of attention and care. The households themselves were often quite large — involving extended family and servants.

In ancient societies, families generally conducted their economic activity from within the household. Though personal space, households were more open and less private than are contemporary homes. In addition, there were more public or community spaces in which the stranger could first be encountered. Several of the stories begin with an initial encounter at the town gate where people gathered and discussed community business. In this setting, neighbors knew when a stranger came into a particular household.

Guests in these stories were not usually destitute, though they were often in temporary need. Hospitality toward them was generally understood to be a limited, short-term arrangement, the responsibility of the particular family with whom they stayed. But there were other kinds of strangers in Israel, those with limited or no resources and connections. The minimal well-being of these people — sojourners and aliens who resided in Israel — became the responsibility of the larger community.

Old Testament laws, addressed to the entire community, established structural supports to protect aliens from impoverishment and abuse. Minimal economic provision was available through access to privately owned fields for gleaning. As the land was harvested, crops on the borders and what remained after the harvest were to be available to the poor and the sojourner. Tithes of grain were to be set aside for the poor and the aliens living in towns. Judges were instructed to deal impartially in cases that involved conflict between aliens and Israelites. Sabbath rest included sojourners. Employers were forbidden from exploiting alien workers.[8]

---

7. Gen. 18-19; Josh. 2; 1 Sam. 25; 1 Kings 17:8-24; 2 Kings 4:8-37.

8. For gleaning and triennial tithe, see Lev. 19:9-10; 23:22; Deut. 14:28-29; 24:19-22; 26:12. For judging impartially, see Deut. 1:16-17; 24:17. For Sabbath rest, see

Extended economic provision and protection did not depend on the charity of individual families alone, but neither did these structural provisions eliminate the personal dimension of hospitality. Societal and personal responsibility for strangers were interconnected. Faithful Israelites included aliens and the poor in their family celebrations and religious events.[9] Structured, legislated forms of care for sojourners reflected and regularized personal expressions of hospitality without eliminating them. Welcoming strangers was spontaneous and personal as well as institutionalized and corporate.

The Old Testament legacy of hospitality is instructive for us. First, the household into which a stranger was welcomed was the center of both social and family activity. Second, even in the earliest part of the tradition, care for strangers went beyond the household. It involved community responsibility and provision, and depended on legislation as well as on generous individual responses. There was never an assumption that individual households alone could care for large numbers of needy strangers. Third, strangers were often first encountered in a more public space. Such a setting allowed a preliminary interaction that reduced some of their "strangeness" before they entered a household. It also provided the larger community with an opportunity to encounter the stranger.

## The New Testament and Early Church Settings

Households remain the most important location for hospitality in the New Testament period. Fellowship and growth in the earliest churches depended on household-based hospitality among believers.[10] For Greeks and Jews, the household (Greek: *oikos;* Hebrew: *bayith*) was very important and served as a basis for social, political, and religious identity and cohesion. For the early Christians, rooted in both Hebrew and Greek traditions, the church as the household of God was a powerful theological

---

Exod. 20:10; 23:12; Deut. 5:14-15. For nonexploitation of alien workers, see Deut. 24:14-15. See also Exod. 22:21; 23:9.

9. Deut. 26:1-15.

10. See, for example, Acts 2:43-47; 9:42–10:48; 16:14-15; 18:1-11.

and social reality.[11] The church was made up of family households, but it was more than a sum of those individual households. The church was a new household, God's household, and believers became family to one another.

Early Christian hospitality was offered from within this overlap of household and church. A homelike setting provided a natural environment for expressing personal qualities of hospitality. The church as a gathered community required the most immediate connection to God's character and expectations — behaviors suitable to the household of God.

This expanded and transformed household was responsible for imitating God's hospitable and gracious character. God's household represented the welcome of Gentiles into the inheritance together with Israel (Eph. 2:19), and relations within this new household explicitly transcended ethnic boundaries. Worship, care, and hospitality in early Christian households included believers from different political, ethnic, and socioeconomic backgrounds, and early congregations developed a translocal and transethnic identity.

Local Christian communities shared meals together as part of their regular church practice — an important location for hospitality. These agape meals provided a setting for a communal response to the needs of the poor for food while simultaneously reinforcing a distinct Christian identity.[12] They were distinguished from the contemporary practice of offering elaborate banquets that reinforced status boundaries. Although ethnic and socioeconomic differences sometimes surfaced in the context of eating together, these meals were intended to reflect transformed relationships in which worldly status distinctions were transcended, if not disregarded, and formerly alienated persons could view themselves as brothers and sisters at God's table.

For the early Christians, the reconstituted household provided the setting for the three dimensions of hospitality noted in the previous chap-

11. See John Elliott, *A Home for the Homeless* (Philadelphia: Fortress, 1981, 1990), 182, 188, 221. See also discussion in Wayne A. Meeks, *The First Urban Christians* (New Haven: Yale University Press, 1983), 75-76.

12. See Igino Giordani, *The Social Message of the Early Church Fathers* (Paterson, N.J.: St. Anthony Guild Press, 1944), 205, 325; and John Bell Matthews, "Hospitality and the New Testament Church: An Historical and Exegetical Study," Th.D. dissertation (Princeton Theological Seminary, 1965), 285.

ter: hospitality as an expression of respect and recognition — in welcoming persons of different status and background into a single place and often a shared meal; hospitality as a means of meeting the physical needs of strangers, traveling Christians, and the local poor; and hospitality as the hosting of local assemblies of believers. These were overlapping and interrelated practices, all located within the household.

In these first centuries, the church was distinct from the larger political system and often at odds with it. Tension with political authorities shaped some of the distinct characteristics of early Christian hospitality. Believers were often a persecuted minority and the practice of hospitality was important in sustaining identity and in providing care. Even ministry to prisoners was understood as an aspect and an extension of hospitality.[13]

## Fourth- and Fifth-Century Settings

During the fourth century the locations of Christian hospitality expanded in several different directions. In addition to hospitality provided by church and family households, hostels provided care for strangers, hospitals were established for the sick, the poor, and strangers, and monasteries welcomed pilgrims. Great changes in this period were associated with the transition of the church from a persecuted sect to the religion of the empire. Although some development of institutions of care had begun slightly earlier, the major innovations occurred in the fourth century.

When the emperor Constantine gave his support to the Christian faith in the early fourth century, substantial public resources as well as substantial responsibilities flowed to the church. Hospitality as care for the needy came to be viewed as "public service," and by the middle of the fourth century outsiders recognized Christian institutions of care as exemplary. A significant testimony to the importance of charity and hospitality, both within and beyond the Christian community, came from a hostile source — the Emperor Julian (A.D. 362). In his attempt to reestablish Hellenic religion in the empire, Julian instructed the high priest of the Hellenic faith to imitate Christian concern for strangers. Referring to

13. See William L. Lane, "Unexpected Light on Hebrews 13:1-6 from a Second Century Source," *Perspectives in Religious Studies* 9/3 (Fall 1982): 267-74.

Christianity as "atheism," he asked, "Why do we not observe that it is
their benevolence to strangers, their care for the graves of the dead and the
pretended holiness of their lives that have done most to increase atheism?" He therefore instructed the priest to establish hostels for needy
strangers in every city and also ordered a distribution of corn and wine to
the poor, strangers, and beggars.

> For it is disgraceful that, when no Jew ever has to beg, and the impious
> Galilaeans [Christians] support not only their own poor but ours as
> well, all men see that our people lack aid from us. Teach those of the
> Hellenic faith to contribute to public service of this sort.[14]

Julian, in his attempt to withdraw the royal patronage given to the church
by Constantine, attested to the significance of Christian institutions of
care for the society as a whole.[15]

Christians established many hospitals *(xenodochia)* in the fourth
century to care for strangers, but particularly for poor strangers who had
no other resources, and for the local poor. Gradually these hospitals were
differentiated into separate institutions according to the type of person in
need: orphans, widows, strangers, sick, and poor. Often, however, they
served various functions.[16]

The first hospital to receive substantial attention in the literature of
the time was that founded by Basil, bishop of Caesarea, in approximately
370. In response to the enormous suffering caused by a severe famine, Basil gathered the victims of famine and what food he was able to collect,
and supplied the poor and sick with prepared food and physical care,
"combining personal respect with the supply of their necessity, and so giving them a double relief."[17] Shortly thereafter, Basil established a variety
of institutions to provide care for the sick, for travelers, and for the poor.[18]
In a eulogy for Basil, the hospital was described as a "storehouse of piety"

14. *The Works of the Emperor Julian,* LCL, vol. 3, pp. 67-71.
15. See Rowan A. Greer, *Broken Lights and Mended Lives* (University Park: Pennsylvania State University Press, 1986), 132, for further discussion.
16. Gerhard Uhlhorn, *Christian Charity in the Ancient Church,* trans. Sophia Taylor (Edinburgh: T. & T. Clark, 1883), 323-29.
17. Gregory Nazianzen, *Panegyric on St. Basil,* NPNF2, vol. 7, p. 407.
18. See George W. Forell, *History of Christian Ethics,* vol. 1 (Minneapolis:
Augsburg, 1979), 125-26.

and the finest wonder of the world, a place where those decimated by disease could have a city of their own, no longer objects of hatred and exclusion because of their illness.[19]

The enthusiasm of Basil and others for the hospital as an institution of Christian care reflects how closely it was originally connected to the practice of hospitality. It also suggests how little the fourth-century leaders could anticipate the ambiguous long-term consequences of these more anonymous and separated settings for hospitality.

The increasing dependence on differentiated and specialized institutions of care was a response to the increasing scale of need, to the increasing availability of resources given to the church, and to the church's related responsibility to the larger population. Although the development of hospices and hospitals emerged from early Christian impulses toward hospitality, these institutions were unable to capture and express some of the most fundamental, personal dimensions of hospitality. Poor people and strangers were frequently cared for at a distance and in large numbers. Personal hospitality was increasingly reserved for visiting dignitaries.

In the writings of John Chrysostom, from the fourth and early fifth centuries, we can identify multiple settings for hospitality as well as the tensions that emerged out of such diversity. Chrysostom's parishioners seem to have excused themselves from the demands of hospitality by noting that the church had the means to provide hospitality to strangers. He insisted, however, that hospitality remained a personal, individual responsibility as well. Even if the needy person could be fed from common funds, Chrysostom asked, "Can that benefit you? If another man prays, does it follow that you are not bound to pray?" He urged his parishioners to make a guest chamber in their own houses, a place set apart for Christ — a place within which to welcome "the maimed, the beggars, and the homeless." Recognizing that some Christians would hesitate to take strangers into their homes or guest rooms, Chrysostom suggested that they could at least make a place in their household for a local poor person who was known to them.[20]

19. Gregory Nazianzen, *Panegyric on St. Basil,* 416.
20. Chrysostom, Homily 45 on Acts, NPNF1, vol. 11, p. 277. See also Greer's discussion in *Broken Lights,* 129-30.

It was very important to him that hospitality be offered personally, with one's own hands, not left exclusively for the church to provide.[21] This emphasis seems to have emerged from several concerns. Hospitality was an essential part of Christian identity. Welcome, compassion, and equal treatment were all part of a proper Christian response to people in need. Personal hospitality broke down some of the social barriers that were so powerful in the culture. Chrysostom's emphasis also derived from a need to counteract the increasing reliance on the newly formed specialized institutions of hospitality.

Chrysostom himself had an important role in developing these differentiated institutions of care. In Homily 66 on Matthew, he described the work of the church at Antioch. Though not wealthy, the church cared for three thousand widows and virgins daily, and, in addition, cared for those in prison, sick, and disabled, and those away from their homes. The church also provided food and clothing to those who came "casually" everyday.[22] From 400 to 403, Chrysostom built a number of hospitals in Constantinople. These provided care for strangers and orphans, as well as for those who were sick, chronic invalids, old, poor, and destitute.[23]

Also within the fourth century, monasticism took root as an essential expression of the Christian life. From the beginning, hospitality was an integral part of monastic identity and practice. Major figures in early monasticism (e.g., Basil, Chrysostom, Jerome) founded many of the specialized institutions for offering hospitality, so that monasticism, hospices, and hospitals were closely related in their origins. Pilgrimages of pious Christians to monasteries to learn about the ascetic Christian life brought to the monks an increasingly large responsibility to provide food, shelter, and welcome.

Benedict of Nursia (ca. 480–ca. 550), the father of western monasticism, developed a rule for monastic life that gave a central place to hospitality to strangers while protecting other disciplines of the monastery from disturbance. The *Rule of Benedict* required that monks graciously receive clerics, pilgrims, and the poor because of Christ's identification

---

21. Chrysostom, Homily 14 on 1 Timothy, NPNF1, vol. 13, p. 455.

22. Chrysostom, Homily 66 on Matthew, NPNF1, vol. 10, p. 407.

23. *Encyclopedia of Religion and Ethics,* ed. James Hastings (New York: Scribner's, 1913), s.v. "Hospitality: Christian," by G. Bonet-Maury, vol. 6, p. 805.

with the stranger in Matthew 25:35. Hospitality in the monastery was personal and face-to-face, though surrounded by ritual and carefully circumscribed interaction.[24]

The distinctive character of Christian hospitality was most clearly articulated in the fourth century. During this time Jerome, Lactantius, and Chrysostom, among others, defined Christian hospitality as welcoming the "least" with no concern for advantage or ambition. There are, however, some ironies implicit in their strong statements about the distinctive character of Christian hospitality. The distinctives were defined as the church was increasing in wealth, power, and influence. The fourth century was in fact the first time in which Christian hospitality could be used to advantage in the larger society. The relation of the church and individual Christians to sociopolitical institutions was changing, and with it, the significance of hospitality. No longer at odds, the church and political authorities became intertwined and dependent on one another. Hospitality reinforced these relationships.

Another historical irony is noteworthy. As institutions were becoming more differentiated, leaders emphasized the importance of a gracious welcome to persons of different socioeconomic status. One of the key assumptions in many of the normative statements is that there was a single table, in the household, church, or monastery, at which to welcome persons from different backgrounds. However, with the differentiation of care that had already begun, but was to accelerate over the next centuries, there was no longer a single institutional context in which the face-to-face, personal relations of early Christian hospitality would occur among persons from substantially different classes. This was especially the case as the church itself faded as a significant site for hospitality. While developments in differentiated and specialized institutions of hospitality — hospices, hostels, and hospitals — were vitally important to human care, they also made it harder to preserve the very distinctives of hospitality that were most valued.

24. See *The Rule of Benedict,* chap. 53 in *Western Asceticism,* The Library of Christian Classics, vol. 12 (Philadelphia: Westminster Press, 1958).

### *Medieval Settings*

In the Middle Ages (ca. 500–ca. 1500), three institutional settings were important for the practice of hospitality: monasteries and their hospices for pilgrims; hospitals; and the great ecclesial and lay households. Needy pilgrims and the local poor looked to the monasteries for hospitality and relief. When their numbers were large, care was often distant and relatively anonymous (e.g., alms distributed at the monastery gate). Hospitality for travelers, pilgrims, and visitors of higher social status was more personal and grand. Wealthy monastic houses provided important guests with fine quarters and lavish fare, offering a standard of entertainment that was widely regarded. Hospitality to the wealthy and the powerful reinforced important social and political bonds between the monastic authorities and the aristocratic powers. Thus, monastic hospitality in the Middle Ages generally reinforced social boundaries, a clear departure from the vision of the early writers.

Hospitals as institutions of public service increased in importance during the Middle Ages. Care was more impersonal, but also more predictable, and increasingly separate from the church. By the fourteenth and fifteenth centuries, many hospitals in European cities had come under municipal control, a change which further distanced the hospital from its origins in Christian hospitality.[25]

A more distanced and differentiated type of care did not necessarily emerge from a lack of piety or a deliberate distancing from those in need; however, such approaches to care had a variety of unintended consequences. Personal hospitality, while meeting physical needs, had also provided people with the human connections that gave them a place in the world. Specialized institutions with paid staff, by contrast, cared for patients/recipients but extracted them from normal routines and connections, sometimes with devastating results.

Great households belonging to bishops and lay aristocrats (as well as those of the monasteries already noted) were central to the practice of hospitality in the Middle Ages. All were responsible for providing hospitality; but welcome was often fashioned according to the status of the

25. *The Catholic Encyclopedia,* vol. 7 (New York: The Gilmary Society, 1910), s.v. "Hospitals," by James J. Walsh, pp. 481-83, and *Encyclopedia of Religion and Ethics,* s.v. "Hospitality: Christian," p. 805.

guest. While hospitality provided a crucial form of general welfare, it explicitly reinforced existing patterns of wealth and power.

Bishops had a primary role in administering hospitality and poor relief. Although all Christians were responsible for hospitality, the bishop's special role is reflected in comments by Isidore of Seville in the early seventh century: "A layman has fulfilled the duty of hospitality by receiving one or two [guests]; a bishop, however, unless he shall receive everyone . . . is inhuman."[26] The *Decretum,* compiled by Gratian in the twelfth century and providing the basis for much of canon law, stated that "hospitality is so necessary in bishops that if any are found lacking in it the law forbids them to be ordained."[27]

Brian Tierney, in his work on the medieval poor laws, notes the very close connection between clerical hospitality and the relief of the poor:

> The word "hospitality" is of some importance because the phrase most commonly used by the medieval canonists to describe the poor relief responsibilities of the parish clergy was *tenere hospitalitatem* — they were obliged, that is, to "keep hospitality." The primary sense of the word referred to the reception of travelers, the welcoming of guests, but the canonists very often used it in a broader sense to include almsgiving and poor relief in general.[28]

Although the medieval church was a substantial property holder, its resources varied at the local level and some clergy had very minimal resources out of which to offer hospitality. Parishioners were expected, but not forced, to pay tithes to the church (out of which some funds for hospitality and relief were taken), and above that to contribute to poor relief.[29] Clergy were required to provide hospitality, but the record of their work was mixed, and during the later Middle Ages there were many protests against the "diminu-

---

26. *Patrologia Latina* 83.786, quoted in Sherman W. Gray, *The Least of My Brothers: Matthew 25:31-46: A History of Interpretation* (Atlanta: Scholars Press, 1989), 120.

27. *Decretum Gratiani. Distinctio* 82 *ante* c.I, *Dist.* 87 *ante* c.I, *Dist.* 84 *ante* c.I, *Dist.* 85 *ante* c.I, quoted in Brian Tierney, *Medieval Poor Law: A Sketch of Canonical Theory and Its Application in England* (Berkeley: University of California Press, 1959), 68.

28. Tierney, *Medieval Poor Law,* 68.

29. Ibid., 93, 97, 126. On pages 98-101, Tierney gives examples of exhortations to provide adequate hospitality and relief, and examples of concern that pastoral care include feeding the hungry and receiving guests.

tion of hospitality." Complaints about absentee priests, misappropriation of funds, and inadequately endowed vicarages suggest that the administration of poor relief was uneven.[30] Hospitality to the poor was at times limited to and equated with indiscriminate almsgiving.

As a result of social and economic changes in this period, vagabondage in the countryside increased tremendously, and from the mid-fourteenth century forward, in the minds of the authorities, "the problem of relieving poverty became inextricably intertwined with the problem of suppressing vagrancy." The large number of vagabonds or "masterless men" made "keeping hospitality" much more complex.[31]

In the late Middle Ages, among the great ecclesiastical and lay households, hospitality was explicitly and intentionally connected to power, influence, and grand displays of wealth and status. To retain authority and influence, the great householder had "to show himself the source of all good things for his dependents, and to equal, or preferably surpass, the magnificence of his allies and enemies."[32] Despite the enormous expense of entertaining visiting dignitaries, it was an essential demonstration of one's status; to abandon entertaining, to lose the capacity to offer hospitality, or to be forced to depend on the hospitality of other great households, was clear evidence of a person's waning power and influence.[33] Without much moveable wealth (a money economy as such did not yet exist), the nobility consumed its excess on its estates in the form of strategic hospitality. This forged and reinforced the complex bonds of interdependence between lord and vassal, church and nobility, which were characteristic of feudal life.

In early fifteenth-century England, households of bishops, as well as those of lay aristocrats, were concerned with displays of power often evidenced through the size and the magnificence of their entertainment. Such hospitality involved an "elaborate deference to rank and power."[34]

---

30. Ibid., 71-72, 107.

31. Ibid., 111-14.

32. Bridget Ann Henisch, *Fast and Feast: Food in Medieval Society* (University Park: Pennsylvania State University Press, 1976), 11.

33. Ibid., 12.

34. Felicity Heal, "The Archbishops of Canterbury and the Practice of Hospitality," *Journal of Ecclesiastical History* 33 (Oct. 1982): 551. Heal's work is exceptionally helpful on English hospitality. See also: "The Idea of Hospitality in Early Modern England," *Past and Present* 102 (Feb. 1984): 66-93.

Grand hospitality was "perceived as a means of securing good neighborliness, of ensuring communal stability and promoting the general well-being of the commonwealth."[35] When all were welcomed, those of lower status were received at a different table, fed different and coarser food, and housed in different lodgings. Distinctions in bread, table linens, and seating arrangements were intended to reflect status differences.[36] Except for hospitality to household servants and their dependents, most provision for the poor was done at the gate, not within the house.

By the end of the Middle Ages, two trajectories of hospitality — hospitality as material care for strangers and the local poor and hospitality as personal welcome and entertainment — had developed along largely separate tracks. In the diversity of institutions, in the loss of the worshiping community as a significant site for hospitality, and in the differentiation of care among recipients, the socially transformative potential of hospitality was lost.

## Reformation and Early Modern Settings

During the sixteenth century, discussions of hospitality continued in the midst of great social dislocations and significant economic and political changes. Many of the great households — monastic, clerical, and lay — were under siege; the feudal and manorial systems were crumbling. Problems of vagabondage peaked. Mobility, urbanization, plague, war, and increased trade contributed to the breakdown of rural communities and to the growing group of "masterless men" — persons severed from any sustaining social network. Traditional practices of hospitality were increasingly ineffective in addressing the needs of vagabonds and the local poor.

35. Heal, "The Archbishops," 547.
36. Henisch, *Fast and Feast,* 12, 157-59, 194. Also, "John Russell's Book of Nurture" (ca. 1460) gives fascinating insight into the complexities of serving dinner to clergy and nobility of different ranks. It includes explanations of how ushers and marshals were to seat strangers, clergy, and men and women of high rank but no wealth, and those in reverse circumstances. See "John Russell's Book of Nurture" and "The Book of Courtesy" in *The Babees' Book: Medieval Manners for the Young Done into Modern English from Dr. Furnivall's Texts,* ed. Edith Rickert (New York: Coopers Square Publishers, 1966), esp. 70-73.

Sixteenth-century Protestant reformers redefined the practice of hospitality. They offered unrelenting critiques of the extravagance, indulgence, and waste associated with late medieval hospitality. Rejecting both elaborate welcome to the rich and indiscriminate aid to the poor, they called for a return to biblical and patristic understandings of hospitality which had focused on care for poor persons and needy exiles. They emphasized frugality, discernment, and orderliness in the practice of hospitality — a reflection of the significant connection between the rise of the middle class and the impact of the Reformation.

Because of the large numbers of Protestant refugees fleeing persecution during the sixteenth century, there was a significant resurgence of the moral credibility and practical relevance of hospitality to needy strangers. Welcoming these persons, Calvin asserted, was the most "sacred" kind of hospitality. He commended the civic leaders of Geneva and Frankfurt for their hospitality in opening up their cities to refugees.[37] Hospitality was an important practice for the early Protestants as they attempted both to survive and to prevail in the religious and political upheavals of that time. It was also significant in the early Anabaptist experience as believers sought refuge from persecution and cared for families of martyrs.[38]

In their studies of Scripture, Luther and Calvin gave limited but explicit attention to hospitality and to how it should be practiced in their own day. For both of them, the primary practitioners of hospitality were civic leaders and godly Christian families. With the Reformation, there was a new appreciation for the value of ordinary life, and Luther and Calvin provided theological support for the importance of faithful labor in the world.

They did not recover from the ancient sources an appreciation for the church as an important location for hospitality; instead, they identified hospitality with the civic and the domestic spheres. Luther viewed

---

37. Calvin, *Commentary on the Gospel According to John,* vol. 1 (Grand Rapids: Wm. B. Eerdmans, 1949), 15-16, and *Commentary on the Harmony of the Evangelists, Matthew, Mark, and Luke* (Grand Rapids: Wm. B. Eerdmans, 1949), 1:xxix-xxx.

38. Anabaptist writers generally subsume hospitality under the category of mutual aid. See, for example, Jeni Hiett Umble, "Mutual Aid Among the Augsburg Anabaptists, 1526-1528," in *Building Communities of Compassion: Mennonite Mutual Aid in Theory and Practice,* ed. Willard M. Swartley and Donald B. Kraybill (Scottdale, Pa.: Herald Press, 1998).

these spheres as essential to the way God ordered society; and hospitality within the home and civic context, though important, was emptied of its potential leveling or socially transformative impact. Hosts were firmly established in their household space, and hospitality, though helpful, did not challenge social roles or relations. Godly hosts offered hospitality as an act of obedience, a practical response to human need. They did not expect reward or special encounters with God as they welcomed strangers. The sacramental character of hospitality was diminished and it became mostly an ordinary but valued expression of human care.

Although the reformers acknowledged that hospitality was a "sacred" act,[39] they allowed no sacred space for it. In emphasizing the value of ordinary life, they simultaneously undermined some of the mystery that had undergirded the potent earlier understandings of Christian hospitality. Only the church of the first several centuries had been able to sustain transformed social relations by keeping the practice of hospitality tied to the church where all members recognized their own guest status.

The long-term consequences of identifying hospitality with the civic and domestic spheres were significant. The public and civic dimensions of hospitality — from hospitals, poor relief, and responsibility to refugees, to later concerns about human rights and equality — became detached from their Christian roots as the public sphere was increasingly secularized. At the same time, the domestic sphere became more privatized; households became smaller, more intimate, and less able or willing to receive strangers. With little attention to the church as a key site for hospitality, the institutional settings for Christian hospitality diminished and the understanding of hospitality as a significant dimension of church practice nearly disappeared. As Protestant denominations increased, their diversity and their voluntary character meant that there was no institutional setting in which Protestants were pressed to welcome persons who were significantly different from themselves.

John Wesley and the eighteenth-century English Methodists have a significant but ambiguous role in the history of Christian hospitality. At a time when community ties were weakening, Methodist small group meetings offered regular opportunities for intense personal interaction,

---

39. Calvin wrote that hospitality was a "sacred kind of humanity," in *Commentaries on the Catholic Epistles* (Grand Rapids: Wm. B. Eerdmans, 1948), 130.

relationship building, and oversight of new believers. Many of these meetings took place in the modest homes of Methodist believers, thus reintegrating church and household. These structures were essential to Wesley's ministry and provided the organizational context for spiritual growth, care for the sick and wayward, and collections for those in need.

To accomplish social and spiritual transformation, Wesley deliberately employed early church and patristic institutional models. He viewed close community as "the very thing which was from the beginning of Christianity."[40] He recovered the practice of shared meals when he instituted love feasts ("so we termed them, retaining the name, as well as the thing, which was in use from the beginning"). The food was simple; the love feasts and other regular meetings provided a context which allowed a close union of the believers with each other.

Wesley described the formation of special homes for widows and others unable to provide for themselves. He and the stewards of the local Methodist group found homes, furnished them comfortably, and took in as many widows as there was room available. Wesley wrote that in addition to the widows, infirm, and children who were cared for in these homes, four or five preachers regularly ate their meals there.

> For I myself, as well as the other preachers who are in town, diet with the poor on the same food and at the same table. And we rejoice herein as a comfortable earnest of our eating bread together in our Father's kingdom.[41]

This blending of poor and weak persons with influential leaders was another significant return to early Christian understandings of hospitality. Although a separate institution was founded to care for the poor, there was a simultaneous, conscious effort to undermine boundaries that such a house might help to maintain. Table fellowship that included different sorts of people brought all closer, and reflected the diversity of the anticipated heavenly banquet. Wesley rejoiced that these homes for widows reflected apostolic institutions as well as the Kingdom.

40. See Wesley, *Works of John Wesley,* vol. 9: *The Methodist Societies* (Nashville: Abingdon, 1989), "General Rules of the Societies, 1743," 70; "A Plain Account of the People Called Methodists," 256, 258.

41. Wesley, "Plain Account of the People Called Methodists," 267-68.

I have blessed God for this house ever since it began; . . . So that it is not in vain that, without any design of so doing, we have copied after another of the institutions of the apostolic age. I can now say to all the world, "Come, and see how these Christians love one another!"[42]

This home, like the group meetings and the common meals, created a distinctive space in which participants transcended some of their social differences. Wesley had drunk deep of the early church writings, and his institutions and concerns reflected their commitments. He did not, however, identify the work as "hospitality."

Wesley frequently encouraged parishioners to visit the poor and sick in their homes and to help as much as possible with the physical, social, and spiritual needs they encountered. The early Methodists created many small-scale institutions to help care for the needs of strangers, poor people, children, and others. Wesley insisted on close face-to-face relations among different kinds of people — another return to much earlier practices. Without using the term, the early Methodists created places and practices that recaptured some of the dynamism and transformative power of early Christian hospitality. However, by not calling their work "hospitality," they actually contributed to the loss of the historical tradition. Subsequent generations of Protestants thus seldom recognized how important hospitality had been to their own founders and theologians.

Some dimensions of hospitality were captured in the work of benevolence organizations which proliferated in nineteenth-century America. Devout Christians developed programs and projects to meet the needs of immigrants and migrants in the cities; sometimes they understood their work as offering hospitality to strangers. Inner-city missions helped ease newcomers' adjustments to urban life and rescued its castoffs, addressing problems of poverty, disease, and illiteracy. These institutions were often staffed by individuals who united around a particular concern. They were rarely congregational undertakings, and so there was no fundamental community base that could support multiple and reciprocal moral bonds. This meant, in part, that there was no internal press for equality or even for a real connection between hospitality providers and recipients. Voluntary associations allowed participants to focus on particular needs in a

42. Ibid., 277.

systematic and efficient way, but as they addressed needs for food, cloth-ing, or shelter, rarely was the need for a place in the community fully met.

This brief overview of the historical settings of Christian hospitality reveals that the most transformative practices of hospitality occurred in the overlap of institutions. Here roles are more fluid and a person's status is less defined by conventional understandings. Victor Turner, the anthro-pologist, calls this liminal (betwixt and between) space.[43] This is also where the most intense community occurs. The overlap of household and church combines the most personal level of interaction with the most sig-nificant institutional base for transcending social difference and creating community.

Because of the biblical claim that in Christ all believers are equal, equality in the church is normative, though not often lived out in daily practice. When in the context of guest/host relations or in the gathered church this ascribed equality was given flesh, it provided a compelling vi-sion and, at times, challenged prevailing social arrangements. It was often in the context of shared meals that social boundaries were redrawn or re-shaped. The meal combined the ordinary with the sacred and challenged conventional relationships with heavenly expectation.

One of the most significant changes in the history of hospitality came after the patristic period with the eclipse of the gathered church as a primary location for hospitality. In addition to its practice within differen-tiated institutions, hospitality became associated with the bishop and his household rather than with the church. Over the centuries, the episcopal household gained material wealth and political power and tended to re-flect and reinforce prevailing social arrangements.

### Contemporary Settings and the Practice of Hospitality

Significant changes in the last two centuries have made modern expres-sions of hospitality both important and difficult. Activities that were origi-nally located in the household — work, religious observance, protection,

43. Victor Turner, *The Ritual Process* (Ithaca, N.Y.: Cornell University Press, 1969), 94-130.

education, care for the sick, provision for the aging, and care for strangers
— are now located in their own spheres and separate institutions. Each
sphere has its own culture, rules, and specialists. Professionals within
each sphere are paid to provide a service. When we want to respond personally to the needs of a stranger, we often face distinct institutional pressures that push us toward relying on specialists.

Welcoming strangers into a family or church household brings them
into functioning, living communities with reciprocal relations and commitments. In specialized institutions, maintaining social networks is
much more problematic; the bond between provider and recipient is
much more limited. Although physical needs might be met, needs for a
social identity and connection are not only overlooked but sometimes intensified.

Hospitality is a personal but institutionally rooted practice. It requires institutions with an identity, history, and purpose, whether family,
church, or larger community. Effective practices of hospitality are dependent, in part, on the viability of the institutions in which the practice
is embedded. Contemporary attempts to recover the practice of hospitality are made more complex by the modern realities of highly specialized,
large-scale institutions, cultural pluralism, and concerns about the institutional viability of the family and the church.

With urbanization and industrialization, the household has become smaller and more private. It is a cherished retreat from the world
into which one admits few strangers. Privacy increases the risk involved
in offering hospitality to strangers. Both hosts and guests are more vulnerable when hidden from view. Few institutions provide the needed
"threshold" or city gate for an initial encounter with strangers that could
make them slightly more familiar.

The problem may be as much related to the loss of local community
as it is to privatization of the household. Some modern cultures are hospitable; they tend to be ones in which neighborly interaction is more vibrant
and in which personal space is not as private. In these settings, hosts can
turn to neighbors if the stranger turns out to be a dangerous guest; guests
can be more confident that the host's actions will not be hidden from
view.

While it is clear that the household has been crucial to hospitality
throughout almost all of human history, it is also clear that households

today are in trouble. Families are unstable; often no one is at home. The future of Christian hospitality is partly tied to the future of the home and family. Recovering hospitality will involve reclaiming the household as a key site for ministry and then reconnecting the household and the church, so that the two institutions can work in partnership for the sake of the world.

The future of hospitality will also require some creative reconceptualization of our relation to the economic sphere and to daily work. To provide significant household-based hospitality, someone has to be home. Given the small size of most households in our society, it will also be important to explore joining households together and forming small communities that can provide a more substantial base for hospitality.

Contemporary communities of hospitality have created settings that foster rich hospitality practices. They welcome strangers into functioning, full households that are more extensive than a single family and that include many activities usually located in the economic sphere. In some ways, as one visitor observed, these communities have reconstructed a preindustrial household where entire families are home, and economic activity is performed within the household. These communities are rich with stories, shared commitments, and rituals. In addition, they sustain a flourishing spiritual life; in many ways they have recovered the overlap of household and church.

It is crucial for us to recover both household and church as key settings for hospitality. However, some hospitality concerns cannot be handled adequately by home or church; we must also recognize the important role government and large institutions now play in provision and protection. Nor should we minimize the necessity of some structural supports for poor people and aliens. But personal hospitality has an important place in contemporary life, and the central tenets of Christian hospitality still challenge contemporary institutions to make their practices more humane and person-oriented.

# II. RECONSIDERING
# THE TRADITION

# 4. HOSPITALITY, DIGNITY, AND THE POWER OF RECOGNITION

*"And the Pharisees and their scribes murmured*
*against his disciples, saying, 'Why do you eat*
*and drink with tax collectors and sinners?'"*

LUKE 5:30

ALTHOUGH WE OFTEN THINK OF HOSPITALITY AS A TAME and pleasant practice, Christian hospitality has always had a subversive, countercultural dimension. "Hospitality is resistance," as one person from the Catholic Worker observed.[1] Especially when the larger society disregards or dishonors certain persons, small acts of respect and welcome are potent far beyond themselves. They point to a different system of valuing and an alternate model of relationships.

Today, some of the most complex political and ethical tensions center around recognizing or treating people as equals. Recognition involves respecting the dignity and equal worth of every person and valuing their contributions, or at least their potential contributions, to the larger community. Struggles over recognition also encompass questions about what it means to value distinctive cultural traditions, especially when a particular tradition has been tied to social disadvantage and exclusion.[2] Central

---

1. Bernard Connaughton, *Catholic Worker,* June/July 1996, p. 2.
2. See Charles Taylor, *Multiculturalism: Examining the Politics of Recognition* (Princeton, N.J.: Princeton University Press, 1994).

to discussions of recognition and dignity are concerns about basic human rights and identity.

For much of church history, Christians addressed concerns about recognition and human dignity within their discussions and practices of hospitality. Especially in relation to strangers, hospitality was a basic category for dealing with the importance of transcending social differences and breaking social boundaries that excluded certain categories or kinds of persons. Hospitality provided a context for recognizing the worth of persons who seemed to have little when assessed by worldly standards.

Because the practice of hospitality is so significant in establishing and reinforcing social relationships and moral bonds, we notice its more subversive character only when socially undervalued persons are welcomed. In contrast to a more tame hospitality that welcomes persons already well situated in a community, hospitality that welcomes "the least" and recognizes their equal value can be an act of resistance and defiance, a challenge to the values and expectations of the larger community.

People view hospitality as quaint and tame partly because they do not understand the power of recognition. When a person who is not valued by society is received by a socially respected person or group as a human being with dignity and worth, small transformations occur. The person's self-assessment, so often tied to societal assessment, is enhanced. Because such actions are countercultural, they are a witness to the larger community, which is then challenged to reassess its standards and methods of valuing. Many persons who are not valued by the larger community are essentially invisible to it. When people are socially invisible, their needs and concerns are not acknowledged and no one even notices the injustices they suffer. Hospitality can begin a journey toward visibility and respect.

Michael Walzer, a political philosopher, comments that the notion of free recognition or equal dignity was conceivable for the Judeo-Christian tradition because God provided a model, "judging men and women without regard to their worldly standing and inspiring a certain social skepticism" among the faithful. However, he also notes that often "religious doctrine ratified, and religious institutions quickly duplicated, the existing hierarchy."[3] The history of hospitality reflects this ambiguity

3. Michael Walzer, *Spheres of Justice* (New York: Basic Books, 1983), 251.

— at times its practice challenged and transformed hierarchies and at times it reinforced them.

Understanding the historical connection between hospitality and recognition is important for several reasons. Within the practice of hospitality, past generations of Christians struggled with some of the same issues that trouble us today — problems such as socioeconomic and racial/ethnic injustices, and neglect of poor, disabled, orphaned, and elderly people. They succeeded and failed at different times, but most of their story has been missed and their resources have been overlooked.

There is another reason to note the long connection between hospitality and recognition. Some Christians are wary of discussions of equality, human rights, and recognition, assuming that these concerns have been imported from secular philosophies, political theory, and sociology. But these concerns have deep roots in ancient Hebrew and Christian commitments and practices. By realizing this, we can claim a responsible though chastened place in political discussions — with relevant contributions to offer from our theological tradition and historical practice.

Recognition and respect cannot be sustained at the level of abstract claims or commitments. To have any meaning, they must be lived out in concrete everyday relations — in the family, church, community, and political sphere. Individual recognition and welcome into homes and close communities are essential. But so is recognition at the larger and more anonymous level of the state. Although impersonal and distant, political recognition and protection of individual worth and rights is crucial, and reduces the dangers of too narrowly bounded personal hospitality.[4]

Christian hospitality has always been partly remedial, counteracting the social stratification of the larger society by providing a more modest and equal welcome to all. It often works within structural constraints to protect and to rescue some of the people adversely affected by prevailing social and economic arrangements. Although at times it distinctly calls into question the arrangements, hospitality is often carried on within those arrangements, blunting the worst consequences, and rescuing some

4. I am indebted to Michael Walzer's arguments regarding the necessary interplay between particular communities with their "thick" meanings and moral practices and more minimal universal commitments and universal community, a "thinner" but equally necessary common morality and practice. See *Thick and Thin: Moral Argument at Home and Abroad* (Notre Dame: University of Notre Dame Press, 1994) and *Spheres of Justice*.

of the neediest from their distress. Hospitality resists boundaries that endanger persons by denying their humanness. It saves others from the invisibility that comes from social abandonment. Sometimes, by the very acting out of welcome, a vision for a whole society is offered, a small evidence that transformed relations are possible.

In the more extreme cases of political and religious persecution, hospitality has afforded an important response to the needs of refugees. Hospitable households, cities of refuge, the underground railroad, and the sanctuary tradition have sometimes made the difference between life and death for those fleeing danger. In its resistance to the dominant powers, this kind of hospitality has cost some hosts their lives.

## The Basis for Recognition

What theological understandings help Christians to transcend difference, resist indifference, and welcome inconvenient strangers? John Calvin, writing in the sixteenth century, developed one of the most comprehensive foundations for a generous response to strangers:

> Therefore, whatever man you meet who needs your aid, you have no reason to refuse to help him. Say, "He is a stranger"; but the Lord has given him a mark that ought to be familiar to you, by virtue of the fact that he forbids you to despise your own flesh (Isa. 58:7, Vg.). Say, "He is contemptible and worthless"; but the Lord shows him to be one to whom he has deigned to give the beauty of his image. Say that you owe nothing for any service of his; but God, as it were, has put him in his own place in order that you may recognize toward him the many and great benefits with which God has bound you to himself. Say that he does not deserve even your least effort for his sake; but the image of God, which recommends him to you, is worthy of your giving yourself and all your possessions.[5]

More than anything else, the conviction that all human beings were marked with the image of God undergirded Calvin's response to the

---

5. Calvin, *Institutes of the Christian Religion,* 2 vols., ed. John T. McNeill (Philadelphia: Westminster Press, 1960), 3.7.6.

stranger. Bearing God's image establishes for every person a fundamental dignity which cannot be undermined either by wrongdoing or neediness. But, for Calvin, the simple fact of our common humanity also provided a basis for recognition and respect. Humanness itself requires that persons recognize others as like themselves. Each person is made for others and depends on others; therefore, each should sympathize with the sufferings and needs of another:

> We should not regard what a man is and what he deserves: but we should go higher — that it is God who has placed us in the world for such a purpose that we be united and joined together. He has impressed his image in us and has given us a common nature, which should incite us to providing one for the other. The man who wishes to exempt himself from providing for his neighbors should deface himself and declare that he no longer wishes to be a man, for as long as we are human creatures we must contemplate as in a mirror our face in those who are poor, despised, exhausted, who groan under their burdens. . . . If there come some Moor or barbarian, since he is a man, he brings a mirror in which we are able to contemplate that he is our brother and our neighbor: for we cannot abolish the order of nature which God has established as inviolable.[6]

Deep sensitivity to the suffering of those in need comes from our ability to put ourselves in their position, and from remembering our own experiences of vulnerability and dependence. This sense of shared human experience extends even to those most foreign to us. Calvin wrote that when seeing a poor person, we should think "now I have been in that condition and certainly wanted to be helped; indeed it seemed to me that people ought to have pitied me in order to help me":

> But what [is the usual case]? When we are comfortable, it is not a matter of our remembering our human poverty, rather we imagine that we are exempt from that and that we are no longer part of the common

6. *Corpus Reformatorum: Joannis Calvini Opera Quae Supersunt Omnia,* ed. Guilielmus Baum, Eduardus Cunitz, and Eduardus Reuss (Brunswick: C. A. Schwetschke et Filium, 1863-1897), vol. 51, column 105. Quoted in John H. Leith, *John Calvin's Doctrine of the Christian Life* (Louisville: Westminster/John Knox Press, 1989), 186.

class. And that is the reason why we forget, and no longer have any compassion for our neighbors or for all that they endure.[7]

Calvin wrote within the traditions of biblical, classical, patristic, and humanist understandings of the stranger. But he shaped his insights from those various traditions into a theological interpretation which is somewhat distinct from earlier understandings of hospitality and strangers. His descriptions of the stranger stressed the dangers of social disconnection and the harm that comes from the absence of relationships that give people a place in the community. In his theological reflections he met these concerns by emphasizing human connection through the shared image of God and the shared experience of suffering and vulnerability. This broad basis for mutual human respect and care allowed concerns about recognition that had been integral to Christian hospitality to provide a significant foundation for early modern political discourse about recognition and human rights.

In the eighteenth century, John Wesley addressed these same concerns from a slightly different angle. He explained that when the scriptural instructions to honor and love every person are taken together, the effect should transform our earthly assessments of a person's value.

> A poor wretch cries to me for an alms: I look and see him covered with dirt and rags. But through these I see one that has an immortal spirit, made to know and love and dwell with God to eternity: I honour him for his Creator's sake. I see through all these rags that he is purpled over with the blood of Christ. I love him for the sake of his Redeemer. The courtesy therefore which I feel and show toward him is a mixture of the honour and love which I bear to the offspring of God, the purchase of his Son's blood, and the candidate for immortality. This courtesy let us feel and show toward all men; and we shall please all men to their edification.[8]

7. Calvin, *John Calvin's Sermons on the Ten Commandments* (Grand Rapids: Baker Book House, 1980), 127. See also his *Commentaries on the Epistle of Paul the Apostle to the Hebrews* (Grand Rapids: Wm. B. Eerdmans, 1948), 340-41, and *Commentaries on the Four Last Books of Moses* (Grand Rapids: Wm. B. Eerdmans, 1950), 3:125.

8. Wesley, *Works of John Wesley*, vol. 3: *Sermons 3:71-114* (Nashville: Abingdon, 1986), Sermon 100: "On Pleasing All Men," pp. 424-25.

Every person is worthy of respect because of the work of God in them and for them.

Wesley broadened patristic and reformed understandings of respect and recognition. Every human being was created by God for eternity and redeemed by Christ. Therefore, every person was due fundamental respect regardless of her or his condition or position in the world. In addition, every person, despite religious profession or life-style, deserved the care prompted by Jesus' identification with "the least of these."

Calvin and Wesley condensed many of the rich resources of the Christian tradition on respect and recognition. Their emphases — on human commonality in creation, on the image of God, on our mutual experience of dependence and suffering, and on the universal need for redemption — offer a comprehensive framework for recognition and compassionate response to other human beings.

## Recognizing Jesus in Every Stranger

Matthew 25:31-46, a crucial text in the history and practice of Christian hospitality, is startling in its implications for recognition and misrecognition. To some of the gathered crowd, Jesus will say, "Come . . . inherit the kingdom prepared for you . . . for I was hungry and you gave me food . . . thirsty and you gave me drink . . . a stranger and you welcomed me." To others, Jesus will say, "I was hungry and you gave me no food . . . a stranger and you did not welcome me." Both groups will respond similarly — Lord, when did we see *YOU* and respond that way? The connection between particular needy persons and Jesus comes as a total surprise.

The possibility that it is Christ coming to us in "the stranger's guise"[9] powerfully intensifies and broadens concerns about care and respect for those most likely to be overlooked. This possibility undergirded the practice of Christian hospitality to strangers for centuries and it sus-

9. From an anonymous poem (Celtic rune) posted in the dining room of the Open Door Community, and quoted in Peter Gathje, *Christ Comes in the Stranger's Guise: A History of the Open Door Community* (Atlanta: The Open Door, 1991), p. 59. It is also quoted in *Moral Fragments and Moral Community,* by Larry L. Rasmussen (Minneapolis: Fortress, 1993), 155.

tains much of the practice today. Fifteen-hundred years ago, John Chrysostom taught his parishioners, "By how much the brother may be least, so much the more does Christ come to thee through him."[10]

Contemporary practitioners explain what it means to them to see Christ in every guest. For some it is a very literal experience. As one woman commented, "Well, if they're hungry, I see Christ hungry. If they're suffering, I see Christ on the cross." For others, it provides a framework for their ministry. One community founder explained, "I don't know that I'm conscious of [Christ in every guest] as I open the door. I think that certainly is very present to me when I think . . . of what feeds me and allows me to remain here. That sense that these are the Christ, present in flesh . . . once again." Another reported that while he attempts to see Jesus in every guest, "mostly what we are referring to is that every person is worthy of all the love we can give them. And Jesus will elicit that from us." Seeing Jesus in every guest also reduces the inclination to try to calculate the importance of one guest over another. Every person deserves the most gracious and generous welcome possible.

If, when we open the door, we are oriented toward seeing Jesus in the guest, then we welcome that person with some sense that God is already at work in his or her life. This can fundamentally change our perspective and our sense of the dimensions of the relationship. We are more sensitive to what the guest is bringing to us, to what God might be saying or doing through her or him.

For several practitioners, the experience of seeing Jesus in every guest was intensified when they participated in the Hispanic Christmas tradition of *Las Posadas*. For several nights, congregations of Christians reenact the story of Mary and Joseph going from door to door to find shelter. They are turned away many times before finding a place where Jesus can be born. One practitioner working with Spanish-speaking people explained:

> After Christmas we realized that the people who come here ask us for exactly what Mary and Joseph were asking for in Bethlehem. For me, I didn't connect it until someone came and said, "Posada." And I'm just

10. Chrysostom, Homily 45 on Acts, NPNF1, vol. 11, pp. 275-76.

thinking, oh my gosh, that's Jesus. . . . Thank you God for making me aware of your presence.

## Recognizing Dignity as Well as Need

Hospitality is a practice that integrates respect and care. Finding ways to respond to the needs of persons while simultaneously respecting their dignity is an ancient concern. In his sermons, John Chrysostom gave exceptional attention to the importance of recognition and respect without overlooking or spiritualizing physical needs. He was convinced that within the practice of hospitality, Christians could meet the needs of poor people and strangers while still respecting their dignity as persons.

He repeatedly warned his parishioners against holding a grudging spirit in the exercise of hospitality. Such an attitude is "cruel and inhuman" for it causes the recipient great pain. Chrysostom was particularly sensitive to the fragility of the stranger's identity — a fragility resulting from his or her dependence on others. In a number of homilies, he developed this theme and warned his congregation to show "excessive joy" when offering hospitality in order to avoid shaming the recipient:[11]

> The stranger requires much attendance, much encouragement, and with all this it is difficult for him not to feel abashed; for so delicate is his position that whilst he receives the favor, he is ashamed. That shame we ought to remove by the most attentive service, and to show by words and actions, that we do not think we are conferring a favor, but receiving one, that we are obliging less than we are obliged.[12]

This was no false performance; in the economy of God, the host was both obliged and blessed in giving hospitality.

Chrysostom stressed the importance of respect and humility in offering hospitality, criticizing those who "think themselves superior to the recipients, and oftentimes despise them for the attention given to them."[13] Here Chrysostom identifies a particularly difficult problem in

11. Chrysostom, Homily 45 on Acts, NPNF1, vol. 11, p. 276.
12. Chrysostom, Homily 14 on 1 Timothy, NPNF1, vol. 13, p. 455.
13. Chrysostom, Homily 41 on Genesis, in *Homilies on Genesis 18–45*, trans.

ministry: that practitioners, while offering a service, can come to disrespect those who receive it, simply because of their weakness and need.

Chrysostom also recognized the terrible power of those with resources who could choose to humiliate even as they provided help. His insight offers appropriate warning to contemporary practitioners to consider the destructive aspects of too-rigorous needs tests that can seem designed to shame and embarrass applicants. Those forced to depend on others do not deserve abuse, Chrysostom warned, especially from those who would have to give an account for their lavish tables and excess resources from which nothing had been shared.[14]

Sensitive to the disrespect implicit in insisting on knowing all the details of someone's life before helping them, Chrysostom warned that the extreme of stinginess is "for one loaf to be exact about a man's entire life." Even if persons were robbers or murderers, they still deserved "a loaf and a few pence," because God caused the sun to rise on them like everyone else. If Christ forgave and healed those who had injured him and welcomed into paradise those who had scorned him, how could Christians neglect even a starving murderer, Chrysostom wondered.[15]

Chrysostom stressed the importance of a proactive approach to hospitality. In commenting on Romans 12:13, he noted that the phrase "given to hospitality" suggests "not waiting for those that shall ask for it . . . but to run to them, and be given to finding them":

> Not as we do, if we happen to see a stranger or a poor man, knitting our brows, and not deigning even to speak to them. And if after thousands of entreaties we are softened, and bid the servant give them a trifle, we think we have done our duty.[16]

Alms and physical assistance were not sufficient to define hospitality; true hospitality involved face-to-face, gracious relationships of encouragement and respect.

---

Robert C. Hill, The Fathers of the Church, vol. 82 (Washington, D.C.: Catholic University of America Press, 1990), 413.

14. Chrysostom, Homily 41 on Genesis, pp. 416-17. See also Homily 21 on Romans, NPNF1, vol. 11, p. 506.

15. Chrysostom, Homily 21 on Romans, NPNF1, vol. 11, p. 505.

16. Ibid., 504.

Combining care and respect remained a concern throughout the Christian tradition. Calvin recognized that the "vile and abject condition" of strangers can cause us to "injure them the more wantonly, because they seem altogether deserted."[17] Strangers — alone, unprotected, and in need — were vulnerable to every form of injustice and disrespect. But, Calvin believed, putting oneself in the place of the person in need would prompt a compassionate response and would keep the giver from arrogance and insolence. It was not enough, Calvin wrote, "to perform acts of kindness towards men, if our disposition towards them were not warm and affectionate."[18] Liberal donations were made "reprehensible" if they were given "with a proud countenance or . . . insolent words."[19]

Similarly, John Wesley insisted that those responsible for the temporal affairs of the Methodist societies treat the poor with respect and kindness. His warnings show his sensitivity to the tendency to be disrespectful to those forced to ask for help:

> If you cannot relieve, do not grieve, the poor. Give them soft words, if nothing else. Abstain from either sour looks or harsh words. Let them be glad to come, even though they should go empty away. Put yourselves in the place of every poor man; and deal with him as you would God should deal with you.[20]

Combining care with respect — seeing the dignity as well as the need of the person — is also a distinctive feature of contemporary ministries of hospitality. At the personal level, hospitality communicates to guests and strangers that they are valued; respect and recognition are expressed in giving someone our full attention. Because so much of "helping" has been turned into a profession with paid specialists, it is very unusual when someone gives focused attention to a needy stranger outside of a paid relationship. Giving a stranger full attention communicates that he or she is interesting and worthwhile; we pay attention to the people we value.

Those who offer hospitality are not so much providing a service as

17. Calvin, *Commentaries on the Four Last Books of Moses,* 3:118.
18. Calvin, *Commentary on the Prophet Isaiah,* (Grand Rapids: Wm. B. Eerdmans, 1948), 4:237.
19. Calvin, *Institutes,* 3.7.7.
20. Wesley, *Works of John Wesley,* vol. 12: *Letters* (Grand Rapids: Baker Book House, 1978), "Directions to the Stewards of the Methodist Society in London," p. 516.

they are sharing their lives with the people who come to them. This is an important distinction because it affects the nature of the relationship. One practitioner explains, "I believe that hospitality . . . means to give of yourself. . . . [In] other types of services you can give of your talents or . . . skills or . . . resources. . . . The tasks aren't what hospitality is about, hospitality is giving of yourself." If hospitality involves sharing your life and sharing in the lives of others, guests/strangers are not first defined by their need. Lives and resources are much more complexly intertwined, and roles are much less predictable.

Respect is sustained in the relationships in two related ways — by recognizing the gifts that guests bring to the relationship and by recognizing the neediness of the hosts. Often these themes surfaced in the interviews. Many practitioners commented on their joy and surprise in discovering how much they learned from the guests and how much the guests ministered to them. From their meager material resources, refugees frequently and joyfully found ways to offer hospitality to their hosts. Volunteers commented that they were learning hospitality skills from the people they welcomed. One worker reflected on the day he learned of his father's death. As word spread through the community of homeless people with whom he shared his life, they reached out to him with sympathy and care. He particularly recalled one man who suffered from deep mental illness but was able to escape the tormenting voices long enough to provide tender and insightful pastoral care. Experiences such as these remind practitioners daily that the gifts of hospitality do not flow in one direction only; hospitality is a "two-way street."

Practitioners are also deeply aware of their own needs, frailties, and dependence on others. Several insisted that this is the starting point of hospitality — a conversion of sorts when they recognize, "I'm not here because I'm helping them. I'm here because we're helping each other." In the midst of the hard work of hospitality, one person described his fresh understanding that "I myself am poor, that I myself am needy. That I walk the same pilgrimage that many of these people walk, just in a different format." Hospitality reminds us that respect does not have to be drained out of a relationship in which one person has substantial needs. Respect and care can be united in a response that truly values the other person.

## Recognizing One Another in Shared Meals

In a society in which even family members eat alone and on the run, we are often not aware of the significance of shared meals. But, in most cultures, eating together expresses mutuality, recognition, acceptance, and equal regard. Even in our own society, eating together remains quite bounded.[21] Unless we intentionally break patterns, we usually eat with people who are similar to ourselves. When strangers and hosts are from different backgrounds, the intimacy of a shared meal can forge relationships which cross significant social boundaries.

Offers of food or a meal together are central to almost all biblical stories of hospitality, to most historical discussions of hospitality, and to almost every contemporary practice of hospitality. In the context of shared meals, Jesus frequently challenged the prevailing religious and cultural boundaries by the company he kept and exposed the hidden patterns of social exclusion. He was a guest in the home of tax collectors, dined with sinners, and taught hosts to welcome those most likely to be excluded.

Many of the early church's struggles over recognition and inclusion surfaced in the context of eating together. Peter, at God's instruction, visited Cornelius and ate with his household — a powerful demonstration of the acceptance of Gentiles into the Christian community (Acts 10–11). Paul addressed the tensions between rich and poor believers that became apparent in the common meals when the poor were "humiliated" by believers with higher status and wealth. In a community that declared ethnic and social boundaries irrelevant, some poor believers were being treated as less significant members (1 Cor. 11:17-34).[22]

Shared meals are central to every community of hospitality — central to sustaining the life of the community and to expressing welcome to strangers. For many participants, it is the high point of their day and a return to an earlier time when families regularly ate together. Jean Vanier explains that when he first began sharing his daily meals with men with serious mental disabilities, he started to understand the force of Jesus'

21. See Mary Douglas, "Deciphering a Meal," in *Myth, Symbol and Culture,* ed. C. Geertz (New York: W. W. Norton, 1971), 61-81.

22. See John Koenig, *New Testament Hospitality* (Philadelphia: Fortress, 1985), 65-71.

words in Luke 14 about who should be invited to the banquet. "Sitting down at the same table meant becoming friends with them, creating a family. It was a way of life absolutely opposed to the values of a competitive, hierarchical society in which the weak are pushed aside."[23]

Because eating is something every person must do, meal-time has a profoundly egalitarian dimension. As one woman from the Catholic Worker commented, no matter what our backgrounds or assets, we are all eaters and drinkers. "It's the great leveler." Meal-time, when people sit down together, is the clearest time of being with others, rather than doing for others. It is the time when hospitality looks least like social services.

Often we maintain significant boundaries when offering help to persons in need. Many churches prepare and serve meals to hungry neighbors, but few church members find it easy to sit and eat with those who need the meal. When people are very different from ourselves, we often find it more comfortable to cook and clean for them than to share in a meal and conversation. We are familiar with roles as helpers but are less certain about being equals eating together. Many of us struggle with simply being present with people in need; our helping roles give definition to the relationship but they also keep it decidedly hierarchical. As one practitioner observed, eating together is "the most enriching part but also the hardest part. When we were first here it was so hard. We didn't have any specific things to do, just be with people."

Practitioners recognize the relation between justice and shared meals. Ed Loring, of the Open Door Community in Atlanta, observed that "justice is important, but supper is essential." His comment in no way reduces the importance of sustained efforts at social justice, to which the entire community is committed. But, as Murphy Davis, cofounder of the Open Door, explained, "Without supper, without love, without table companionship, justice can become a program that we *do* to other people."[24]

In many settings the line between the shared meal and the Eucharist is blurred; the two flow into each other much as was the case in the

23. Jean Vanier, *The Heart of L'Arche: A Spirituality for Every Day* (New York: Crossroad, 1995), 29.

24. Murphy Davis, "Dorothy Day: The Only Solution Is Love," *Hospitality* 17/1 (January 1988): 8.

early church. The sacramental aspects of meals become clearest in these settings, but even separate from the Eucharist, one often senses a divine mystery in dining together at a table of welcome.

## Recognizing the Stranger, Redefining the Neighbor

In the parable of the Good Samaritan (Luke 10:29-37), Jesus redefines neighbor and love for neighbor. The scope of our responsibility to care includes anyone in need. This expands more tightly bounded definitions of neighbor that tend to limit responsibility to those we like or those like us. Jesus also broadens our moral obligation to others when he explicitly includes the well-being of our enemies in our circle of responsibility (Matt. 5:43-48). This universalizing of the neighbor to include anyone in need connects with other theological commitments (e.g., God as common creator, and our shared human flesh) — to shape the groundwork for recognition and care.

The practice of hospitality forces abstract commitments to loving the neighbor, stranger, and enemy into practical and personal expressions of respect and care for actual neighbors, strangers, and enemies. The twin moves of universalizing the neighbor and personalizing the stranger are at the core of hospitality. Claims of loving all humankind, of welcoming "the other," have to be accompanied by the hard work of actually welcoming a human being into a real place.[25]

Both Calvin and Wesley addressed aspects of the meaning of neighbor and stranger. For Calvin, the obligation to care for the stranger was "a mutual obligation between all men." His more universal motivations for care were directed to a very universal interpretation of the neighbor — "the whole human race."[26] In addressing the question, "Who is my neighbor?" Calvin asserted that "Christ has shown in the parable of the Samaritan that the term 'neighbor' includes even the most remote person (Luke 10:36)," and therefore "we are not expected to limit the precept of

25. Riggins R. Earl, Jr., in slightly different language, develops this theme and its significance in the black church tradition. See "Under Their Own Vine and Fig Tree: The Ethics of Social and Spiritual Hospitality in Black Church Worship," *Journal of the Interdenominational Theological Center* 14/1-2 (Fall 86–Spring 87): 181-93.

26. Calvin, *John Calvin's Sermons on the Ten Commandments*, 126.

love to those in close relationships."[27] For Calvin, "to make any person our neighbour, therefore, it is enough that he be a man; for it is not in our power to blot out our common nature." The parable of the Good Samaritan, Calvin believed, conveyed the truth that "the greatest stranger is *our neighbour,* because God has bound all men together, for the purpose of assisting each other."[28]

Defining anyone in need as our neighbor, as it seems the tradition requires, can elicit two problematic responses. Because it is such a broad claim, it can remain an abstract commitment, something related to an attitude of care or compassion rarely translated into action. Another danger is that our responses to large numbers of "neighbors" can become general, superficial, and less personal. On the other hand, universal claims are an important corrective to personal one-to-one care that, though intense, can also be very limited and private. The challenge has been to allow these various impulses to shape one another.

Wesley also insisted that love of neighbor meant "universal benevolence," "embracing neighbours and strangers, friends and enemies . . . the good and gentle, but also . . . the evil and unthankful . . . every soul that God has made."[29] In a sermon written a few years before his death, Wesley reflected on the social distance that insulated those who could help from those in need:

> One great reason why the rich in general have so little sympathy for the poor is because they so seldom visit them. Hence it is that [according to the common observation] one part of the world does not know what the other suffers. Many of them do not know, because they do not care to know: they keep out of the way of knowing it — and then plead their voluntary ignorance as an excuse for their hardness of heart.[30]

27. Calvin, *Institutes,* 2.8.54. See also *Commentaries on the Four Last Books of Moses,* 3:118.

28. Calvin, *Commentary on the Harmony of the Evangelists, Matthew, Mark, and Luke* (Grand Rapids: Wm. B. Eerdmans, 1949), 3:61-62.

29. Wesley, *Works of John Wesley,* vol. 10: *Letters, Essays, Dialogs, Addresses* (Grand Rapids: Baker Book House, 1978), "Letter to the Rev. Dr. Middleton," p. 68. Wesley repeated this in "A Letter to the Right Reverend the Lord Bishop of Gloucester," vol. 11, p. 528.

30. Wesley, *Works of John Wesley,* vol. 3: *Sermons 3: 71-114* (Nashville: Abingdon, 1986), Sermon 98: "On Visiting the Sick," pp. 387-88.

Wesley recognized the importance of relationships that crossed boundaries. When believers had personal connections with their poor neighbors, they could understand the situations better and respond effectively. Wesley understood clearly the necessity of holding together the qualities of universal love and particular, personal care. Lofty statements about loving every person as one's neighbor had to be accompanied by acts which brought the Christian face-to-face with those persons most commonly excluded from the "neighborhood."

The comments of one contemporary practitioner of hospitality reflect Wesley's insight into the dangers of social distance between Christians and the most vulnerable: "I see us quickly developing into, not a society of bad people, but a society with people out of touch with the suffering of the vast majority of the world's population today — including the poor within our own country." He continued, "The distance that wealthy people are now able to put between them and the poor makes them less likely to appreciate the need for hospitality." In his community, members deliberately structure settings and produce newsletters that help people connect more closely with the humanness of persons in need.

Several contemporary communities that welcome refugees and homeless people hold together a universal concern for the neighbor and personal relations with strangers. They resist the temptation to work exclusively at a distant level for social change, but they also resist the tendency to get caught up with a very small group of strangers and lose sight of larger concerns. While these practitioners live close to human need, they simultaneously work on the structural issues that contribute to the continual flow of needy guests.

Aware that their small acts of welcome are acts of recognition and valuing, practitioners also know that recognition and rights must be acknowledged and protected by other institutions, especially governments. Because practitioners have close relationships with persons in need, they live alongside the daily injustices and indignities such people often endure. Their voices in the public forum carry a wisdom, integrity, and authenticity that come from living out their commitments. As one worker commented, "if it is not a genuine thing here on a small scale, then we don't really have anything to say on this larger scale."

## Tensions in Hospitality, Failures in Recognition

The actual story of Christian hospitality as an expression of care, respect, recognition, and equality is not without serious problems, failures, and ambiguities. In past centuries, hospitality was an important way of addressing issues of respect and equality in nonegalitarian societies. The association of hospitality with charity and entertainment has often hidden its historic relation to concerns about recognition. The problem, however, is more complex. Hospitality is a voluntary act, a gift. Today, people claim rights and demand recognition,[31] and hospitality concerns can seem both anachronistic and paternalistic.

The emphasis on rights is partly an attempt to move away from a charity model that reinforces "the donor's distance and the recipients' dependency."[32] Individual rights provide an important framework for concerns about justice, equality, protection, and provision. The cost of our emphasis on rights, however, includes a devaluation of personal care and social connection.

Today, equality, inclusion, and minimal provision are viewed as rights, but serious concerns remain. Inclusion mandated by law and provision gathered through taxes cannot guarantee that people will experience the kinds of human connections and rootedness that give us a safe and meaning-filled place in the world. On the other hand, modern experience suggests strongly that there are few safe places when laws and governments do not protect fundamental human rights.

Ironically, concerns about recognition and respect were partly undermined by the very institutions that grew out of the desire to provide hospitality. When much of hospitality to the poor and sick became located in specialized institutions — hospitals and hospices — significant unintended consequences followed. Hospitals, especially for the indigent, provided more organized relief, more predictability and efficiency, but they also removed the needy populations from the larger community,

31. See Charles Taylor, *Multiculturalism,* for a full discussion on rights, recognition, and difference.
32. Helen Fein, *Congregational Sponsors of Indochinese Refugees in the United States, 1979-1981* (Rutherford, N.J.: Fairleigh Dickinson University Press, 1987), 20.

leaving their care to persons paid for rendering a service. Commitments to respect and recognition often fade when needy persons are segregated out, grouped together, and hidden from view. Such populations are easily overlooked and quickly forgotten. Without close human relationships, the vulnerability of these people is actually heightened — apart from those paid to care, no one in particular cares about them, and they have no place in the world to make any contribution. John Boswell's history of the origins of the foundling hospital, and its deadly consequences for most of its "patients," gives powerful evidence of the ambiguous role of some of these institutions.[33] We continue to struggle with some of these same tensions as we recognize the destructive human consequences of institutionalizing people who are elderly, mentally ill, or seriously disabled.

Hospitality can easily reflect contemporary social distinctions so that some guests are seen as deserving hospitality and other guests are not seen at all. This may be the most dangerous form of nonrecognition — some persons are rendered invisible by the values and arrangements of the larger society. There are no explicit discussions about excluding them, they are simply overlooked. Historically, this often happened to the poor and infirm. Today we face this danger as many churches ignore the urban poor or never notice the elderly or disabled people in their own communities.

In responding to the needs of the stranger/guest, hospitality sometimes intensified the vulnerability of powerless persons already in the community, especially in the family. Historically, hospitality did not function as a critique of distorted family relations or hierarchy, and at times it aggravated and justified injustices. This is an important feature of two Old Testament stories and the later commentaries on them — the account of Lot's willingness to sacrifice his daughters for the well-being of his male guests (Gen. 19) and the account of the concubine who was not treated as guest or as family member, but rather offered to a hostile crowd in place of her master (Judg. 19). Although commentaries on hospitality provided piercing critiques of exclusionary practices in certain settings, they did not address domination and exclusion within families. This should warn us against overlooking the protection and well-being of those closest to us and the vulnerable ones among us as we offer hospitality to strangers.

33. John Boswell, *The Kindness of Strangers* (New York: Pantheon Books, 1988).

Because of the importance of hospitality in human relationships and in church practice, denials of hospitality are a significant means for expressing rejection of behaviors or teachings. Early Christians denied welcome and hospitality to two categories of people; both claimed to be believers. One category included those who persisted in immoral life-styles (1 Cor. 5:9-11) and the other included those who propagated false teaching (2 John 9-11).

While it is essential for Christians to be able to maintain a distinct identity and practice within our churches, it is also important to recognize how much power is condensed in the authority to exclude persons on the basis of their deviation from belief or practice. Such power involves the capacity to define a community and the capacity to affect negatively the well-being of persons who threaten that definition. Denials of hospitality in the early church were applied to those already self-defined as Christians. It was an intracommunal form of discipline by exclusion — tied to the hope for repentance and reintegration. In these early communities, exclusion would not have threatened the temporal life or well-being of offenders.

A profound danger results when enforcement of religious boundaries is tied to political power. Terrible examples of this weave through church history, but the sixteenth century provides some potent cases. The persecution of Anabaptists affords appalling testimony to the overwhelming destructiveness of combined religious/political forces that choose to exclude some persons from land and life. Another disturbing example comes from the writings of Martin Luther against the Jews in Germany. Claiming the authority of "host" in order to relegate other persons to "guest" status and then to deny them welcome is a particularly virulent form of injustice. Describing the Jews as unwanted and ungrateful guests of the German people, Luther urged their removal from the land. He portrayed them as plundering their hosts' goods and blaspheming their hosts' God. He complained:

> We suffer more from them [the Jews] than the Italians do from the Spaniards, who plunder the host's kitchen, cellar, chest, and purse, and, in addition, curse him and threaten him with death. Thus the Jews, our guests, also treat us: for we are their hosts. They rob and fleece us and hang about our necks, these lazy weaklings and indolent

bellies; they swill and feast, enjoy good times in our homes, and by way of reward they curse our Lord Christ, our churches, our princes, and all of us, threatening us and unceasingly wishing us death and every evil.[34]

To be rid of the "unbearable, devilish burden of the Jews," Luther recommended that their homes, schools, and synagogues be razed, that they be forced to live in barns and to do manual work, if not expelled or cut off like a gangrenous limb.[35] He continued:

> Now let me commend these Jews sincerely to whoever feels the desire to shelter and feed them, to honor them, to be fleeced, robbed, plundered, defamed, vilified, and cursed by them, and to suffer every evil at their hands — these venomous serpents and devil's children, who are the most vehement enemies of Christ our Lord and of us all. . . . Then he will be a perfect Christian, filled with works of mercy — for which Christ will reward him on the day of judgment, together with the Jews — in the eternal fire of hell![36]

Luther turns the expectations of Matthew 25:31-46 inside out, claiming that hospitality to Jews could only bring judgment for Christians. Assigning German Christians the role of hosts, Luther then announced a responsibility, a duty, to exclude certain "guests." By choosing guest/host language, Luther was able to reinforce already existing patterns of social exclusion.

It is clear from these passages that when basic societal membership is at stake, the status of "guest" leaves persons vulnerable to the arbitrary whims of the "hosts," especially if the latter have the power of the sword and feel threatened economically or politically. Expulsion from the civic sphere, in which the basic rights of citizens are protected, is the most dangerous form of expulsion, but the danger is intensified when particular religious, ethnic, and cultural identities are singled out for exclusion.

It is important to note that Luther's harsh words belie his own practices of sacrificial hospitality toward some in need, as well as other significant passages about the importance of Christian hospitality. And he is far

34. *Luther's Works,* vol. 47: *The Christian and Society IV* (Philadelphia: Fortress, 1971), "On the Jews and Their Lies," pp. 275-76.

35. Ibid., 269-75, 285-92.

36. Ibid., 278.

from alone in contributing to a dreadful legacy of exclusion: Christian history is splattered with failures in hospitality and terrible expressions of nonrecognition.[37] But Luther is important for several reasons. He used language which denied basic humanness to the Jews — the most total and dangerous form of nonrecognition, a form which allows any abuse to follow. His rhetoric defined abuse of human beings as a form of Christian responsibility and he made care for them an expression of disloyalty to Christ. Such rhetoric is evil in itself, but when it is tied to political power, it unleashes unbounded religiously sanctioned cruelty. The twentieth century provides us with the most terrible confirmation of the reality of these dangers. Protection of basic human rights, a protection located in the political/civic sphere, must always transcend religious and ethnic identity.

## Maintaining Distinctions, Protecting Difference

John Wesley, writing during a century wearied by religious wars, offers relevant insight on dealing with religious differences. Critical of the Roman Catholic church of his day, his words speak to the broader Christian community today. By its "bitter . . . anathemas" the church commended to utter destruction all who differed from its teaching. Wesley argued that because the church's view of people was often seen as God's view, the results could be very dangerous. "Anathemas" had a "natural tendency to utterly destroy neighbour love," mercy, and justice.[38] Wesley recognized the dangers of religious exclusivism for basic human rights and civil justice; for him, benevolence did not require conformity.

Christians have a significant stake in being able to maintain distinctions while not allowing differences to be translated into liabilities in

37. Chrysostom, the champion of hospitality in the Christian tradition, wrote very harshly and inhospitably about the Jews and the Judaizing Christians of his own day. See John Chrysostom, *Discourses Against Judaizing Christians,* trans. Paul W. Harkins, The Fathers of the Church, vol. 68 (Washington, D.C.: Catholic University of America Press, 1977).

48. Wesley, *Works of John Wesley,* vol. 10: *Letters, Essays, Dialogs, Addresses* (Grand Rapids: Baker Book House, 1978), "Popery Calmly Considered," p. 156.

terms of basic rights, entitlements, and protections. It is critical to have the freedom to define a Christian identity and Christian community with distinctive beliefs and practices. But, to welcome strangers into a distinctly Christian environment without coercing them into conformity requires that their basic well-being not be dependent on sharing certain commitments. When basic well-being is under attack by the larger society, Christians have a responsibility to welcome endangered persons into their lives, churches, and communities.

The story of the village of Le Chambon is a powerful example of the meaning of difference in the practice of hospitality. This small community of French Protestants rescued Jews during World War II. Opening their homes, schools, and church to strangers with quiet, steady hospitality, they made Le Chambon the safest place in Europe for Jews. They acknowledged and valued the Jewish identity of their guests and understood their need for protection. Defining as neighbor anyone who dearly needed help,[39] they saved the lives of thousands of Jews. When the police asked the pastor of the community to turn in the Jews, André Trocmé responded, "We do not know what a Jew is. We know only men."[40] His response is profoundly illuminating. When, by acknowledging difference, we only endanger, then we must only acknowledge our common human identity.

Some of the original concerns of hospitality were related to providing safety and refuge to persecuted, endangered, or needy persons. Today hospitality, rights, and entitlements are separate, and they should be. Requiring particular commitments or beliefs in order for people to receive material help or protection is very dangerous; some boundaries are properly removed for the sake of fundamental human well-being. On the other hand, entitlements and rights are necessary but not sufficient for human well-being. Although persons need provision, they also need connection to living communities; otherwise, they remain anonymous and vulnerable. We need a constant, complex interaction between identity-defining, bounded communities and a larger community with minimal boundaries that offers basic protection of individuals.[41]

39. Philip Hallie, *Lest Innocent Blood Be Shed* (New York: Harper & Row, 1979), 170.

40. Ibid., 103, 160.

41. See the discussion in Michael Ignatieff, *The Needs of Strangers* (London: Chatto & Windus/The Hogarth Press, 1984), 136-42.

The opportunities for personal, face-to-face relations that can give people a place and a social network are found within churches, families, neighborhoods, and voluntary associations. These are bounded communities to which detached strangers need connection. However, many social groups find it very difficult to accept people different from their prevailing membership. Therefore, the more anonymous care of the state is essential in that it protects basic human rights while it avoids the coercion often present in very local ties; it helps to control the impact of more parochial hospitality which chooses its guests and the needs it will meet.

Christians who live and work alongside poor and vulnerable people have rediscovered the importance of hospitality for full human identity. Gustavo Gutiérrez, the Latin American theologian, identifies three dimensions of liberation: transformation at the social-structural level, at the personal level, and at the level of estrangement from God and others.[42] Historically, the concerns of hospitality were related to all three dimensions. Recent attempts to recover hospitality have tended to connect it with transformation at the middle, more personal level, which recognizes the particular importance of solidarity, gestures, eating together, and friendship with the poor. The polarization between attention to large-scale structural change and to individual, personal change that has characterized so much contemporary discussion has often eclipsed the importance of friendship and hospitality with poor people and strangers. Simple acts of respect and appreciation, presence and friendship are indispensable parts of the affirmation of human personhood.

A century ago, William Booth recognized the importance of friendship with the poor when he wrote, "One of the secrets of the success of the Salvation Army is that the friendless of the world find friends in it."[43] True hospitality involves friendship which "brings to the other what no law or revolution can do: understanding and acceptance."[44] Hospitality, while certainly insufficient in efforts for justice and transformation, is essential, very essential.

42. Gustavo Gutiérrez, *A Theology of Liberation,* rev. ed. (Maryknoll, N.Y.: Orbis, 1988), xxxviii.

43. William Booth, *In Darkest England and the Way Out* (Chicago: H. Seigel and Co., 1890), 271.

44. Ed Loring, "Bandaids and Beyond," *Hospitality* 8/2 (March 1989): 2.

# 5. THE STRANGERS
# IN OUR MIDST

---

*"We always treat guests as angels —*
*just in case."*

BROTHER JEREMIAH[1]

IF WELCOMING STRANGERS IS A SIGNIFICANT CHRISTIAN
practice with a strong claim on us as believers, then who are the strangers
we should welcome? Where do we find them? Does every stranger need
hospitality?

## Different Kinds of Strangers

Is someone a stranger simply because he or she is unknown to me or to
my particular communities? Are there different ways of being unknown?
While I am unlikely to bring a homeless man to my home for a meal, I am
certainly less hesitant about inviting a visiting lecturer to dinner at my
house. I know neither of these people, but they are strange to me in different ways.

In the case of the homeless man, I know nothing about him or his

---

1. Brother Jeremiah, an Egyptian monk, quoted in Alan Jones, *Soul Making: The
Desert Way of Spirituality* (San Francisco: HarperSanFrancisco, 1985), 13.

life, except what he might tell me. His homelessness is symptomatic of his distance from almost every conventionally significant relationship — family, friends, employment, even church. He has lost most ties to the things that give people an identity and a place in the world. This man has few connections with which I can intersect — and there may well be no one in my world of acquaintances who could readily vouch for him. Compare the description of the homeless man with the situation of the visiting lecturer — someone I also don't know but someone who works for an institution I do know of and respect. I assume that if he is employed there, he's probably OK. Without much difficulty, I can learn about his family, his academic and religious affiliations. He comes into my life with a set of connections which make him more readily known — connections that keep him from being as strange to me as another person might be. Any hospitality to strangers has some risks, but the risks and uncertainties seem lessened when, although we don't know the person, we can readily know about them and find easy points of connection with them.

Obviously there are other reasons that I might more readily invite a college professor into my home than a homeless person, and the contrast between their social situations is extreme. But the difference helps illustrate the point that they are unknown to me in different ways. Well over three hundred years ago, the Puritan John Owen expressed some of these distinctions in his discussion of hospitality. Noting that in his day, hospitality had come to mean entertaining family, friends, and acquaintances, he contrasted that meaning to the biblical and historical understandings. In the past, Owen said, hospitality had applied to welcoming "such as are strangers indeed, and unknown unto us as unto other circumstances, and so such as really stand in need of help and refreshment."[2]

While making clear the distinction between hospitality to needy strangers (those who "really stand in need of help") and entertaining people with whom we have some ties, Owen also suggested a distinction between different kinds of strangers. He described strangers as those "whose circumstances we know not but from themselves" — effectively capturing

---

2. *Works of John Owen,* ed. William H. Goold and Charles W. Quick (Philadelphia: Leighton Publications, 1869), "An Exposition of the Epistle to the Hebrews," vol. 7, pp. 386-87.

the quality of being most fully a stranger — detached from relationships that characterize and locate a human life. He further described hospitality as the ancient virtue of "entertaining of unknown strangers." While "unknown strangers" certainly seems redundant, it expresses a more total strangeness and social distance.

Strangers are "people without a place."[3] To be without a place means to be detached from basic, life-supporting institutions — family, work, polity, religious community, and to be without networks of relations that sustain and support human beings. People without a place who are also without financial resources are the most vulnerable people. This is the condition in which homeless people, displaced poor people, refugees, and undocumented persons find themselves. They not only lack supportive connections with other human beings, but they also are unable to purchase many of the basic necessities of life. In our world money opens many doors, and strangers with resources, even if foreign born, do not find themselves vulnerable in the same way as those who are impoverished.

Through most of its history, the Christian hospitality tradition has expressed a normative concern for strangers who could not provide for or defend themselves. Calvin's various descriptions of the conditions of strangers identify key characteristics of their vulnerability. Defining strangers by their distance from social networks of support, Calvin described them as "for the most part destitute of all things, being far away from their friends."[4] Because strangers had "no one who would submit to ill-will in their defense, they were more exposed to the violence and various oppressions of the ungodly, than as if they were under the shelter of domestic securities."[5] People tend to favor and protect others who are familiar, but strangers, widows, and orphans were "exposed as it were to plunder" because they were not fortified by strong defenses.[6]

---

3. Walter Brueggemann, *Interpretation and Obedience* (Minneapolis: Fortress, 1991), 294.

4. Calvin, *Commentaries on the Epistle of Paul the Apostle to the Romans* (Grand Rapids: Wm. B. Eerdmans, 1948), 467.

5. Calvin, *Commentaries on the Four Last Books of Moses, Arranged in the Form of a Harmony* (Grand Rapids: Wm. B. Eerdmans, 1950), 3:116.

6. Calvin, *Commentary on the Book of Psalms* (Grand Rapids: Wm. B. Eerdmans, 1949), 5:290. See also *Commentaries on the Twelve Minor Prophets* (Grand Rapids: Wm. B. Eerdmans, 1950), 5:179.

Calvin's portrayal of the stranger captures the vulnerability and need of the person who is without support. It is a definition that has less to do with being foreign than with lack of power and loss of home. These persons are vulnerable to abuse, exploitation, or social invisibility, and depend on others to respect their lives and provide for their immediate needs.

In contemporary society, severe poverty is often tied to rootlessness and detachment from family and other key institutions. However, in past centuries, one could be poor but still situated in a community. Describing that person as a stranger would not have been accurate. Although poor, he or she would have had a place within the immediate society. It is in eighteenth-century England that we first catch a glimpse of the devastating conditions of the new urban poor that marked them out as strangers in their own society.

In 1785 a group of Methodists, with the support of John Wesley, founded the Strangers' Friend Society in London, dedicated to ministry among the urban poor. Wesley described the Society as "instituted wholly for the relief not of our society, but for poor, sick, friendless strangers."[7] Societies were quickly established in a number of cities in England and Ireland. In a letter to Adam Clarke, Wesley wrote, "you have done right in setting up the Strangers' (Friend) Society. It is an excellent institution."[8] According to Clarke, the Society was founded as a response to the extraordinary human misery and poverty he had seen among the hidden poor of Dublin. Describing the local poor as "strangers" because of their "sore affliction" and their inability to find relief in the traditional sources, he characterized them as persons who had "no helper" in society. The only criterion for help was "sufficiency of evident distress."[9]

Across the centuries, the identity of strangers in need of welcome has varied somewhat — but the most vulnerable have included religious and political refugees, widows, orphans, pilgrims, and the local poor. For those without the protection and support that would ordinarily be associ-

7. Wesley, *Works of John Wesley,* vol. 4: *Journals* (Grand Rapids: Baker Book House, repr. 1979), 481.

8. Wesley, *Works of John Wesley,* vol. 13: *Letters* (Grand Rapids: Baker Book House, repr. 1979), Letter 823, p. 105.

9. See Adam Clarke, *The Nature, Design, Rules and Regulations of a Charitable Institution Termed the Stranger's Friend: Begun in Dublin, in 1791* (London, 1798), 5.

ated with natural bonds of affection and responsibility, an absence of hospitable welcome could be both dangerous and cruel.

For some refugees and homeless people, a lack of welcome can literally mean death. When their "placelessness" is compounded by mental or physical illness, disability, or old age, their vulnerability is most severe. Some of the most desperate and heart-breaking human stories shared by hospitality practitioners were accounts of people who had been sick enough to be hospitalized but, upon release, had nowhere to go. Still ill, their convalescence would have been on the street if not for a welcoming community. One woman, undergoing chemotherapy, asked a Christian community for help because she had been returning to the street after each treatment. Such desolation and need are nearly incomprehensible for most Americans but disturbingly familiar to those who live close to the needs of the most vulnerable strangers.

## "Relative" Strangers and Contemporary Society

In daily life we cross paths with many strangers and interact regularly with other persons we barely know. Most do not strike us as particularly vulnerable or detached; neither do they immediately present themselves as in need of Christian hospitality. Most strangers are able to provide for and obtain what they need. While they may be unknown to us, they are not without connections or resources. For those away from home, the hospitality industry supplies hotel rooms and restaurants to meet the needs of persons with sufficient resources to pay for the services they require.

Sometimes we describe our nation as a society of relative strangers — millions of people minimally attached to home and community, highly mobile, independently pursuing our own projects, contentedly leaving one another alone to pursue our own tasks.[10] We value autonomy and independence and are wary of tight community bonds. We often feel like strangers ourselves, somewhat rootless and disconnected, unsure of how to offer welcome or to whom it should be given.

10. See Jon P. Gunnemann, "Justice with Strangers: The Ethics of Exchange," *Prism* 2/2 (Fall 1987): 74-88.

This is a confusing social situation in which to think about strangers. In describing ourselves as strangers, we underestimate some significant connections — most of us have economic and civic ties; we have familial and social networks that protect us from anonymity and powerlessness. Even if family and home are less sturdy today than in the past, we have multiple relationships which give us some places of connection or belonging.

Sometimes we choose to characterize ourselves as strangers involved in mutual welcoming — a "partnership among strangers."[11] We do this in part to avoid the language of host and guest because such terms and the relations they represent seem anachronistic and hierarchical. While there is legitimacy to this concern, and while we need to be careful in recovering guest/host language, there are serious problems with losing it altogether. When we describe everyone as a stranger, we wash out some of the crucial distinctions between socially situated persons and persons who are truly disconnected from social relations. If we see ourselves only as strangers, and reject the responsibility associated with being hosts, then we squander opportunities to create hospitable environments and situations.

In our economically driven society, to be outside of, or irrelevant to, the economic system is a very significant vulnerability. To be outside the market marks one off as a stranger. If that condition is tied to physical or mental disability, severely fractured family relations, or ethnic or racial differences, persons are profoundly vulnerable and are "strangers" by some of the classic criteria. They are without a place, and without the resources to gain one.

What makes these people especially vulnerable is that without significant human connections, they become essentially invisible to the larger society. Such invisibility is compounded by contemporary living arrangements that allow many of us to choose carefully who will enter our private worlds. Communities or neighborhoods developed around particular "life-styles"[12] help assure that the people we and our children en-

11. See, for example, Parker J. Palmer, *The Company of Strangers* (New York: Crossroad, 1986), and John Koenig, *New Testament Hospitality* (Philadelphia: Fortress, 1985).

12. See *Habits of the Heart,* by Robert N. Bellah, Richard Madsen, William M. Sullivan, Ann Swidler, and Steven M. Tipton (New York: Harper & Row, 1985), 71-75, 335. The authors describe such places as "lifestyle enclaves."

counter on a daily basis are much like ourselves in education, race, and socioeconomic background. Many of us drive to work each day from carefully defined neighborhoods to carefully controlled work environments, and can effectively avoid encountering most strangers, particularly those that might be troublesome. For many of us, it takes intentional effort to intersect meaningfully and personally with strangers different from ourselves.

At times we deliberately turn away from vulnerable strangers, choosing not to see them, quietly steeling ourselves to resist their intrusions into our lives. This is not only a contemporary problem; Chrysostom and Wesley criticized parishioners who ignored the poor and the strangers they encountered. They had strong words for Christians who pled ignorance when they had actually chosen not to see.[13]

A peculiar feature of contemporary life is that while we are able to screen out actual persons from our lives, the media provide us with images of needy strangers who walk into our living rooms every evening. News reports and documentaries broadcast the most terrible details of the lives of refugees or famine victims thousands of miles away, and regularly bring their faces and stories into the most intimate spaces of our homes. We are saddened, sometimes overwhelmed, and wonder at such desperation. However, these people and the reports about them rarely make any claim on our personal response and we quickly move on to the next report or family task. We can know more about a woman in Rwanda or Kosovo whose family was decimated in the latest outbreak of ethnic cleansing than we do about the homeless man we walk by daily on the way to the office, or the elderly woman who lives two doors down from us.

A steady exposure to distant human need that is beyond our personal response can gradually inoculate us against particular action. It can also delude us into thinking that by simply knowing about it we are somehow sharing in the suffering of others. Isolation from local need, and overexposure to overwhelming but distant need, make our responses to strangers uncertain and tentative at best.

---

13. Chrysostom, Homily 21 on Romans, NPNF1, vol. 11, p. 504, and Wesley, *Works of John Wesley,* vol. 3 (Nashville: Abingdon, 1986), Sermon 98: "On Visiting the Sick," pp. 387-88.

## "Unknown" Strangers and Personal Responses

When most of the ancient hospitality traditions were shaped, every stranger was dependent on someone else's hospitality — inns were rarely available and often had a bad reputation. Dependence on personal hospitality, then, had little to do with lack of resources. Strangers were not necessarily destitute, only away from home and in immediate need of food and shelter. Providing hospitality to them was the customary practice.

Inns provided minimal accommodation primarily for merchants and traders away from home. As commerce developed so also did commercially provided hospitality. Noting the increasing dependence on inns by the mid-seventeenth century (as trade was also increasing), John Owen wrote, "It must also be acknowledged, that whereas provision is now made in all civilized nations for the entertainment of strangers, though at their own cost, things are somewhat in this case altered from what they were in the younger days of the world."[14] Today, we can hardly imagine travel without hotels and restaurants, and would find it quite uncomfortable to be regularly dependent on the hospitality of strangers.

So today, strangers with resources take care of their own needs, and we usually assume that people without resources can turn to benevolence institutions, service agencies, and the state for help. Personal hospitality, in home and in church, tends to be reserved for people with whom we already have some connections. It is hard for us to think of offering personal hospitality to strangers.

Strangers that we do invite into our homes are rarely complete strangers to us. Complex educational, socioeconomic, familial, and religious networks reduce the strangeness, the "unknownness" of such people. We seldom notice how substantially bounded our private worlds are — how few "unknown" strangers we welcome, nor do we recognize how frequently the boundaries are socioeconomic.

But strangers — with or without resources — continue to need hospitality. Those with financial resources still need human connections; professors far from home are enriched by the food and friendship of hospitality. Strangers without resources need more than the minimal food, clothing, and shelter that might come through institutional provision. They need friendships and opportunities to contribute their gifts to a community.

14. Owen, *Works,* 7:387-88.

We may be willing to acknowledge that needy strangers can benefit from personal hospitality, but we are unlikely to offer welcome without reducing "strangeness" and risk. Overcoming strangeness is necessary when our responses are personal and when strangers are welcomed into personal, valued places. The very private character of the contemporary home makes hospitality more difficult and more risky. Both hosts and guests are more afraid of being victimized when hospitality is completely hidden from the view of others. That is why we depend on finding ways to reduce strangeness and why we are much more likely to welcome work associates, church members, and distant relations than total strangers.

Obviously, there are risks in welcoming strangers. It is not necessarily the case that strangers only bring blessing and gifts, though sometimes they do. In a fallen, disordered world, strangers may be needy, but they occasionally take advantage, bring unanticipated trouble, or intend harm.

## "Risky" Strangers and Worried Hosts

In almost every conversation and discussion about hospitality to strangers, someone raises a question about risks and danger. Some people have compelling horror stories about troubled guests who set their host's house on fire, stole the family's food money, or molested a child. Others tell of guests who came but then would not leave, or took over the house. Still others tell of encountering corrupt hosts who used their hospitality as a cover for predatory behavior. While these incidents are very infrequent, they are very serious and occasionally devastating. We worry about risk and danger not only because of concerns about our own safety. Because of responsibilities to protect others in our families and communities from harm, especially children and other vulnerable persons, we must attend to the possible dangers.

People have always worried about the risks and danger in welcoming strangers. Frequently, we look back to the old days as a time when hospitality to strangers was easier and safer. Many of us are convinced that our grandparents or great-grandparents had an easier time with hospitality back on the farm or in their tight ethnic community.

Martin Luther was sure that the Old Testament patriarchs and their children had found it safer and easier to offer hospitality to strangers than was the case for the Christians of the sixteenth century, for "there was not such a large number of vagabonds and scoundrels in the world as there is today." He warned households to be cautious "lest through lack of discretion they invite dangers for themselves." While patriarchs could receive "strangers as reverently as if God Himself were coming," "in our age, in these dregs of the world, there is such great wickedness, and there are such manifold instances of fraud and deceit that you do not know what to do for anyone."[15]

Calvin also believed that in Abraham's day it was safer to exercise hospitality than it was in his own situation. "At that time, there was greater honesty than is, at present, to be found among the prevailing perfidy of mankind; so that the right of hospitality might be exercised with less danger." Calvin associated the increased dependence on commercially provided hospitality in his own day with increased sinfulness.[16]

Concern about the risks in offering hospitality to strangers is evident even in an ancient rule governing monastic life from the fifth or sixth centuries. The writer feared that guests welcomed into the monastery might be thieves or mischief-makers, "parasites," or "loafers."[17] Nevertheless, none of these writers saw the risk as sufficient reason for excluding strangers or neglecting hospitality; only that the risks had to be acknowledged and reduced. Thus, Luther recommended that hosts get references for strangers from persons that were trusted. The monastic rule included instructions to keep a watchful eye on guests and to require that they share in the work of the community. Although some of the language and strategies might strike us as overly suspicious, we can learn from those who worked to reduce risks in times when hospitality was more commonly practiced.

One of the ways to reduce risk is to make hospitality more public. This is not to suggest making hospitality less personal, but rather that welcome be initiated in a more public setting and sustained in less private places. Several Old Testament accounts show hospitality beginning in a

15. *Luther's Works* (Philadelphia: Fortress, 1955-), vol. 4, "Lectures on Genesis Chapters 21–25," p. 282; vol. 3, "Lectures on Genesis Chapters 15–20," p. 245.

16. Calvin, *Commentaries on the First Book of Moses Called Genesis,* vol. 1 (Grand Rapids: Wm. B. Eerdmans, 1948), 470.

17. *The Rule of the Master,* 78:1-9, trans. Luke Eberle (Kalamazoo: Cistercian Publications, 1977), 240.

public place where the community gathered regularly. The stranger was first encountered there, and then invited into an individual household. Welcoming total strangers is difficult when there is no community setting in which initial minimal relations can be established. When there is no way to mediate strangeness, when there is no space or means by which people can safely and comfortably engage in initial encounters with one another, then potential hosts worry about danger and deception and strangers are less frequently welcomed in.

Hospitality begins at the gate, in the doorway, on the bridges between public and private space. Finding and creating threshold places is important for contemporary expressions of hospitality. Several communities of hospitality approach this issue in creative ways. In one case they established a large urban household easily accessible to strangers. In that house, several families welcomed strangers and in ongoing, informal relations were able eventually to discern who among them might benefit from extended hospitality in their community's rural household. Another community uses its main house to welcome homeless people; after a person has lived with them for a month or two, he or she might then be invited into a more intimate family setting in which to live for several years.

In these transitions, bridge or threshold people are very important. Such persons understand both the world of the stranger and the world of the welcoming community. Often they are persons who were previously welcomed as strangers and then eventually became part of the community, assuming the role of host with newer strangers. Such persons can interpret and discern situations, needs, and resources effectively.

In previous centuries, welcoming households were often quite large and active with many tasks. In fact, hospitality may have been easier for Abraham and our great-grandparents, not because people were less sinful in those days, but because the practice had a stronger moral claim and because households were larger. Never have households been so small, so frequently empty, and so separated from a larger community as they are today. Smaller households make the need to reduce strangeness and risk more acute. Contemporary communities of hospitality have intentionally constructed households that include more people and are more active than most in our society. This enables them to welcome full strangers with less worry about risk and danger.

Other ways of reducing risk are evident in early Christian practices.

When Christians offered substantial hospitality to Christians from other places, they developed structural arrangements and institutional settings that helped reduce strangeness. In the early church, they used letters of reference from other believers.[18] They also employed simple tests — warmly welcoming strangers and then observing their behavior. If they stayed too long, were idle, or revealed by their life or conversation that they were false or immoral, then hospitality was withdrawn.[19] Strangers were welcomed into the community's rituals of worship, shared meals, and the Eucharist — practices which helped incorporate people from very different backgrounds and helped in reducing their differences. In the first centuries, deacons acted as patrons of the local poor, seeking out those in need, identifying the details of their circumstances, and bringing their condition to the attention of the bishop.[20] They employed an almost proactive approach to hospitality.

When monastic communities welcomed strangers into their midst, they welcomed them into a very structured environment. *The Rule of Benedict* provides a significant model for this. The stranger was received as Christ, welcomed warmly, and invited into a number of the daily rituals of monastic life. During prayer, the reading of Scripture, and a shared meal, strangers could become known and some of their character and intent could be discerned.[21]

A later example of a way of reducing the strangeness of strangers comes from eighteenth-century Methodism's emphasis on small group meetings. Their intimate small-group structuring provided a setting in which strangers could become known to several persons who lived nearby to them. This arrangement provided for mutual accountability and help as persons moved from being strangers toward being members.

Without intentionally building some minimal connections, it is unlikely that we will welcome the most vulnerable people into our homes or churches, even if we accept responsibility to offer hospitality to strangers and recognize its significance for them. We need to find or create contem-

18. See Acts 18:27; Rom. 16:1-2; 1 Cor. 16:3; Phil. 2:29-30; Philem. 8-17; 3 John 12.

19. See *Didache* 11:1-6; 12:2-5; Shepherd of Hermas, *Mandate* 11:12-13.

20. Gerhard Uhlhorn, *Christian Charity in the Early Church,* trans. Sophia Taylor (Edinburgh: T. & T. Clark, 1883), 160.

21. See *Rule of Benedict,* chaps. 53 and 61.

porary equivalents of the city gate, community rituals, and small group meetings in which we can build preliminary relations with strangers.

Christians also used theological arguments to reduce resistance to welcoming strangers and to minimize concerns about risk. Welcome involved identifying common ground with strangers; the stranger was never welcomed as "other." Exhortations to extend hospitality recognized that the stranger was created in the image of God and was made of the same human flesh. Almost every sermon insisted that Christ was to be recognized and welcomed in the needy stranger. The force of Matthew 25:35, "I was a stranger and you welcomed me," was profound in providing common ground between strangers and hosts. Jesus, the most desired guest, comes in the form of the vulnerable stranger. The possibility that hosts are welcoming Jesus can overcome resistance and fear.

Recognizing shared human experience also provided common ground. To be welcomed as guests, strangers had to be viewed as similar to the hosts, "like us" in needs, experiences, and expectations. It was not sufficient that strangers be vulnerable; hosts had to identify with their experiences of vulnerability and suffering before they welcomed them. Old Testament texts reminded the Israelites that they knew the heart of the stranger from their own experience (Exod. 23:9) and therefore had to treat strangers well. Responses of care depend significantly on empathy.

It is important to reduce strangeness because it takes work and courage to offer substantial hospitality. Welcome to persons very different from ourselves is demanding. When persons are different, inconvenient, or their needs are substantial, we have to work at finding connections and sustaining commitment.

A very potent way to exclude strangers from even the most basic provision and safety, not to mention our homes, is to focus on their difference and to exaggerate their strangeness. Nazi forces made Jews into strangers by wildly exaggerating their "otherness." The logic of ethnic cleansing depends on seeing another culture or community as totally other and alien. The current hostile rhetoric about immigrants and refugees portrays strangers as dangerous and other.

A close reading of the hospitality tradition suggests that we should carefully consider current philosophical discussions which emphasize and celebrate the "otherness" of persons. While we certainly want to appreciate difference and affirm particular identity, and while we often need to take the focus off ourselves and our own distinctives, we must remember that actual care for strangers has been tied to seeing them fundamentally as like ourselves. Hospitality has depended on recognizing our commonalities rather than our differences, seeing strangers as neighbors, brothers, and sisters.

## Desperate Strangers and Hesitant Welcome

Many of the historical figures who have written so eloquently on the importance of hospitality also help us to see that certain situations make hospitality much more difficult or overwhelm hospitality practices entirely. Commitments to welcome can be overwhelmed by large numbers of strangers or by the magnitude of their needs. Three groups of strangers have often strained the limits of hospitality, though their need for hospitable responses has typically been desperate. Partly because of their numbers and partly because of their detachment from institutions and relationships, pilgrims, the displaced poor, and refugees strained the limits of hospitality.

Pilgrims were among the first masses of people who were detached from place and social relationships; few had significant connections with hosts along the way. Many were beggars, combining the vulnerabilities of the poor and the stranger; some pilgrims were criminals and adventurers. Such a mixture made hospitality within the household dangerous and unwieldy. Thus in the Middle Ages, hosts — whether in great lay or monastic households — differentiated the welcome they offered to pilgrims. The quality of welcome was based not on the pilgrim's character, but on his or her wealth and social rank. Poor pilgrims, especially, were handled at a distance, at the gate or in institutions set up for them; rarely were they welcomed into the center of the household.

An example of how harshly communities could deal with masses of impoverished and uprooted people comes from sixteenth-century England. As much as fifty percent of the population faced grinding poverty in that period.[22] Vagabondage and vagrancy were widespread and sometimes orga-

22. Christopher Hill, *Society and Puritanism in Pre-Revolutionary England* (New York: Schocken Books, 1964), 274.

nized. Communities were hard-pressed to deal with this new category of poor persons — strangers detached from community responsibilities, mobile and "masterless."[23] The vagrant bands could be frightening — able to demand alms or lodging by virtue of their size and sometimes their lawlessness. English monarchs feared them as ungovernable, unsettled, and ready to join in rebellions. Authorities dealt with them by harsh and utterly unsympathetic legislation and with severe punishments.

Later, the impact of urbanization and industrialization turned many poor people into strangers, persons detached from the land and from old obligations that connected lord and tenant. The poor who migrated to the cities became a permanent mass of "strangers." Their needs and numbers were far greater than could be addressed by the dying practices of medieval hospitality.

Large numbers of refugees also strained the limits of hospitality. Sustained welcome to refugees seems to have been closely tied to their economic impact on the settled population. Hospitable responses waned when refugee needs were substantial and were perceived as a drain on local resources. They also waned when refugee skills and successes threatened local business, agriculture, and general social and political arrangements. This was evident in the Geneva of Calvin's day, a small city which struggled to absorb thousands of persecuted Protestants. The local population was often less enthusiastic than Calvin about a "sacred duty" to welcome refugees. Similar complaints surface today in communities in the United States that perceive immigrants or refugees as threats to the local economy or community identity. People proclaim that there is "no more room" when they feel overwhelmed by cultural difference or socioeconomic need, or when they feel threatened by the increasing power of strangers who have come. Strangers are then recast as enemies, threats to the community.

Today hospitality can also be overwhelmed by the unpredictability and violence sometimes associated with addictions and severe mental illness. In some situations, given the numbers of needy persons or the gravity of their distress, we properly turn to more specialized institutions to meet needs. The Catholic principle of subsidiarity can be helpful in dis-

23. See A. L. Beier, "Vagrants in Elizabethan England," *Past and Present* 64 (August 1974): 27.

cerning these situations. It is best to care for strangers and to meet needs at the most personal, unstructured level possible; when necessary, we can move to more structured environments and responses.[24]

Certain characteristics or perceptions of characteristics of strangers and their situations make welcome easier or more difficult. Strangers whose needs and difficulties seem beyond their control are perceived as "deserving" of help and are more readily welcomed. These strangers, using Philip Hallie's image, are persons who need to be and can be "rescued" from a "hurricane" — some externally caused problem or disaster. Those who bring the "hurricane" with them in the form of addictions or severe mental illness also need welcome, but informal personal hospitality alone is rarely sufficient.[25]

Those strangers who are part of a mass of desperate people often find a hesitant welcome because hosts fear that the task will never end, that the "flow" will continue indefinitely. Strangers whose needs are short-term, even if substantial, are easier to welcome than those whose need for assistance remains ongoing. In the first case, there is the potential that once the need is addressed or the crisis has been survived, persons can quickly return to self-sufficiency. Those with complex and long-term needs present greater challenges for hospitality.

Strangers with some resources such as marketable skills, supportive family, or finances are usually easier to welcome than those who have no resources or connections. Strangers who bring with them a history, values, and commitments that are shared by their hosts usually find a more ready welcome.

Recognizing that some characteristics of strangers make welcome easier or more difficult is not to suggest that ease or difficulty is tied to whether people deserve welcome or whether others have an obligation to welcome them. It does suggest, however, that in the practice of hospitality, there are varying degrees of commitment required and levels of challenge experienced, depending on the needs and the resources strangers bring with them.

24. See *The New Catholic Encyclopedia* (New York: McGraw-Hill, 1967), vol. 13, s.v. "Subsidiarity," by R. E. Mulcahy, p. 762.
25. Philip Hallie, *Tales of Good and Evil, Help and Harm* (New York: HarperCollins, 1997), 204.

## The Strangers Nearest to Us

Gracious welcome to those with significant needs and vulnerabilities (e.g., homeless people, refugees and migrants, and persons with severe disabilities) includes material and physical help, inclusion in community, and a respect for them that values their identities, stories, and contributions. Hospitality to such persons, especially if welcoming involves more than an individual or single family in need, often requires the resources of a community organized around hospitality. But there are many other strangers and neighbors for whom hospitality can also have incalculable benefits. Neglected children or those with special needs, abused women, pregnant teens, and persons recovering from severe illness or in the later stages of terminal disease can be welcomed by individuals or single families. We do not have to choose the very hardest scenario to offer life-giving or life-sustaining hospitality.

For strangers with adequate material resources, hospitality can bring connections, community, comfort, and a place. People who are isolated or distant from family and friends need a welcoming place, the warmth of a shared meal, a family that will adopt them. International students, foreign workers, college students, and soldiers far from home can easily be drawn into a welcoming household or church. We can give hospitality to elderly neighbors, families who have recently relocated, individuals whose families are destructive, and persons recovering from some traumatic experience. These people are often first encountered in church, work, school, or neighborhood — and welcome, though important, is not particularly complicated, sustained, or risky.

Some of the strangers most in need of the companionship, recognition, and care characteristic of hospitality are hidden in prisons and in facilities for extended care. Visiting prisoners and the sick was viewed by the ancient church as an extension of hospitality. To reach these people requires a willingness to enter their world, and to accept the role of the stranger who brings friendship and comfort. In a similar way, persons who serve on hospice teams enter homes as strangers but enable the family of the dying person to provide hospitality to their loved one.

In emphasizing the moral responsibility to welcome strangers, especially vulnerable strangers, it is possible to overlook opportunities for hospitality much closer to home. In fact, the hospitality we give to strangers is an extension of the welcome we offer the members of our households and churches.[26] The risk, however, in focusing our hospitality on those closest to us is that our welcome can easily slide into entertainment, or become so oriented to friends and family that there is no room or time for others who have few friendship and family networks to sustain them.

We should never trivialize the importance of welcoming family and friends into a loving place. Grace-filled hospitality to a relative or a friend who needs some time and a place to recover from weariness or wounds is a tremendous gift. Welcoming and incorporating an aging parent into one's home is a wonderful expression of hospitality. Providing hospitality to those who work on the front lines of ministry in difficult or exhausting circumstances is a ministry in itself. Those who are primary caregivers to an elderly relative or a seriously disabled child can be renewed through simple acts of welcome and kindness. Many of these workers do not themselves have sufficient resources to arrange a needed vacation, and a welcoming household in a peaceful setting can provide much needed respite and relief. Even beyond these possibilities, hospitality is simply a joy of life. As we welcome family, friends, and coworkers into loving places, we find mutual refreshment in shared meals, in conversations, and in the shelter of each other.

Most communities of hospitality actually welcome different kinds of strangers, and their hospitality is multilayered. Some of the strangers, such as homeless people or refugees, have multiple needs and are the primary focus of the community's ministry. But in almost every case there are other groups of strangers who also receive significant welcome. Many of these people come hungering for a vision of an authentic Christian life or for a taste of Christian community. Some are looking for meaning, purpose, or an opportunity to contribute their gifts to others. In some communities, the numbers of visitors and volunteers far exceed the numbers of persons around whom the ministry was originally shaped.

Don Mosley of Jubilee Partners describes the welcome they provide beyond their care for refugees. "And then we do another type of hospitality . . . to middle class, North Americans, Europeans, who have it . . . materially but come here because they sense there is a chance to touch something that will make their lives more meaningful." Another worker, noting their vari-

---

26. See Jean Vanier, *Community and Growth*, rev. ed. (New York: Paulist Press, 1989), 272.

ous kinds of guests, commented, "I think each one is just as valuable. The volunteers, the guests, the refugees are all just as valuable." At L'Arche, people with disabilities are the core community but many other visitors and seekers are welcomed because of the founding mission to be an expression of hope in the world, to be a living demonstration that love is possible.

One community that cares for homeless people defines its ministry more broadly to include other strangers and neighbors as well. It welcomes the social worker struggling with cancer or with a sick child, convinced that she is a "person equally valuable to us as the homeless Bob." In the neighborhood, workers reach out to local children through "kids clubs," and guests assist their elderly neighbors with home repair and maintenance. The founder of the community stresses the importance of making time to visit with neighbors and realizing "that your time with them is equally valuable as time with the homeless. Because ultimately, it's all ministry to the Lord." On Friday nights, they offer supper to elderly and mentally ill people from a nearby housing complex and to others in the area who had formerly lived in the house. Often, the meal is prepared and served by some of the homeless people who recently found help and shelter in the community.

In the context of hospitality, strangers with questions about faith and meaning can find answers. Monasteries which are never without guests[27] welcome seekers and inquirers looking for a fuller Christian life. For forty years, L'Abri households have welcomed students and seekers from around the world. In both settings, hospitable welcome embodies the answers; it gives flesh to the content of the gospel.

When hospitality is a way of life, the strangers and guests we welcome seem to become increasingly diverse. A life that is open to surprise and contingency has room for the refugee family and the elderly woman down the street recovering from surgery. The door is open to the teenager with developmental disabilities and to the student with questions about life's meaning and purpose. The hospitable church finds room for the homeless man and for the family that has just arrived from a distant state. Obviously, as finite persons, there are limits to how much we can do, but welcoming different kinds of strangers usually equips us to open the door wider and more often, with less fear and more confidence.

27. *Rule of Benedict* 53:16.

# 6. HOSPITALITY FROM THE MARGINS

*"I was a stranger and you welcomed me."*

MATTHEW 25:35

"I WAS AN ORPHAN AT THIRTEEN. NO ONE SHOULD EVER be alone." These two simple sentences provided a window into my ninety-one-year-old grandmother's determination that, once again, we would take Christmas dinner to an elderly acquaintance of hers who lived several towns away. For all of her long life, my grandmother welcomed countless acquaintances and strangers, but never before had she or I connected this consistent practice of hospitality to her own childhood experience of having been left alone, raised in an unfamiliar and sometimes unkind household. Her distant but still vivid memory of having been an orphan and stranger sustained a lifelong passion for hospitality.

Impatient with her descendants who did not always share her hospitable bent, she chided us when we tried to remind her that Mr. Arthur often seemed to have more food than he needed when we brought the holiday dinners. With obvious frustration she explained, "It's not just about food, you know, it's about knowing someone cares."

My grandmother's comments express a fundamental truth about hospitality — that the experience of having been a stranger, or of being a vulnerable person on the margins of society, is often connected with *offer-*

*ing* hospitality. When hospitality involves more than entertaining family and friends, when it crosses social boundaries and builds community, when it meets significant human needs and reflects divine generosity, we often find hosts who see themselves in some way as marginal to the larger society.

## The Connection Between Marginality and Hospitality

Vulnerable strangers in need of welcome are usually marginal to the society because they are detached from significant human relationships and social institutions; often they are overlooked and undervalued by people more centrally situated. The marginality of hosts is somewhat different; it most often involves a certain distance rather than detachment from important social institutions. It may also involve a deliberate withdrawal from prevailing understandings of power, status, and possessions. Such hosts are often distinguished from the larger society by their practices, commitments, and distinctive ways of life.

The Bible makes the experience of marginality normative for the people of God. For the Israelites and the early Christians, understanding themselves as aliens and sojourners was a reminder of their dependence on God. It provided a basis for gratitude and obedience. For the Israelites, especially, it was also connected to recognizing the feelings and vulnerabilities of the literal aliens who lived among them. Alien status for the early Christians suggested a basis for a different way of life and loyalties to a different order, which in turn challenged conventional boundaries and relationships. In emphasizing that both provision and welcome came as grace, the early Christians shared their lives and possessions with one another and transcended significant social and ethnic differences. Alien status allowed them to recognize the importance of making a home on earth and of nurturing the practice of hospitality, but it also relativized and transformed the experience of "home." While home was important, it was also provisional.

Jesus makes hospitality more complicated for Christians. We offer hospitality within the context of knowing Jesus as both our greater host and our potential guest. The grace we experience in receiving Jesus' welcome energizes our hospitality while it undermines our pride and self-righteousness. The possibility of welcoming Christ as our guest strengthens our kindness and fortitude in responding to strangers.

The periods in church history when hospitality has been most vibrantly practiced have been times when the hosts were themselves marginal to their larger society. The basis for their marginality varied. For example, the early Christians were a persecuted minority, literal aliens in some cases. In the patristic period, when persecutions were over, some Christians deliberately re-created marginality through their ascetic practices and monastic life. Among the early Methodists, many of those who cared for poor people and strangers were themselves poor and of low social status.

Victor Turner's work on liminality and community is helpful in interpreting the distinctive characteristics of these periods. These were times when Christians were more intentional about equality, when there was more ambiguity within the Christian community as to status and rank, and when there was more fluidity in property relations than was common in the larger society. Liminal persons and communities, as Turner describes them, "slip through the network of classifications that normally locate states and positions in cultural space. Liminal entities are neither here nor there; they are betwixt and between the positions assigned and arrayed by law, custom. . . ."[1]

In Turner's analysis of liminal persons across cultures and time periods, he notes that all share certain characteristics. They either "1) fall in the interstices of social structure, 2) are on its margins, or 3) occupy its lowest rungs." Turner associates the most intense forms of community with situations of liminality, marginality, and inferiority.[2]

The most transformative expressions of hospitality, both historically and in our own time, are associated with hosts who are liminal, marginal, or at the lower end of the social order. These hosts are essentially threshold or bridge people, connected in some ways to the larger society but distinct from it either in actual social situation or in self-imposed distance. Without these crucial dimensions of marginality and

1. Victor Turner, *The Ritual Process* (Ithaca, N.Y.: Cornell University Press, 1969), 95.

2. Ibid., 125, 128, 130.

liminality, the relations between hosts and guests often serve the more conservative function of reinforcing existing social relations and status hierarchies.

When Christians were well connected to wealth, power, and influence, some deliberately chose to construct a marginal identity and context. An excellent example comes from ancient Christian monasticism. With its strict rules on simplicity, dress, obedience, and chastity, monasteries created a setting highly distinguished from the larger society. With their daily practices and rituals, and their separation from the world, monks were able to create a distinct way of life. Some became shining examples of Christian hospitality.

Many of the Christian leaders and writers of the fourth and fifth centuries who helped shape monasticism had themselves been very wealthy and influential in the world. Renouncing their wealth and status, they created monastic communities, or, as in the case of Chrysostom, encouraged faithful Christians to adopt monastic intensity in their ordinary lives. During this period a number of Christian women were celebrated for their exceptional hospitality. Most were very wealthy widows who gave away large parts of their fortunes and personally turned away from privilege and status. They adopted very strict disciplines for their own lives, renouncing family, sexuality, and wealth. In Turner's language, they became liminal persons — betwixt and between. The roles they played in offering hospitality and forming communities were unusual for women of their day — they found a freedom to work, minister, and travel not available to most women in the church or the culture.

From historical records we know that women such as Melania, Marcella, Paula, and Eustochium offered generous hospitality to the poor, often exhausting their family's resources. Jerome provides a long testimony to Fabiola's charity and hospitality. She was a Roman matron (d. 399) with enormous wealth who had spent time in Bethlehem with Jerome, Paula, and Eustochium. Fabiola later returned to Rome where she continued her vast charitable works. Jerome described her return: she "who only had her traveling baggage and was a stranger in every land, returned to her native city to live in poverty where she had been rich, to lodge in the house of another, she who had once entertained many guests." Jerome praised her generosity, humility, simple dress, and intensity of faith. His description of her work shows how closely her liminal status was tied to her generous hospitality. He writes that she had broken up and sold "all that she could lay her hands on of her property":

> It was a large one and suitable to her rank, and when she had turned it into money she disposed of everything for the benefit of the poor. First of all she founded an infirmary and gathered into it sufferers from the streets, giving their poor bodies worn with sickness and hunger all a nurse's care. Need I describe here the diverse troubles from which human beings suffer, the maimed noses, the lost eye, the scorched feet, the leprous arms . . . ? How often did she carry on her own shoulders poor filthy wretches tortured by epilepsy? How often did she wash away the purulent matter from wounds which others could not even endure to look upon! She gave food with her own hand. . . . I know that many wealthy and devout persons by reason of their weak stomachs carry on this work of mercy by the agency of others, and show mercy with the purse, not with the hand. I do not blame nor do I by any means construe their lack of fortitude as lack of faith. But while I excuse their weakness, I extol to the skies the ardent zeal that perfect courage possesses.[3]

Jerome was deeply affected by the contrast between Fabiola's former status and her present ascetic and charitable life. He considered her willingness to give personal service as particularly exemplary. Although Jerome and other leaders denied the significance of social status, its voluntary rejection was still very compelling. He wrote that Fabiola was generous to the poor, indigent, and sick, as well as to clergy, monks, and virgins. Rome, Jerome concluded, "was not large enough for her compassionate kindness."[4]

Fabiola founded the first hospital in the west, in Rome. Along with Pammachius, a fellow Christian of significant wealth and status, she established and maintained a hostel for pilgrims and strangers at Ostia. Jerome wrote that they contended for the "privilege of setting up Abraham's tent in the harbour of Rome":

> Not only did they relieve the wants of the destitute; their generosity was at everyone's service and provided even for those who possessed

---

3. Jerome, Letter 77, "On the Death of Fabiola," in *Select Letters,* LCL, pp. 311, 323-25.
4. Ibid., 325.

something themselves. The whole world heard that a Home for
Strangers . . . had been founded in the port of Rome. . . .[5]

Olympias (ca. 365–ca. 410), a deaconess in the church at Constantinople, worked closely with John Chrysostom. A woman of great wealth
and status, she was well known for her hospitality and charity. Out of her
personal resources, she maintained church leaders in their work, supported the poor of Constantinople, and provided for virgins and ascetics.
The writer of a fifth-century account of Olympias' life noted that "she
distributed all of her unlimited and immense wealth and assisted everyone, simply and without distinction." The author described her practice
of hospitality as "the crown of perfections," and went on to claim that no
place "remained without a share in the benevolence of this famous
woman" who supported churches, monasteries, convents, beggars, prisoners, and exiles. Olympias founded and led a community of women associated with the church in Constantinople, and from that base provided
charity and hospitality.[6]

Although in theory associated with the private sphere of the household, these wealthy women actually functioned in the ambiguous space
between public and private life. They, and the hospitality associated with
them, flourished in the institutional interstices, or overlaps of household
and church, while they simultaneously helped to create new institutions.
They achieved a liminal existence in their acceptance of the severities of
an ascetic lifestyle. In their renunciation of family ties and traditional
roles, they created an alternative to the ordinary household.

For these women, the practice of hospitality combined servanthood
with influence. Hospitality entailed the deepest acts of humility and service when offered to the poor, sick, or strangers, but it also provided close
connections with church leaders and their authority and power. When

5. Ibid., 333. Gerhard Uhlhorn, in *Christian Charity in the Early Church*, trans.
Sophia Taylor (Edinburgh: T. &T. Clark, 1883), suggests that the circle of people associated with Jerome were instrumental in bringing the hospital as an institution from the
east, where it had begun, to the west (pp. 328-29).

6. Elizabeth A. Clark, *Jerome, Chrysostom, and Friends: Essays and Translations,*
Studies in Women and Religion, vol. 2 (New York: Edwin Mellen Press, 1979), 68, 127,
130, 137. See also *Encyclopedia of Early Christianity,* 2nd ed., ed. Everett Ferguson (New
York: Garland Publishing, 1997), vol. 2, s.v. "Olympias," by William Babcock, 830.

hospitality later became separated into very defined public and private expressions, women's roles became more constrained.

Wealthy Christian women in many periods of history found opportunities to offer significant hospitality from within their large households. Safely located within a "woman's sphere," they welcomed the poor and the powerful, and had roles far greater and more influential than the rhetoric of the day often permitted women.

An interesting example from a much later time is that of Catherine Livingston Garrettson (1752-1849). An intensely devout Christian from a very prominent and wealthy New York family, she eventually married a Methodist evangelist. Their household, called "Traveler's Rest," was a center of hospitality where she welcomed "itinerant clergy, . . . ecclesiastical dignitaries, and any other persons who happened by the house needing a comfortable place to stay." In her account of Catherine Livingston Garrettson's life, Diane Lobody notes:

> Traveler's Rest was, of course, very much a public household: men and women, clergy and laity, famous personages and common folk were continually trekking in and out of this home. Catherine, though, saw this as a private household, with herself as the wife and mother, and as a good early nineteenth-century matron she took charge of the moral and religious life in her domestic sphere. Within this home that was both public and private, Catherine constructed a ministry that was entirely acceptable as a feminine enterprise and yet as vibrantly pastoral as any man's ministry. She organized and presided over regular services of worship (barring only the celebration of the sacraments), she taught Bible and theology to children, young people, and adults; she mobilized and conducted prayer groups; she expounded the scriptures within the setting of home worship . . . and she functioned, both in person and in correspondence, as a pastoral counselor and spiritual director for a great variety of persons.[7]

One of the complexities in recounting the story of hospitality is that, because many of the hosts were marginal, their particular stories were

---

7. Diane H. Lobody, "A Wren Just Bursting Its Shell: Catherine Livingston Garrettson's Ministry of Public Domesticity," in *Spirituality and Social Responsibility,* ed. Rosemary Skinner Keller (Nashville: Abingdon, 1993), 29.

overlooked in the recorded histories. Although we have some marvelous accounts of wealthy Christian women's practices of hospitality, ordinary women are invisible in significant portions of the story. While they must have done much of the work of welcome, that work along with their status was not highly valued. While we know from experience that some of the most gracious and self-sacrificing hosts are poor people, rarely were accounts of their hospitality recorded, except as we find them in miracle stories and folk tales.

In the eighteenth century, the practices of welcome were briefly but closely identified with marginal hosts and liminal places. John Wesley and the early Methodists were decidedly marginal to the English religious establishment, and many were also marginal in a socioeconomic sense. With these people, Wesley recovered ancient Christian practices that had created liminal space in which believers could offer mutual encouragement and experience personal transformation. By reintegrating household and church, the small group meetings of early Methodism recovered the most liminal setting for hospitality.

One of the ironies of Methodist history is how quickly, even in a single generation, most abandoned their marginal identity. As converts moved toward a more respectable and settled status, they lost their willingness to reach out to the most vulnerable strangers of early industrial society. Wesley had sharp words for the "gentleman" and "gentlewoman" and for those who aspired to such roles. Those who clutched the symbols of new-found respectability (fancier clothes, elegant food, and grander houses) quickly and deliberately left their poor neighbors behind.[8]

In the nineteenth century, Salvation Army workers deliberately took on a marginal and liminal identity so that they could become friends with the urban poor. An offshoot of the Methodist revival, the Army expected its workers to live among the poor, resisting what the founders called a distant "mechanical charity." They adopted the very monastic practices of distinctive dress (their special uniforms), strict discipline, and rules restricting marriage and private property. In doing this, they recovered the

8. See Wesley, *Works of John Wesley,* vol. 12: *Letters* (Grand Rapids: Baker Book House, 1978), Letters 269, 270, 271; pp. 300-302. See also *Works,* vol. 9: *The Methodist Societies: History, Nature and Design* (Nashville: Abingdon, 1989), "A Plain Account of the People Called Methodists," 271.

importance of assuming a liminal identity and of stripping away symbols
of social distinctions in the work of hospitality.[9]

Contemporary communities of hospitality vividly illustrate the
close relation between marginality, liminality, and welcoming strangers.
Leaders in a number of these communities, much like the fourth-century
women previously mentioned, have deliberately distanced themselves
from the more privileged positions in society available to them and have
chosen to place themselves on the margins of society. Almost every practitioner I spoke with had significant personal experience with being a
stranger for a time in another culture or with exposure to other kinds of
disorienting situations.

These hospitality communities embody a decidedly different set of
values; their view of possessions and attitudes toward position and work
differ from those of the larger culture. They explicitly distance themselves
from contemporary emphases on efficiency, measurable results, and bureaucratic organization. Their lives together are intentionally less individualistic, materialistic, and task-driven than most in our society. In ally-
ing themselves with needy strangers, they come face-to-face with the
limits of a "problem-solving" or a "success" orientation. In situations of
severe disability, terminal illness, or overwhelming need, the problem
cannot necessarily be "solved." But practitioners understand the crucial
ministry of presence: it may not fix a problem but it provides relationships
which open up a new kind of healing and hope.

Roles within these communities are complex and quite fluid. Recently arrived refugees make nourishing meals for their families and the
volunteers, and people with disabilities welcome visitors to their community. Members of these communities work out distinct relations to property and possessions. More things are held in common and there is a
lighter hold on property in general. In these communities there is little di-
vision between home, work, and church; hospitality happens in their dynamic overlap. Meals slide into communion or Bible study; transforming
conversations occur as the garden is weeded or as supper is prepared.

Most, though not all, of the communities have a precarious financial existence. Guests and hosts share a minimal economic security. Some

9. Maude Booth, *Beneath Two Flags* (New York: Funk & Wagnalls, 1890), 260; William Booth, *In Darkest England and the Way Out* (Chicago: H. Seigel and Co., 1890), 271.

of the workers have little or no personal income; several depend on the same clothing donations as are available to their guests.

Contemporary members of monastic communities clearly live on the margins of the larger society. But in their distinct identity and tradition, they offer a refreshing alternative to life-styles centered in consumption, immediate gratification, and unrelenting busyness. Their long tradition can teach us about the peculiar freedoms that come with a cultivated marginality.

Communities of hospitality provide persons with more conventional life-styles an opportunity to experiment with close community and hospitality to strangers. Short-term volunteers or guests of the community can assume a temporary liminal state. Leaving most of their possessions in safe storage, they can be relatively untroubled about protecting their things. They are able to put aside careers and school though they can anticipate picking them up again after their time in the community. Without having to make a permanent commitment, they are free to give graciously of their time and energy to strangers.

The experience for volunteers is often life-changing. They share in the intense and vibrant life of community and in the mysteries of hospitality to strangers. While it is possible that they will romanticize strangers, hospitality, and community, usually the work is hard enough and the relationships sufficiently challenging that they go away knowing both the difficulties and the blessings. They leave with glimpses of how they can incorporate hospitality into their regular lives. They recognize personal practices that they will need to change in order to make welcoming strangers more possible.

Certain decisions and situations contribute to a loss of marginality; often the result is more settled hosts and a much more conservative function for hospitality. Several phenomena are worth noting from history because they remain so relevant today. The first is evident within the first five centuries of the church. After the church ceased being a persecuted sect and was embraced by earthly powers, Christians moved into influential public positions. During that time, the social carriers of hospitality, persons within the Christian communities who acted as hosts, moved from the margins of institutions into more central institutional locations. As Christians became more established in positions of influence and wealth, their marginal status was diminished and their hospitality was more likely to reflect and reinforce social distinctions than to undermine them.

Later, when Christians moved their expressions of hospitality into places like hospitals, hospices, and orphanages, the "hosts" were assigned specific roles and were often paid for their work. As a result, they experienced little encouragement to develop normal relationships or to find things in common with the "guests." Specialized institutions tend to flatten social relations to one dimension — that of caregiver and recipient, or professional and client. These roles are not interchangeable, and the bonds among people are very narrowly defined.

Another factor which seems to have undermined the important connection between marginality and hospitality is the change in the primary location of Christian hospitality. In the earliest centuries of Christianity, the gathered church, in their shared meals and household-based fellowship, had provided an important site for hospitality. The setting and practices of these assemblies reminded Christians that they were all guests of the divine host, adding a certain richness and paradoxical complexity to human guest/host relations. Over the centuries, the church's role in hospitality eroded, and any expressions of ecclesiastical hospitality were centered in the bishop's household, not in the gathered church.

Hospitality was later associated primarily with the smaller individual household, entirely separate from the church. The liminal dimensions of hospitality were lost as hosts were firmly settled in private household space which they owned. Roles for guests and hosts were sharply defined and hospitality lost many of its most interesting and mysterious dimensions.

## Marginality and Possessions

Recognizing our status as aliens in the world is important for attitudes toward resources and property. Although for most of church history private property was taken for granted, its use among Christians was sometimes moderated by the teaching that everything beyond necessity belonged to the poor. Most of the normative discussions of hospitality assumed that God had loaned property and resources to hosts so they could pass them on to those in need.[10]

10. See, for example, Augustine's sermons on almsgiving and Wesley's on the dangers of riches. A similar commitment is evident in the "Aims and Means of the Catholic

Hospitality requires some material resources. In theory, the more resources available, the more hosts can supply hospitality. However, substantial resources also bring hosts into intimate connections with the larger society and its power and status arrangements. This often undermines an alien identity important for provoking a generous and personal response to need. In fact, the relation between hospitality and resources is far from simple.

In the second-century writing of Hermas we can see an important connection between alien residence and the use of resources. The *Similitudes* begin with the claim that servants of God are living in a "strange country," far from their true home of heaven. Given their alien status, it makes little sense for believers to collect possessions, fields, or dwellings. Christians live under another law; whatever they have beyond what is sufficient for their needs is for widows, orphans, and other afflicted persons. God gives more than sufficiency for that purpose, not for making believers comfortable and vulnerable to the enticements of a strange land (*Sim.* 1:1-11).[11]

For John Chrysostom, likewise, the images of stranger, pilgrim, and alien served to critique the wrong use of wealth. When Christians understand their life on earth as residing in a foreign land, where they are "strangers and sojourners," they can more readily recognize how uncertain their stay is. If Christians live "in a strange land as though in [their] home country," they build "extravagant mansions," and indulge in "countless other luxuries," wasting their substance on "inanities." Because, when forced to leave the land of their sojourn they will be unable to take their possessions and buildings with them, Christians should instead use their wealth to benefit those in need.[12]

---

Worker Movement," which states that "Houses of hospitality are centers for learning to do the acts of love, so that the poor can receive what is, in justice, theirs; the second coat in our closet, the spare room in our home, a place at our table. Anything beyond what we immediately need belongs to those who go without" (*The Catholic Worker* 65/3 [May 1998]: 3).

11. Shepherd of Hermas, *Similitudes, The Apostolic Fathers,* vol. 2, LCL.

12. See Chrysostom, Homily 2: "Concerning the Statutes," NPNF1, vol. 9, p. 350; Homily 12 on Matt. 3:13, NPNF1, vol. 10, pp. 78-79; Homily 16 on 2 Corinthians, NPNF1, vol. 12, pp. 358-59; Homily 42 and Homily 45 on Genesis, in *Homilies on Genesis 18–45,* trans. Robert C. Hill, The Fathers of the Church, vol. 82 (Washington, D.C.: Catholic University of America Press, 1990), pp. 432-33, 471. See also Rowan Greer's excellent discussion of the paradox of alien citizenship in *Broken Lights and Mended Lives* (University Park: Pennsylvania State University Press, 1986), 141-61.

Hospitality does not require many resources; it does require a willingness to share what we have, whether food, time, space, or money. It often seems that the most gracious hosts are themselves quite poor. In his book describing his recent trip across America with no money and entirely dependent on the kindness of strangers, the journalist Mike McIntyre comments, "I walk on, wondering how it is that the people who have the least to give are often the ones who give the most." He tells of a woman with very little who provided him with a generous meal and said, "We don't have much, but we don't mind sharing what we have." She explained further, "I know what it's like to be hungry. There've been times when I've been down to my last ten cents, but people have always helped me." After benefiting from another stranger's generosity, McIntyre observed, "Once again I'm amazed at how often it's the ones with little to eat who are quick to share their food."[13]

Dorothy Day, in her book *House of Hospitality,* wrote that "The ideal, of course, would be that each Christian . . . should take in one of the homeless as an honored guest, remembering Christ's words: 'Inasmuch as ye have done it unto the least of these, ye have done it to me.'" She noted that in her experience "the poor are more conscious of this obligation than those who are comfortably off." Day described families she knew who were already overburdened but readily took in "orphaned children, homeless aged, poor who were not members of their families but who were akin to them because they were fellow sufferers in this disordered world."[14]

If it is the case that poor people provide hospitality more readily than those with more resources, there are some factors that could help account for the difference. Poor people often know what it is like to need food, shelter, and help from someone else. Often their lives are less private than those of middle-class people, and more family and neighbors are around on an ordinary day. Many have a lighter hold on property and possessions. Some of their lives are less dominated by an unyielding routine and so they are able and willing to accommodate more interruptions. Traditional African-American and Hispanic cultures value hospitality highly, and have a long history of practicing it graciously even when re-

13. Mike McIntyre, *The Kindness of Strangers: Penniless Across America* (New York: Berkley Books, 1996), 42, 51, 183.
14. Dorothy Day, *House of Hospitality* (New York: Sheed & Ward, 1939), 236-37.

sources are very limited. Whether or not families have many material assets they find ways to make room for one more person — no matter how many people are already at the table.

Perhaps there is, as some suggest, an inverse relation between wealth and hospitality. But certainly, concerns about possessions can make us hesitate to offer hospitality to strangers. We worry about damage, theft, or misuse. Those of us with substantial material wealth can also be embarrassed by our abundance, especially when we live close to others in need. Rather than deal with our discomfort by making changes, we sometimes choose to keep our distance or to find new friends whose resources more closely match our own.

It is not as difficult to let go of some possessions if the people around us who have great need are people we know and love. It is easier to open ourselves to strangers when our lives are less encumbered by things. Tensions are reduced when the differences in resources are more minimal.

In communities of hospitality we see a deep intertwining of lives and resources. In those communities most influenced by the Catholic Worker tradition, workers and guests live out of the same resources — sharing the same food and space, and choosing their clothes from the same donations. Guests and hosts are sometimes nearly indistinguishable in these settings. As hosts voluntarily increase their marginal status, the marginal condition of the strangers they welcome is reduced. Often needy strangers find this voluntary simplicity surprising, if not bewildering, but they know that in their welcome into the community, they "aren't being marginalized one more time."

But the challenge to learn to hold possessions more lightly is a tough one. As one practitioner noted, after he had given up his expensive stereo he found himself trying to hold onto the nice pair of running shoes he had found in the community clothes closet. Gradually he learned that in order to see God's remarkable work of provision, he had to hold onto things with a lighter grasp.

## Marginality and Weakness

Although as a society we seem enamored with those who project self-confidence and offer ready answers to even the most complex questions, the best hosts are people who recognize their own frailties and weaknesses. When we offer hospitality, our faults as well as our possessions are open to scrutiny. If we need to hide either, we are unlikely to offer much hospitality. Hospitality to strangers, especially when practiced in community, has a way of laying bare our lives and surfacing our inadequacies.

As one practitioner commented, "There's not one day that goes by that I feel adequate to do this." Such feelings, she explained, force her to "reckon with God's grace daily." "All of us workers have weaknesses," she said, "the difference is that we can suspend . . . addressing those weaknesses for the sake of listening to other people and what their needs are." Without a healthy acknowledgment of their own frailties and needs, hosts can take on very patronizing attitudes. But hosts must also be able to move through their own brokenness in order to welcome others. The same practitioner who acknowledged her sense of inadequacy also noted that a good host is one who is "not fragile when it comes to other people's needs."

A life of hospitality means a more continual interaction with others, and fewer opportunities to carefully project a "perfect image." One practitioner explained that to try to hide weaknesses within community would be very pompous. "To be so uptight and try to put on a show for eighteen hours a day is unworkable." No one lasts long in a community of hospitality "without acknowledging weakness and frailty." We can't share all of our life "except for our failures."

While recognizing their own poverty and need, the best hosts are not undone by those needs or by the frailties of others. By locating their strength and sufficiency outside themselves, hosts are able to absorb some of the pain guests bring and are able to bear some of their burdens.

An awareness of one's own needs and weaknesses is no guarantee against self-absorption, however. Hosts who are self-focused are stifling. Hospitality requires a dynamic mix of honest assessments of adequacy, need, and God's sufficiency.

When we try to hide from the reality of human vulnerability and weakness, whether our own or others', we shut out the people who manifest that condition most acutely. We certainly find it hard to imagine that we can receive help from the most marginalized people. Hosts who recognize the "woundedness" in themselves and their ongoing need for

grace and mercy, but continue to care for others, find in God their sufficiency. Like Jesus, the best hosts are not completely "at home" themselves, but still make a place of welcome for others.

## Hospitality and Power

Persons who have never experienced need or marginality, or who are
uncomfortable with their own vulnerability, often find it easier to be
hosts than guests. Sometimes they insist on taking the role of hosts,
even in the domain of another. Giving the appearance of generosity,
they reinforce existing patterns of status and wealth and avoid questions
about distributions of power and resources. They make others, especially poor people, passive recipients in their own families, churches, or
communities. Recipients of such "hospitality" thus become guests in
their own house.

I witnessed a powerful expression of this phenomenon when I regularly attended a mission church. Although there was potential for some
leadership from within the congregation, the resources almost always
came from outside. One holiday season in particular, I watched with
deepening dismay as waves of well-meaning suburban congregations
came to the mission to help — they provided dinners, brought gifts, and
led the worship programs. There was, in fact, nothing that the local congregation needed to do. Everyone assumed that the local people had
nothing to offer. They became guests in their own church building. And
despite the festive trimmings, disempowerment would be a generous description of what had happened.

There is a complex dance between recognizing our own need, ministering to those in need, and recognizing their ministry to us. The helper
must also be able to receive — especially from those who look as if they
have little to offer. Gracious hosts are open to the gifts of others and allow
themselves to accept and enjoy their expressions of generosity. In his work
on issues in contemporary missions, Anthony Gittins offers an important
insight.

> Unless the person who sometimes *extends* hospitality is also able some-
> times to be a gracious recipient, and unless the one who receives *the*

*other* as stranger is also able to *become* the stranger received by another, then, far from "relationships," we are merely creating unidirectional lines of power flow, however unintended this may be. And that is quite antithetical to mission in the spirit of Jesus.[15]

The deepest condescension may be expressed in a person's unwillingness to be a guest — reflecting an unwillingness to recognize another person's capacity to help us. Allan Boesak, the South African theologian, wrote that the pinnacle of lovelessness is not our unwillingness to be a neighbor to someone, but our unwillingness to allow them to be a neighbor to us.[16]

There is a kind of hospitality that keeps people needy strangers while fostering an illusion of relationship and connection. It both disempowers and domesticates guests while it reinforces the hosts' power, control, and sense of generosity. It is profoundly destructive to the people it welcomes. It is the kind of help which, in Philip Hallie's words, "fills their hands but breaks their hearts."[17]

When hosts recognize their own need and inadequacy, even as they minister to others who are in need, the power differential between hosts and guests is reduced. Humility is a crucial virtue for hospitality, and especially important in keeping hosts' power in check. Power is a complicated dimension of hospitality.

In an effort to find common ground and develop community among hosts and guests, it is possible to overlook some profound differences.[18] When we emphasize the alien status of hosts, we must recognize that for many it is a chosen identity. If chosen, it can also be left behind. Most hosts can reconnect with the larger society with minimal difficulty. Most needy strangers have not chosen their marginal identity and cannot easily abandon it. The ability to leave marginality behind means the person has a certain power in relationships. As one man from the Catholic

15. Anthony J. Gittins, "Beyond Hospitality? The Missionary Status and Role Revisited," *International Review of Mission* 83/330 (July 1994): 399.

16. Allan Aubrey Boesak, *Farewell to Innocence* (Maryknoll, N.Y.: Orbis, 1977), 5.

17. Philip Hallie, *Tales of Good and Evil, Help and Harm* (New York: Harper-Collins, 1997), 207.

18. Michael Garvey, in *Confessions of a Catholic Worker* (Chicago: Thomas More Press, 1978), 96, discusses the significance of these differences.

Worker observed, "We have the power to walk away. I could find something else to do, but I want to be here. They don't have those freedoms. [With] that power we have to be so careful."

## Empowered by Offering Welcome

The role of host is empowering because it is an acknowledgment that one has rightful access to a place of meaning and value, and that one has the authority to welcome other persons into it. The host role affirms that what you have and what you offer are valuable. An important transformation occurs when people without power or status have the opportunity to be more than guests, when they, too, can be hosts. It is a time when their contributions can be recognized and when they are not defined first by their need.

We see a wonderful example of this in the story of Zacchaeus' encounter with Jesus (Luke 19:1-10). Jesus calls out to Zacchaeus the tax collector and informs him, "I must stay at your house today." Jesus chooses Zacchaeus from the crowd to be his host and Zacchaeus, welcoming him joyfully, is transformed.

Especially when working with refugees who come from cultures in which offering hospitality remains a fundamental moral practice, it is crucial to recognize and value their expressions of hospitality. Going to their homes, sharing in their food, learning hospitality practices from them is a crucial recognition of the gifts they bring and the cultures they represent.

Some contemporary writers, in their concerns for justice and equality, argue that there is no moral requirement for oppressed groups to offer hospitality to strangers.[19] In suggesting this, however, they overlook the

19. For example, Thomas Ogletree writes in *Hospitality to the Stranger* (Philadelphia: Fortress, 1985): "For the oppressed, the moral imperative is not to display hospitality to strangers. The oppressed are daily subjected to an alien world quite against their wills. . . . Their challenge is to secure social space within which an alternative world of meaning can be established and nurtured, generating resistance to oppression" (p. 4). While I understand Ogletree's point, I would emphasize the fact that many of the poor already have alternative worlds of meaning which can be nurtured if they are recognized. One form of this recognition is respecting their ability to be hosts, to offer hospitality.

recognition and power associated with being a host. Many of the important modern expressions of hospitality and self-sacrifice come from those on the margins of society, those who, in spite of their vulnerable and minimally respected positions, share their gifts and resources with others. As hosts, they have opportunity to teach others the skills they have learned for keeping hope and meaning alive in the midst of suffering and injustice. Being their guest involves recognition of their unique assets. As hosts, they subtly challenge the assumption of the larger society about where grace and strength are actually located.

Consider the "host" role African-American churches and individuals took during the civil rights campaign. Historically, hospitality was highly valued in the black church, a marginal institution in the larger society but clearly central in African-American communities. Black churches welcomed strangers, black and white, even when there was no reciprocity in the white church. According to Riggins R. Earl, an African-American ethicist, in the civil rights movement, black people literally offered themselves as embodied symbols of moral energy to turn Southerners' notions of hospitality inside out and to challenge them on their own terms. Through their nonviolence and inclusivity, protesters acted as hosts and claimed their rightful place at the table.[20]

Moral communities in which roles of host and guest are not tightly defined but allow for mutuality are communities that recognize a multiplicity of gifts. By their existence and practices they challenge societal patterns of stratification and valuing. In the various L'Arche locations, people with serious disabilities are the heart and center of the community. Many have lived in L'Arche much longer than most of the assistants who help them with daily tasks; they and the assistants make a home together. Because L'Arche households welcome an extraordinary number of visitors, core members have ongoing opportunities to be hosts and to welcome people into their place.

In other communities there is a significant reconfiguration of roles

20. I am grateful to Dr. Riggins R. Earl, Jr., of the Interdenominational Theological Center in Atlanta for our extended conversation about hospitality in the black church tradition. Some of his insights in this area are developed in his article, "Under Their Own Vine and Fig Tree: The Ethics of Social and Spiritual Hospitality in Black Church Worship," *Journal of the Interdenominational Theological Center* 14/1-2 (Fall 1986-Spring 1987): 181-93.

when guests do some or all of the cooking. Shared tasks break down barriers and have the potential for equalizing some relations. There is a sense of camaraderie that emerges and spills over as all sit down to eat together.

There are situations in which everyone is a stranger and some of the strangers must take on the role of host in order to establish any community or relationships. In groups of displaced persons such as refugees or migrants, no one feels "home." Part of the transformation of a camp or settlement into a community requires that some people become hosts, an act of courage when they are strangers themselves. But someone must begin the welcoming, the formation of a community, the forging of new relationships. A similar challenge faces persons in urban areas where community and neighborhood identity are shattered and persons have no connections with others who live nearby.

## Experience at the Margins

Many of us are situated so centrally that we have to make conscious decisions to experience marginality in our lives. I am reminded of a friend who has directed a home for homeless people for the past fifteen years. Every year he takes several days to live on the street, far from home, so that he will understand something of what it means to be marginal, treated as if he were invisible. He is determined to experience some of the disconnection and loneliness of the street. His brief sojourns as a homeless person have a profound impact on the humane way in which he runs the home and on the sensitivity with which he befriends the guests.

Describing the impact of his voluntary homelessness, he explains, "What I experience in those journeys is replenishing the reservoir of compassion. I tend to not realize how hardened I've become until I get out there. And when I see someone mistreating the homeless — a professional — it's a prophetic voice. It's the most effective teaching method for me." Experiences show him what he does and does not want to be like, and they help him to understand some of the deep-seated fears in the guests he welcomes.

Many situations can help us to experience the marginality that might make us better and more gracious hosts. Being poor and in need is one, but experience with disability is also a powerful teacher. Living as an alien in another society is also illuminating, as is being marked as different in one's own community. Such experiences can make us hard and closed, but they can also make us tender and open toward others, more ready to recognize needs, hurts, and gifts.

We can also cultivate a constructive marginality through deliberate decisions to become part of churches and communities which are sufficiently heterogeneous to challenge our own sense of being settled. In such settings we can develop friendships with persons quite different from ourselves. As guests and hosts to one another, and as hosts together to persons outside the community, we can learn new ways of hospitality.

Most gracious hosts are, in some way, marginal to the larger society, but they are not alone. Households, churches, and intentional communities can cultivate a countercultural identity that nurtures a distinct way of life,[21] a vibrant and welcoming environment, and clear reasons for welcoming strangers. Transformative hospitality still finds its most effective location on the edges of society, where it is offered by hosts who have a sense of their own alien status.

---

21. Stanley Hauerwas and William H. Willimon have developed this theme in their book, *Resident Aliens* (Nashville: Abingdon, 1989).

# III. RECOVERING THE PRACTICE

# 7. THE FRAGILITY OF HOSPITALITY: LIMITS, BOUNDARIES, TEMPTATIONS

*"The peculiar beauty of human*
*excellence just is its vulnerability."*

MARTHA NUSSBAUM[1]

WE CANNOT SEPARATE THE GOODNESS AND THE BEAUTY of hospitality from its difficulty. In a paradoxical way, hospitality is simultaneously mundane and sturdy, mysterious and fragile. As a practice it involves soup and bread, blankets and beds. But it always involves more than these, and certain tensions internal to hospitality make it fragile — vulnerable to distortion and misuse.

Hospitality depends on defined communities but it always presses those communities outward to make the circle of care larger. It requires the crossing of significant social boundaries and the simultaneous affirmation of certain distinctions. Hospitality should be offered with grace and enthusiasm, yet it is often provided in the context of limited resources. Although the practice is undermined when it is used instrumentally or for gaining advantage, hospitality often benefits both hosts and guests.

Hospitality will never be free from difficulty, but to sustain the prac-

1. Martha C. Nussbaum, *The Fragility of Goodness* (Cambridge: Cambridge University Press, 1986), 2.

tice, it is crucial to consider the well-being of hosts as well as guests. It is here that we quickly encounter struggles with limits and boundaries because physical and emotional strength, space, food, and other resources are finite. While God often supplies these miraculously, hosts still must make hard choices about how to distribute resources, expend energy, and focus ministry.

A number of years ago I was part of a church that decided to make hospitality central to its identity and life. We welcomed hundreds of refugees and many local poor and homeless people into our lives and worship. We shared homes, church, finances, meals, and energy. We attempted to respond to every person's need. It was an incredibly fruitful and blessed time. Within only a few years, however, the church itself had collapsed under the weight of ministry, the leaders worn out from the unrelenting numbers of needy strangers, the parishioners wary of any further commitments.

We were unwilling to close the door, to tell anyone there was no room. Deeply troubled by the inhospitality of many Christians during the Nazi holocaust, we were determined to welcome the refugees and strangers of our own day. Under the pressure of needs all around us, we were not careful to nourish our own lives, or to put guidelines in place that made sure workers had adequate rest and renewal. Eventually, we were only able to move from crisis to crisis, and gradually the quality of hospitality weakened.

People who become known for their generous response to strangers often find increasing numbers of strangers at their door — whether it is the door to a home, church, or community. Sometimes, as the numbers or the frequency of guests increase, hosts find themselves stretched to their limits. Energy, resources, space, identity, and cohesion of the family or the community are strained. Faced with such pressures, host communities either work out guidelines or give up hospitality, or the community itself gradually disintegrates.

Conversations with practitioners of hospitality about boundaries and limits reveal similar experiences. Most communities started out resistant to boundaries and were committed to as broad a welcome as possible. Along the way, most also decided that certain guidelines, certain boundaries were necessary to be able to continue offering hospitality. But practitioners also remained ambivalent about the boundaries — they were a concession to human finiteness, and they were never imposed without regret for the cost and loss involved.

Communities struggle with boundaries and they struggle without them. All households and communities have some boundaries, although some are more explicit about them than others. Some communities, as a matter of principle, work with minimal boundaries while others establish a significant number of guidelines for both hosts and guests. Boundaries can be literal doors and walls, but they can also be rules, policies, or mission statements. They are shaped in relation to space, resources, relationships, roles, commitments, and identity.

A closed door is the most tangible kind of boundary, but boundary issues are worked out at various levels. Some communities by their rural or isolated location deal with boundaries before people get to the door; strangers must somehow know about the place and make a significant effort to find it. Other communities welcome strangers only through referrals; in that way they make advance choices about which strangers, how many, and when they will receive them. Some communities live in the midst of need and must make decisions every time a person comes to the door.

Boundaries are troublesome in the context of hospitality for a number of reasons. By definition, hospitality is gracious and generous. Limiting hospitality seems to undermine what is fundamental to the practice. But boundaries are also a problem because so many of them are hidden. While we are likely to notice the most obvious ones — for example, turning someone away or saying there is no room — we are unlikely to notice how even our own occupations, neighborhoods, and churches can, in themselves, create boundaries that shut out most strangers, especially needy ones.

Because Christian hospitality reflects divine hospitality, when it fails it is especially devastating. Claims to have run out of resources or to have "no more room" are particularly problematic when we reflect on the abundance of God's household. There is a certain moral horror associated with turning persons away; when refugees are excluded and left in danger, or when homeless persons are left outside on freezing nights, it is rarely morally sufficient to say that there was not enough room.

The wideness of God's mercy and the generosity of God's welcome must frame our thinking about limits and boundaries. God's kindness continually challenges us to reconsider our commitments. Jesus and the stranger stand outside, asking our communities to enlarge their borders and to share their resources. As we welcome the poor, the stranger, or the marginal person, they help us to remember that each of us is an alien and a stranger, welcome only by God's generous invitation. The practice of hospitality challenges the boundaries of a community while it simultaneously depends on that community's identity to make a space that nourishes life.

Sometimes welcome must be limited and distinctions made, however, if only for the sake of other guests or members already within the community. The amount of space available and the physical and emotional capacity of the hosts and guests impose certain limits. For example, hospitable families must face the challenge of balancing their commitment to welcome with their responsibility both to preserve the marital bond and to care for their own children.

## Limited Resources

In offering hospitality, we regularly come face-to-face with difficulties posed by limited resources. In the Christian hospitality tradition, most writers did not assume that there was a problem of scarcity; they assumed that the problem was with distribution. They argued that if people who had more than they needed shared their surplus with those in need, then there would be enough for everyone. Hospitality, however, is generally practiced in the context of scarcity — a scarcity which is often the result of human injustice — and its relation to God's abundance is quite complex.

At three o'clock one morning I woke to the sound of pouring rain. I was staying in the guest room of one of the communities of hospitality. Just outside my window I could hear a chorus of coughing. Because the city had become exceedingly harsh in how it dealt with homeless people, about thirty men and women found refuge in the yard of this community every night. They must have been cold and getting wetter by the minute. An overwhelming combination of sadness and horror engulfed me — I looked around at my large and sparsely furnished room and realized that the only thing between thirty cold, wet people and a dry room was a locked front door.

I know about issues of homelessness; I teach the details to my classes. But I had never lived this close to a person's basic needs for warmth and shelter. These people — outside the door, coughing and wet — these people had names and faces. They were known to the people inside the house. They came into the house for meals during the day. How could we leave them outside when there were still corners of open space inside? Of course I have lots of space in my own home, but I had never before felt so awkward about keeping it for myself. At home, during an ordinary day, I do not encounter any homeless people, and no one ever camps in my backyard because they have no other shelter.

The next day I spoke with one of the women who had lived and worked in the community for eleven years. I asked her how she survived, knowing that the house could not take in everyone, knowing that although they provided a home for many people, some people were always left outside. How did she make peace with it and keep going? She responded that you never make peace with it, but you do what you can.

In offering hospitality, practitioners live between the vision of God's Kingdom in which there is enough, even abundance, and the hard realities of human life in which doors are closed and locked, and some needy people are turned away or left outside. A door — open or closed — is one of the most powerful images of hospitality. Responses of "Yes, of course we have room — please, come in," and "No, there's no room tonight," may be daily fare for hosts and guests, but these phrases also distill difficult questions about boundaries, scarce resources, and a place within community.

We rarely see the consequences of life-styles that have little room for strangers. Most of the time we do not live close enough to the needs of strangers, much less to our limits, to have no choice but to close the door on a particular person. We do not encounter the same soaked person the next morning, or know that the one who is coughing at breakfast slept in the rain the past night. And although we might feel some dismay at leaving someone outside or hungry, our lives are sufficiently insulated that we do not feel such pain very often.

If we are genuinely concerned about the needs of strangers, offering hospitality requires courage. It involves not only a willingness to take some risks in welcoming others, but it also requires the kind of courage that lives close to our limits, continually pressing against the possible, yet

always aware of the incompleteness and the inadequacy of our own responses. At the same time, living so close to the edge of sufficient resources increases our dependence on, and our awareness of, God's inter-
ventions and provision.

Can we say yes to everyone who comes to us? If we limit our hospitality do we risk turning Jesus away? If we say yes to everyone, how will
we keep what we offer from becoming diluted, more and more inadequate and impersonal? If we welcome a very troubled person, how will
the people we have already welcomed into our lives be affected? Do we
have a special responsibility to them? Do we have to be careful about our
own needs — will our strength be sufficient for the task, no matter how
much we take on? If we burn out in six months, what then?

Edith Schaeffer of L'Abri Fellowship captures some of the tension
with which many practitioners live when she writes that "because there
are more people than we have time or strength to see personally and care
for, it is imperative to remember that it is not sinful to be finite and limited."[2] When hospitality is not practiced widely in the larger society, or
when resources are not distributed fairly or adequately, personal hospitality cannot respond to every need. It can, however, meet some needs; it can
be a living demonstration of what is possible when people care.

Today when hospitality is freely offered, it is sometimes overwhelmed by need. An individual person or family, church, or state, which
has limited resources yet offers them to those who have less, can find itself
unable — and eventually unwilling — to meet the needs of strangers who
come in increasing numbers. We see disturbing examples of this on the
international and national level. The limits to hospitality are being pro-
claimed in many places as societies receive large numbers of refugees
from impoverished or war-torn countries. Fears of economic scarcity
combine with old nationalisms to encourage discrimination against, and
resistance to, recently arrived refugees. The economic and political injustices within countries and within the world economy cannot, of course, be
addressed by welcoming refugees, though, for the few, such welcome is a
form of rescue. For many others fleeing hunger and poverty, an uncertain
guest status locks them into an oppressive, marginalized existence in

2. Edith Schaeffer, *What Is a Family?* (Grand Rapids: Baker Book House, 1975,
1994), 201.

which they remain strangers indefinitely, kept far outside the ordinary benefits of participation in the host community.[3]

Although the practice of hospitality rarely results in major changes in the patterns of wealth or power within a society, it is at times very demanding and costly. Without directly confronting the prevailing property and power relations in the larger society, hosts sometimes share substantially from their own resources. Because hospitality is a voluntary act, it is important to take seriously concerns about limited resources and energy. Charitable impulses can fade as hosts grow weary or overwhelmed, increasing the risk of their becoming heartless or cynical about the needs of strangers.

One of the most challenging theological and practical questions raised in the practice of hospitality is whether there is "enough." Are there enough resources to care for the guests we welcome? Practitioners give different answers. One responded that there is never enough because there are always more people needing hospitality than can be accommodated. Another very experienced practitioner said with intense feeling, "There is never enough — never enough time, energy, or space."

On the other hand, every community has wonderful stories of provision. There are accounts of sufficient, sometimes abundant, food, furniture, checks, and clothing. Their experiences echo Paul's words in 2 Corinthians 9:8: "And God is able to provide you with every blessing in abundance, so that by always having enough of everything, you may share abundantly in every good work" (New Revised Standard Version). Their testimonies remind us of the story of the widow of Zarephath who shared her last bits of food with Elijah and was miraculously provided with more than enough for a long time.

Interestingly, almost every practitioner said that there had always been enough food, no matter how many people they had welcomed. There may have been very little variety, and sometimes portions were cut back, but no one went hungry. This may be a reflection of the abundance of inexpensive food in our society, or there may be some mysterious connection with biblical miracles of bread and fish, or both. Perhaps, in some sense, the supply of food is a small sign of the abundance of the Kingdom.

---

3. Consider, for example, the very difficult conditions within which "guest workers" or migrant workers live.

Although notions of how much space a person needs are shaped culturally, there are practical limits to how many people can be absorbed into a single household or community. One person observed that "It's almost an in-built conflict in the Catholic Worker about how many [guests] you take into a house. One theory is that when a stranger comes to the door, it's Christ and you let him in. And the other theory is that if you're going to let Christ in, you don't want to have Christ sleep under the sink, and you don't want Christ to crowd out all the other Christs that are already in there."[4]

Issues of space combine with psychological and emotional limits to influence how many people hosts can welcome. Everyone who offers significant hospitality is overwhelmed at times, facing deep fatigue, feeling as if it is impossible to respond to even one more person.

Although boundaries are difficult to impose and sometimes contested by hosts and guests, ignoring limits can be a form of arrogance, a refusal to recognize finiteness. One practitioner explained that after a while they knew that they could not handle people with severe mental illness at the same time that they welcomed refugees. They had to recognize their lack of structure, skill, and energy for some tasks. He explained that thinking they could handle anyone who came along was a "kind of arrogance — send us anything and we'll take care of it. We learned a long time ago that that is not true."

Many practitioners said that the hardest part of ministry is saying no, closing the door, setting limits. Ed Loring explains:

> In a ministry that is open to the suffering of the neighbor, there is a terrific pain and cost of daily having to say no, of having limits. This cuts deep for those turned away and for those who have to say it. We've gotten angry with each other over this. We have lost volunteers.[5]

Those who practice substantial hospitality live in the tension between finiteness and grace, heartbreak and miracle, tragedy and gift.

---

4. Fr. Richard McSorley, quoted in *Voices from the Catholic Worker*, ed. Rosalie Riegle Troester (Philadelphia: Temple University Press, 1993), 164.

5. Ed Loring, "Community Self-Portrait: The Open Door," in *Fire, Salt, and Peace: Intentional Christian Communities Alive in North America*, by David Janzen (Evanston, Ill.: Shalom Mission Communities/Reba Place Fellowship, 1996), 121.

Some Christians are dismayed at the notion that hospitable families and communities at times close their doors and turn people away. Ironically, some of these same Christians insist that there are limits to how much they themselves can do. Hospitality practitioners know that they cannot do everything, but they are willing to do something. In a hospitable context, any lack of welcome is very painful and very noticeable, but persons and communities are limited in their resources.

It is tempting to look at people for whom hospitality is a way of life and view them as "hospitality professionals" — people who "know how to do it." I vividly remember when my small church was in the middle of receiving hundreds of refugees. We were terribly busy and far beyond any sensible limits on space and energy. A local pastor called and said a homeless family had come to his door for assistance. He was wondering if we would take them since our church was "experienced with that sort of thing." While appreciating that this minister was trying to connect the family with help, our very weary congregation wondered if there wasn't anyone in his church who could learn the skills and graces required for welcome.

Many of us, especially when we compare ourselves with much of the world's population, live with abundance, not scarcity. But we often act as if resources are scarce; we fear there won't be enough, even before we begin sharing what we have. The problem may have much more to do with our willingness to respond than with our resources.

There is almost always more abundance in the actual practice of hospitality than we can anticipate in careful calculations about welcome. Hosts sometimes fear that they cannot possibly receive one more guest, only to find themselves enlivened and blessed as they actually welcome the person. While it is important to recognize our limits, it is equally important to remember Jesus' words that we will save our lives in giving them away (Matt. 16:24-25).

## Community Boundaries

There are other boundary questions that are in some ways even more complicated than concerns about resources. Important tensions arise as we seek to sustain a particular identity and to welcome strangers. A welcoming place is rich with stories, rituals, and a history. It is valued, and it nurtures life. It is never simply a physical space, but a place alive with commitments and relationships.

Boundaries help define what a household, family, church, or community holds precious. However, the modern world is deeply ambivalent about boundaries and community. Although we yearn for home and a place to belong, often we find ourselves more comfortable with empty space where we can "sing our own songs" and pursue our own plans.[6] Hospitality is fundamentally connected to place — to a space bounded by commitments, values, and meanings.[7] Part of the difficulty in recovering hospitality is connected with our uncertainty about community and particular identity.

Hosts value their "place" and are willing to share it; strangers desire welcome into places that contain a rich life of meaning and relationships. By welcoming strangers, however, the community's identity is always being challenged and revised, if only slightly. While this is often enriching, it can occasionally stretch a place beyond recognition.

Within much of the biblical tradition, there are tensions between living a distinctive life, holy to the Lord, and the command to welcome strangers. Their relationship is best understood through the theological framework of covenant — bonds of responsibility and faithfulness connecting guests, hosts, and God. Only in this context can we adequately understand the simultaneous practices of inclusion and separation. Faithful believers who practice hospitality understand themselves to be in a relationship with God whose worship requires holiness, a distinct identity, and attention to the needs of others.[8]

The complex relation between living a holy life and providing hospitality to strangers begins in early Israel. Israel understood itself as chosen by God and owing to God its singular loyalty and obedience. Israel's requirement and capacity to love aliens, to meet its social, economic, and legal obligations to them, was embedded in its relationship

6. Henri Nouwen, *Reaching Out: The Three Movements of the Spiritual Life* (New York: Image Books, 1975), 72.

7. See Walter Brueggemann, *The Land: Place as Gift, Promise and Challenge in Biblical Faith* (Philadelphia: Fortress, 1977), 5.

8. See Paul D. Hanson, *The People Called: The Growth of Community in the Bible* (San Francisco: Harper & Row, 1987), 425-26.

with God.[9] Two interconnected concerns in Israelite law — that of protecting and including the weak, and that of maintaining loyalty to God alone — are not separable because God's holiness includes care for the weak.

Laws concerning care for aliens were closely connected to themes of covenantal love and holiness. Israel was told to love the alien in its midst, to care for the sojourner as it cared for fellow Israelites in need, and to permit certain aliens to participate in its religious life. On the other hand, foreign elements that might subvert undivided commitment to Israel's God were rigorously excluded.[10]

It appears that Israelite response to strangers as inclusion or separation hinged, at least in part, on the capacity of the stranger to threaten Israel's identity and unity.[11] If when they left their country of origin, strangers also left behind familial, religious, and political connections, then they came under Israelite protection and care. Incorporation into membership in Israelite society was possible when strangers identified fully with the social meanings of the Israelite community — participation in festivals, laws, and, for males, identity-defining acts such as circumcision.[12]

The church, likewise, is called to be a distinct community and yet, simultaneously, to welcome strangers.[13] The first generations of Christian believers struggled to define minimal boundaries that would allow good relations among converts from different cultural, socioeconomic, and eth-

9. Norman Porteous writes that "what made Israel unique in the ancient world was that its profoundest thinkers found themselves compelled to the belief that it was the object of the active, loving concern of a God who would not allow Himself to be worshipped in isolation from the relations which men ought to have to one another" ("The Care of the Poor in the Old Testament," in *Living the Mystery* [Oxford: Blackwell, 1967], 144).

10. E.g., Deut. 18:9-16. These distinctions are evident in the four words in the Hebrew text that are generally related to the condition of being a stranger. *Ger* and *toshab* are usually connected with being a sojourner or resident alien. *Nekar/nokri* and *zar* are related more to notions of being a foreigner or foreign, maintaining ties with another home.

11. See Dale Patrick, *Old Testament Law* (Atlanta: John Knox Press, 1985), 258.

12. E.g., Exod. 12:48-49; Num. 15:14-16.

13. See Wayne Meeks' excellent discussion on the early church and its boundaries in *The First Urban Christians* (New Haven: Yale University Press, 1983), 84-107.

nic backgrounds. Certain socially significant boundaries were not to be viewed as relevant in the new community: the usual dividing lines between Jew and Greek, slave and free, male and female no longer applied "in Christ" (Gal. 3:28).

We are given some insight into one of the major struggles the first Christians faced over the issue of circumcising male Gentile converts. Especially significant to Jewish identity, circumcision was declared irrelevant for Christian identity (Gal. 5:6; 6:15). Paul argued in Galatians that if, in fact, Gentiles were to adopt the practice of circumcision, it would make Christ of no benefit to them (Gal. 5:2). However, the issue remained troublesome and was debated by the council at Jerusalem (Acts 15:1-21). Finally, the leaders concluded that "we should not trouble those of the Gentiles who turn to God, but should write to them to abstain from the pollutions of idols and from unchastity and from what is strangled and from blood" (Acts 15:19-20). This was the minimum that Jewish Christians could live with — these minimal boundaries would allow social relations between the two groups. In the greater context of God's "welcome," there was substantial freedom in observing or not observing dietary rules and sacred days, as long as such freedom did not cause weak members to stumble (Rom. 14:3, 13).

Boundaries were also important in protecting the young communities from false teaching and grave misuses of their hospitality. Every person was to be welcomed; if believers by their life or doctrine revealed themselves to be "false" or immoral, then hospitality was withdrawn. In 2 John, believers are warned that if anyone comes to them with a teaching different from the teaching of Christ, "Do not receive him into the house or give him any greeting; for he who greets him shares his wicked work" (2 John 9-11). Just as welcome given to true believers is welcome to both them and their message, and serves to support them and the spread of the message, hospitality to false teachers implicates the hosts in their "wicked work." Hospitality provided false teachers with material and social support, allowing them to undermine authority and morality, and to cause divisions (Jude 4, 8, 12, 19).

In 3 John, Gaius is commended for his hospitality to brothers who were strangers to him. By giving hospitality to these men, believers became "fellow workers in the truth." Diotrephes, on the other hand, is criticized for his evil words and refusal to welcome certain believers. Hospitality and the denial of hospitality became the context for an early struggle over whose authority and teaching would prevail (3 John 5-10).[14]

Later, in the monastic tradition, the "two-fold theme of reception and separation" remains strong. Both are defined in relation to Christ:

> Separation and hospitality are therefore two manifestations of the same love: following Christ and receiving Christ. The following draws us out of the world, but there again he comes to us under the appearances of those who are in the world, and we receive him. Then the love which has provoked the separation is verified in hospitality.[15]

In the history of Christian monasticism, "tensions accompanied every attempt to reconcile spiritual life with the reception of guests." Although guests potentially softened ascetic disciplines and introduced false teaching, they were to be received as Christ and to be provided with care.[16] Both separation from the world and welcome to the stranger were undertaken for Christ's sake.

Boundaries or guidelines protect guests, maintain communal identity and commitments, and preserve workers. They are necessary in defining who we are, and in providing the kind of ordering necessary to life.[17] While we value the uniqueness and importance of every person, we should also be able to acknowledge difference.[18]

Just as families shape their households with varying degrees of freedom and structure, so in hospitality, hosts must find an appropriate balance of boundaries and freedom that allows them to sustain the practice. Boundaries, restrictions, and guidelines will vary with the kinds of guests, type of setting, needs of hosts, and the availability of resources. Jean

---

14. See Abraham Malherbe, "Hospitality and Inhospitality in the Church," in *Social Aspects of Early Christianity* (Philadelphia: Fortress, 1983), for full discussion of this passage.

15. Adalbert deVogüé, *The Rule of Saint Benedict: A Doctrinal and Spiritual Commentary,* trans. J. B. Hasbrouck (Kalamazoo: Cistercian Publications, 1983), 261-62.

16. Aquinata Böckmann, "Openness to the World and Separation from the World According to RB," *American Benedictine Review* 37/3 (September 1986): 319-20.

17. See Miroslav Volf's book, *Exclusion and Embrace: A Theological Exploration of Identity, Otherness, and Reconciliation* (Nashville: Abingdon, 1996), especially chapters 1-3, for an excellent discussion of this entire topic.

18. Jean Vanier, *An Ark for the Poor* (New York: Crossroad, 1995), 14.

Vanier suggests that communities who welcome strangers should ask for minimal conformity and provide maximal space for diversity. In his experience, if a community states its commitments, rules, and expectations clearly from the beginning, some people will choose to exclude themselves without being denied welcome from the community.[19]

Boundaries are an important part of making a place physically and psychologically safe. Many needy strangers (e.g., refugees, homeless people, abused women and children) come from living in chronic states of fear. A safe place gives them a chance to relax, heal, and reconstruct their lives. If hospitality involves providing a safe place — where a person is protected and respected — then certain behaviors are precluded and certain pragmatic structures follow. Violent actions obviously make a place unsafe, but so can violent words. Restrictions regarding alcohol and drug use provide certain safeguards. Minimal orderliness and cleanliness give people security and a sense of respect.

Some of the most difficult questions about boundaries arise not so much in connection with hospitality as with membership in the community. Some guests do not move on but stay in the community. Long-term guest status is disempowering, and in most communities, if the guest stays on, there is eventually a change in role. The situation of Catholic Worker Houses poses this most acutely because hospitality and life in community are so intermixed. In his study on Catholic Worker hospitality, Harry Murray notes that "Guests can become members of the community, and therefore, hosts":

> Conflicts inevitably arise from this mixing of community and hospitality because the guest/community member/host often does not thoroughly internalize the Worker philosophy of hospitality. She or he may reject certain aspects, particularly nonviolence. Nonetheless, as an "equal" community member, she or he cannot be denied the opportunity to play the role of host.[20]

19. Jean Vanier, *Community and Growth,* rev. ed. (New York: Paulist Press, 1989), 275; and Kathryn Mowry, "Do Good Fences Make Good Neighbors?" in *God So Loves the City,* ed. Charles Van Engen and Jude Tiersma (World Vision: MARC, 1994), 120.

20. Harry Murray, *Do Not Neglect Hospitality: The Catholic Worker and the Homeless* (Philadelphia: Temple University Press, 1990), 208-9.

While experiences of having been a stranger/guest enrich a host's sensitivity in offering hospitality, particular frailties can also make offering hospitality to others more difficult. Members who bring with them special needs, such as mental or emotional disabilities or past addictions, often require additional support and consideration. Almost every community struggles with discerning the appropriate level of commitment and shared values necessary for membership.

When strangers are welcomed in, especially if they come in significant numbers or if they are quite different from the welcoming community, there will be strains on identity. The community will be transformed by the people it welcomes. This happens in varying degrees. There is less impact if strangers stay only briefly, but if strangers stay long-term or desire to join the community, then a fairly complex set of questions about beliefs and behaviors emerge.

Boundary issues are always slightly ambiguous when we realize that God is already working in the life of every person who comes. Recognizing this opens each community to what God might be saying, what it can learn from the stranger/guest. It keeps the possibility alive that the boundaries could be redrawn.

## Temptation to Gain or Take Advantage

Hospitality is fragile precisely because it is so potent as a human practice. Because of the human connections it fosters, and because of the significant potential for transfer of resources, hospitality can be misused by hosts and guests. It can be used instrumentally for personal or corporate gain.

In past centuries, hospitality readily served the purposes of hosts by reinforcing particular social bonds which were useful in gaining or maintaining authority, power, or prestige. Lactantius and Chrysostom worried about this in the fourth century; they were concerned that hosts might use hospitality for advantage, and that their hospitality might be "ambitious."

When hosts seek to gain advantage from hospitality, they make careful calculations about whom to include and whom to exclude in welcome. Often those most in need of welcome are overlooked because they seem to have little to offer. Beyond this, though, seeking to gain advantage through hospitality undermines it as a moral practice. If hospitality is calculated, the moral bond between host and guest is destroyed. Rather than caring for guests, and responding to their needs out of kindness or love, hosts use them as a means to another end.[21]

Hospitality is fragile because it is to be offered out of kindness only. Each historical period has provided particular temptations to seek advantage in offering hospitality, and at times hospitality has served such ambition well. While hosts often do benefit from hospitality, they must not seek it.

In the ancient church, Christians could gain advantage by entertaining "some great or distinguished man" because of the attention it brought them and the potential return of the favor. They could also benefit because of the rise in public standing that came with having someone of higher status as one's guest. Chrysostom warned Christians against using hospitality to gain "intimacy" with the powerful. Such calculating hospitality was tempting because it offered gains that were "useful in their own affairs and to their families."[22]

During that same period, Basil (ca. 330-379) worried about seeking advantage in the monastery and urged monks to offer simple and frugal meals to guests. Hospitality was to be free from worldly trappings and ostentation; otherwise it was offered with a "desire to please men" and for "display."[23] Centuries later, Calvin warned that to offer hospitality with the hope of gaining reward was not "generosity, but a system of commercial exchange."[24]

Resistance to advantage-seeking, however, was reshaped following the Reformation when concerns about mutual edification became a significant feature of hospitality. With a new emphasis on mutuality, more

21. See Alasdair MacIntyre's discussion of goods internal and external to practices in *After Virtue* (Notre Dame: University of Notre Dame Press, 1981, 1984), 187-203.

22. Chrysostom, Homily 20 on 1 Corinthians, NPNF1, vol. 12, p. 117.

23. Basil, *The Long Rules,* The Fathers of the Church (New York: Fathers of the Church, 1950), 277-78.

24. Calvin, *Commentary on a Harmony of the Evangelists, Matthew, Mark, and Luke* (Grand Rapids: Wm. B. Eerdmans, 1949), 2:166.

was expected of both guest and host. Especially when guests and hosts shared significant common ground in faith, hospitality was seen as a context for mutually edifying conversation and growth in faith. While this was not an instrumental approach to hospitality, the stress on mutual advantage was a significant shift toward emphasizing a more reciprocal practice.[25]

An even more significant change in attitudes toward hospitality can be found in the writings of Richard Baxter, a seventeenth-century English Puritan. In answering a question about costly entertaining, Baxter wrote that whatever was spent entertaining "great" guests that could have been used to relieve distressed families, was spent sinfully. However, he moved beyond the traditional critique of lavish entertaining, and offered a strikingly prudential argument for a calculating sort of hospitality:

> And yet on the other side, it may fall out that a person of quality, by a seasonable, prudent, handsome, respectful entertainment of his equals or superiors, may do more good than by bestowing that charge upon the poor. He may save more than he expendeth, by avoiding the displeasure of men in power: he may keep up his interest, by which if he be faithful, he may do God and his country more service, than if he had given so much to the poor. And when really it is a needful means to a greater good, it is a duty; and then to omit it, and give that cost to the poor, would be a sin.[26]

The ambiguous character of Baxter's argument is important. Costly entertaining was wasteful and sinful; money was to be used to support the poor, unless it could accomplish a greater good by entertaining the influential. Christians, of course, had been entertaining the influential for centuries, but rarely had that practice been so frankly described as possibly accomplishing a greater good, and never had failure to do it been regarded as a sinful breach of Christian duty. A certain pragmatism and utilitarian calculus are noticeably present in Baxter's thought. Samuel

25. See John Bunyan, *The Pilgrims Progress from this World to that which is to Come,* ed. James Blanton Wharey (Oxford: Clarendon Press, 1960), pp. 47, 52-53, for numerous examples of the "edifying discourse" Christian and his hosts engaged in.

26. Richard Baxter, *The Practical Works of the Rev. Richard Baxter,* ed. William Orme, vol. 6 (London: Duncan, 1830), "The Christian Directory," pt. 4, chap. 21, pp. 367-68.

Johnson's comments about hospitality in eighteenth-century England also show a very significant inclination toward calculation. When he concluded that "promiscuous hospitality is not the way to gain real influence," he was contrasting hospitality's former usefulness to hosts with its contemporary failure to achieve similar advantages.[27]

The temptation to use hospitality for advantage remains an important issue today because we tend to be so instrumental in our thinking, so calculating, so aware of costs and benefits. We continually ask, almost as an expression of good stewardship, "Well, what will it accomplish? How is it useful?" Hospitality is rich with blessing but such benefits come as gifts, and we must be wary of efforts to turn hospitality into some form of commercial exchange.

Most contemporary attention to hospitality links it to entertainment and commerce. Today's "effective hosts," whether perfect hostesses or elegant hotels, offer hospitality that "makes a lasting impression." Entertaining requires presenting one's self and one's place in a particular way. Carefully prepared and planned, it has a great deal to do with creating the right atmosphere and projecting the right image.

As one practitioner explained, entertainment involves "putting on something for people," creating the impression of "perfect people in a perfect house." Hospitality, in her mind, puts the focus elsewhere, asking " 'How can I extend myself for you without having all my things put together first?' . . . It's being willing to say, 'Come in — as we live.' I think it takes a certain amount of self-denial to be able to do that."

Much entertainment, especially in the business world, is tied to gaining advantage. But churches face temptations as well. Faithful Christians are encouraged to entertain neighbors and coworkers because hospitality is a good setting for the latest outreach project. Concerned pastors are challenged to adopt a comprehensive "hospitality program" as a means to church growth. Hospitality sometimes seems little more than another marketing tool.

To view hospitality as a means to an end, to use it instrumentally, is antithetical to seeing it as a way of life, as a tangible expression of love. There is probably no better context for sharing the gospel than in a setting

27. James Boswell, *The Life of Samuel Johnson, L.L.D.* (New York: Modern Library, 1931), 408.

of warm welcome, and people will come in increasing numbers to a church that takes hospitality seriously. But when we use occasional hospitality as a tool, we distort it, and the people we "welcome" know quickly that they are being used. Such misuse of hospitality feeds the loneliness that Henri Nouwen suggests is characteristic of our times. The roots of loneliness "find their food in the suspicion that there is no one who cares and offers love without conditions, and no place where we can be vulnerable without being used."[28]

It is difficult to resist the complex blend of intimacy, commercialization, and instrumental thinking that characterizes much personal entertainment, the hospitality industry, and even therapeutic techniques today. Extra vigilance is required to make sure that we do not misuse hospitality. An expression of this vigilance comes from several communities that explicitly distance their hospitality to strangers from any financial gain. One practitioner explained:

> We don't charge anything for overnight stays or for food. . . . That's the last thing we want to do. . . . It would be like charging your mother. Are you going to charge Jesus? The guests are Jesus personified. . . . For us it's just better to keep that part of our life, our relationship with other people, completely separate from dollars and cents.

By divorcing welcome from any reimbursement, the community distinguishes its hospitality from professional social services and from the hospitality industry. Not every community is as strict in separating hospitality from any reimbursement, but every Christian host must take seriously the influences of the market on gracious hospitality.

But if one of the inherent limitations in the hospitality relationship is in the potential for hosts to use it instrumentally for their own advantage, another is the potential for guests to abuse the host's generosity. If hospitality is provided out of kindness only, then a continuation of the practice requires that recipients not take advantage of their hosts. Gracious and kind hosts can never be comfortable with careful scrutiny of guests. However, unless guests take some responsibility and share some respect for sustaining relationships, the practice dries up or becomes very limited. Early church

---

28. Henri Nouwen, *Reaching Out: The Three Movements of the Spiritual Life* (New York: Image Books, 1975), 26.

documents provide evidence of these tensions when they criticize guests who make a "traffic" of Christ. Complaints that recipients were idle, lazy, or "using" hospitality also reflect these concerns. The tradition alternated between worrying that hosts might use hospitality to gain advantage and concern that guests were using hospitality to take advantage.

Attempts to protect against misuse of hospitality by guests tended to be structural. Hosts turned to letters of reference, simple tests, bureaucratic regulation, and record keeping to control advantage seeking in guests. With the substantial mobility of the early church and the emphasis on welcoming strangers, protections against misuses of hospitality were quickly established. The intention in the New Testament seems to have been to receive all persons hospitably unless their behavior or teaching was clearly destructive.[29] Some in the New Testament church used letters of recommendation to assure welcome to certain strangers, to prevent unfair demands on hospitable households, and to limit the spread of false teaching. The writer of a reference letter identified the bearer as a fellow laborer and asked that the community receive this person with the hospitality they would extend to the writer, or to any faithful worker.[30]

While urging Christians to practice hospitality, and while dependent on it for his own ministry, Paul attempts to correct its abuse and misuse. True leaders, Paul explains, do not take advantage of local communities; only charlatans abuse hospitality. Greed and false teaching are closely linked. In Acts 20:32-35, Paul reminds the leaders of the church at Ephesus that by his own labors he took care of his needs, those of his companions, and those of the weak. In a context where hospitality to strangers and to those in need was so significant, Paul was especially careful to model a role which was responsible and sensitive to the limited resources of the communities.[31]

The demands of hospitality on local households are evident in a number of New Testament passages. In 1 Peter 4:9, the church is instructed to offer hospitality "ungrudgingly" or without grumbling. Why they might have grumbled is not entirely clear from the text. However, in

29. See Donald Wayne Riddle, "Early Christian Hospitality: A Factor in the Gospel Transmission," *Journal of Biblical Literature* 57 (1938): 146-48.

30. See Malherbe, "Hospitality and Inhospitality," 101-3. See also Acts 18:27; Rom. 16:1-2; 1 Cor. 16:3; Phil. 2:29-30; Philem. 8-17; 3 John 12. Also, 2 Cor. 2:17–3:1.

31. See also 2 Thess. 3:6-10.

several other New Testament passages, there is an explicit emphasis on guests not being a burden to the local community. Paul wrote that he, as opposed to false apostles, "did not burden any one" in the Corinthian church (2 Cor. 11:8-9), that in his next visit he would not be a burden for he sought "not what is yours but you" (2 Cor. 12:14). In 1 Thessalonians 2:9, Paul reminded the Thessalonians that he and his coworkers had "worked night and day, that we might not burden any of you, while we preached to you the gospel of God."

In the extracanonical writings of the early church period, significant attention was given to dealing with abuses of hospitality. Because hospitality was the practice within which so much of the message of faith was worked out, writers continued to be concerned about protecting the young communities from those who would misuse hospitality. Their instructions reflected their efforts to establish unity and authority, and to provide for proper use of economic resources. The *Didache,* a very early Christian guide to morals and church practice,[32] offered safeguards against abuses of hospitality. Everyone who came in the name of the Lord was to be received, but also tested (12:1):

> If he who comes is a traveller, help him as much as you can, but he shall not remain with you more than two days, or if need be, three. And if he wishes to settle among you and has a craft, let him work for his bread. But if he has no craft provide for him according to your understanding, so that no man shall live among you in idleness because he is a Christian. But if he will not do so, he is making traffic of Christ; beware of such. (12:2-5)

Christians fleeing from persecution and seeking a new community in which to establish themselves were to be received and helped but they were expected quickly to assume their own responsibilities. Any Christians who depended on the community for physical support when they had no need were profiting from their Christian commitment.

The teachings of the *Didache* were an attempt to control abuses while simultaneously encouraging the practice of hospitality. The most stringent restrictions applied to traveling teachers, apostles, and prophets. The document warned communities that any teacher who perverted the

---

32. *The Oxford Dictionary of the Christian Church,* ed. Frank L. Cross (London: Oxford University Press, 1983), s.v. "Didache," p. 401.

gospel or taught "another doctrine" should not be heard, but every apostle who came and was teaching "for the increase of righteousness and knowledge of the Lord" should be received "as the Lord." However, such persons were not to be permitted to stay for more than one or two days. If someone stayed for three days, he was "a false prophet." "And when an apostle goes forth let him accept nothing but bread till he reach his night's lodging, but if he ask for money, he is a false prophet" (11:1-6). Every true prophet and teacher, however, was "worthy of his food" (13:1), and was to be supported out of the first fruits of the community.

Because hospitality was voluntary but could involve substantial sharing of resources, hosts' inclinations to provide it sacrificially could diminish quickly when they felt they were being used. Partly for this reason, there was a strong tendency in the tradition to discriminate between deserving and undeserving strangers. Even when the decision was made to meet the needs of the "undeserving," the category itself was affirmed, but then overridden by the concern to respond to persons, whatever the cause of their need. Attention to distinguishing between those in need who deserved help and those who did not is less evident in the biblical texts than in the writings which followed. Chrysostom especially took issue with the distinctions while recognizing their salience. Such concerns were part of the long debate over the appropriateness of "indiscriminate" almsgiving to beggars and others in need. The local community was often more sympathetic toward the local "deserving" poor and accepted some responsibility for them, but was less willing to offer sympathy to impoverished strangers or the "able-bodied" unemployed.

Calvin wrote that it was crucial to relieve those who were truly in need, and also that it was entirely appropriate to make inquiries regarding the circumstances of persons in need. Without some scrutiny and discernment, he worried that the boldest poor would take everything. However, Calvin's further warning speaks powerfully to every discussion about deserving and undeserving strangers: "Let us beware that we seek not cover for our stinginess under the shadow of prudence." Inquiry should never be "too exacting"; it should be done with a "humane heart, inclined to pity and compassion."[33]

33. John Calvin, *Sermons from Job* (Grand Rapids: Wm. B. Eerdmans, 1952), 202, 204-6.

The attempt to distinguish deserving from undeserving guests is deeply rooted in the tradition as is a critique of presuming to make those distinctions. Echoes of such concerns ring loudly today in complaints about welfare abuse, in questions about whether some people are "really" homeless, and in distinctions between political and economic refugees.

The potential for misuses of hospitality cannot be eliminated. Most gracious hosts and hospitable communities know that they will sometimes be "used," but they provide welcome anyway. There is no perfect resolution to this issue. Martha Nussbaum's comments on the fragility of goodness remind us that attempts to make hospitality less fragile, less subject to misuse and distortion, often diminish its essential character:

> There is a loss in value whenever the risks involved in specifically human virtue are closed off. There is a beauty in the willingness to love someone in the face of love's instability and worldliness that is absent from a completely trustworthy love. There is a certain valuable quality in social virtue that is lost when social virtue is removed from the domain of uncontrolled happenings.[34]

"The peculiar beauty of *human* excellence," she argues, "just *is* its vulnerability."[35]

Offering hospitality in a world distorted by sin, injustice, and brokenness will rarely be easy. We need a combination of grace and wisdom. Substantial hospitality to strangers involves spiritual and moral intuition, prayer and dependence on the Holy Spirit, the accumulated wisdom of a tradition, and a pragmatic assessment of each situation.

But grace is always primary. As Miroslav Volf writes in *Exclusion and Embrace,* "The will to give ourselves to others and 'welcome' them, to readjust our identities to make space for them, is prior to any judgment about others, except that of identifying them in their humanity."[36] We will need to differentiate and sometimes even exclude but our first priority must always be one of welcome, embrace, hospitality. When we begin with a strong presumption in favor of welcoming the stranger, we will be better equipped to handle the more ambiguous situations.

34. Nussbaum, *Fragility of Goodness,* 420.
35. Ibid., 2.
36. Volf, *Exclusion and Embrace,* 29.

# 8. MAKING A PLACE
# FOR HOSPITALITY

*"If there is room in the heart, there
is room in the house."*

DANISH PROVERB[1]

BECAUSE HOSPITALITY IS BASIC TO WHO WE ARE AS FOL-
lowers of Jesus, every aspect of our lives can be touched by its practice. If
we use hospitality as a lens through which to examine our homes,
churches, jobs, schools, health care, and politics, might we see them dif-
ferently? Can we make the places which shape our lives and in which we
spend our days more hospitable? Do current practices within these settings distort hospitality or shut out strangers?

It is important to look at specific settings for hospitality because
welcome is always offered from within a "place" that combines physical
space, social relationships, and particular meanings and values.[2] Making
a place for hospitality is not only about creating or transforming a physical environment to make room for a few extra people. The human rela-

1. Quoted in Philip Hallie, *Tales of Good and Evil, Help and Harm* (New York:
HarperCollins, 1997), 54.
2. Tim Cresswell, *In Place/Out of Place* (Minneapolis: University of Minnesota
Press, 1996), 157. See also F. W. Dillistone, *Traditional Symbols and the Contemporary
World* (London: Epworth Press, 1973), 85-102, for an excellent discussion of space and
place in the Christian tradition.

tionships and commitments that shape the setting affect whether it is or is not welcoming.

Jesus' words in Matthew 25:35, "I was a stranger and you welcomed me," do not refer to any particular physical location for hospitality. Instead, the verse challenges us to examine our practices of welcome to strangers in every setting. Jesus' words are more closely associated with relationships than with location — I was a stranger and you received me into your group. Whatever the location, unless the invitation is given, it is a setting in which the stranger would not feel free to enter. It is somehow bounded space, a set of relations which convention says does not have to be open to strangers.

The story of Abraham's hospitality to the angels (Gen. 18) is relevant as we reflect on places for hospitality. He and Sarah welcomed the strangers into their household — but households then included economic, political, religious, and familial activities. Because in the households of ancient societies, these aspects of life were not highly differentiated, hospitality was intertwined with all of them. Thinking about hospitality today requires intentionality in applying it to the complex and separate spheres of contemporary life.

The need to make places for hospitality is unquestionable, however. Elie Wiesel writes, "Our century is marked by displacements on the scale of continents. . . . Never before have so many human beings fled from so many homes."[3] Even if we think only about the needs of refugees, we quickly see the necessity of hospitable responses at various levels. Refugees need a compassionate response from the international community; they also depend on individual nations, communities, churches, and families to be willing to make a place for them.

Many of our contemporary responses to the needs of strangers require minimal personal investment and responsibility; we depend on large-scale institutions and specialists in almost every area of life. Assuming some personal responsibility for hospitality to strangers can therefore seem daunting. But hospitality requires both personal and communal commitment, and settings which combine aspects of public and private life.

3. Elie Wiesel, "Longing for Home," in *The Longing for Home,* ed. Leroy S. Rouner (Notre Dame: University of Notre Dame Press, 1996), 19.

A first step in making a place for hospitality may be to make room in our hearts. Whether or not we can always find room in our houses, welcome begins with dispositions characterized by love and generosity. Hearts can be enlarged by praying that God will give us eyes to see the opportunities around us, and by putting ourselves in places where we are likely to encounter strangers in need of welcome.

At different times in our lives our capacity for hospitality will vary, and different kinds of strangers will require different types of responses. Although a particular family may not be able to take a homeless person into their home, that family can participate with others in creating a place that is welcoming to homeless people. When our lives are open to hospitality, opportunities will come to make a place for others. And, in doing so, our places and our lives will be enriched and transformed.

## Characteristics of Hospitable Places

What makes a space inviting? By looking at personal places — small-scale environments like homes and other informal settings — we can identify certain characteristics that are also relevant in larger environments. Hospitable places are comfortable and lived in; they are settings in which people are flourishing. Although not necessarily beautifully maintained or decorated, they are evidently cared for. Such places provide the people that inhabit them with shelter and sanctuary in the deepest sense of these words — not only with the shelter of physical buildings but also with the shelter of relationships. Such places are safe and stable, offering people a setting where "they can rest for awhile to collect themselves." Hospitable places are not frenetic, though people within them may be busy. When sanctuary and a slower pace are combined, there is a sense of peace.

In such places life is celebrated, yet the environment also has room for brokenness and deep disappointments. Such places make faith and a hospitable way of life seem natural, not forced. Hospitable settings are often enhanced by the simple beauty of creation, where body, soul, and spirit are fed by attention to small details such as attractively prepared and good-tasting food, or flowers from a nearby garden. Attention to these details expresses an appreciation for life which has more to do with taking time than with having money.

When we have opportunities to design settings and physical environments, an important consideration should be to identify the types of architecture and arrangements that communicate a sense of welcome and enable hospitality to occur. Inviting entrances and accessible facilities, comfortable furnishings and adequate lighting are important. Designing layouts that are somewhat public yet encourage personal conversation can foster easier interactions among strangers.

Hospitable places are alive with particular commitments and practices; however, guests are not coerced into sharing them. Although the human relationships within such places may demonstrate God's existence, communicate God's love, and invite response, welcome does not violate the stranger's identity and integrity. Kathleen Norris describes the hospitality of Benedictine monasteries as "powerful without being seductive."[4]

Hospitable places allow room for friendships to grow. Food, shelter, and companionship are all interrelated in these settings. In such environments, weary and lonely persons can be restored to life. Jean Vanier writes that when people sense "that they are wanted and loved as they are and that they have a place, then we witness a real transformation — I would even say 'resurrection'."[5] Years ago, John Cogley described the restoration of persons he witnessed in a Catholic Worker House of Hospitality:

> The security of the House, poor as it was, regular meals, a sure place to sleep, work to be done, the knowledge of being useful to others . . . and the casual but very real fellowship of . . . the place — these things were enough. It was often as if you could see a change taking place before your eyes, like something visible happening — color returning to a face after a faint.

As he went on to observe: "Even the crudest hospitality can work miracles."[6]

4. Kathleen Norris, *Dakota* (Boston: Houghton Mifflin Company, 1993), 198.
5. Jean Vanier, *From Brokenness to Community* (New York: Paulist Press, 1992), 15.
6. John Cogley, "House of Hospitality," October 1947, in *A Penny a Copy: Readings from "The Catholic Worker,"* ed. Thomas C. Cornell, Robert Ellsberg, and Jim Forest (Maryknoll, N.Y.: Orbis Books, 1995), 56.

## A Place in Our Homes

The frequency with which people define hospitality as "making someone feel at home" demonstrates the integral connection in our experience between hospitality and home. This connection is also communicated in the common Hispanic expression of welcome, *"mi casa es tu casa"* — "my house is your house." Homes are the most personal settings into which we can invite people.

The possibility of welcoming Jesus into one's home shaped ancient church teachings on home-based hospitality. Chrysostom instructed his parishioners: "Make for yourself a guest-chamber in your own house: set up a bed there, set up a table there and a candlestick. [cp. 2 Kings 4:10]. . . . Have a room to which Christ may come; say, 'This is Christ's cell; this building is set apart for Him.'"[7] Christ's room, Chrysostom wrote, would be for the "maimed, the beggars, and the homeless." Even if it were inadequate, "Christ disdains it not."

Setting aside space for a stranger in the form of a "Christ room" was important to Peter Maurin and Dorothy Day as they turned to ancient church traditions in shaping the hospitality of the Catholic Worker. Day writes that she was moved by Maurin's quotation from St. Jerome "that every house should have a 'Christ room' for our brother who was in need."[8] Viewing our spare beds or guest rooms as belonging to Christ might prompt us to open our homes to some of the "least" with whom Jesus identified.

Homes can be very modest, with little space to spare and few amenities, but they can be the site for wonderful hospitality. Making people feel welcome and "at home" is not the same as entertainment. One couple, with years of experience offering hospitality to countless people every day, commented, "When hospitality is viewed as entertainment, the house is never ready."

Welcoming people, especially strangers, into our homes does require that someone be at home. This is not a minor issue for single people who live alone and work full time and for families in which all the adults are working outside the home. To offer significant hospitality from our homes will require some rethinking of the relation between work and

7. John Chrysostom, Homily 45 on Acts, NPNF1, vol. 11, p. 277.
8. Dorothy Day, *House of Hospitality* (New York: Sheed & Ward, 1939), xxvi.

home, the living arrangements we choose, and the significance we assign to our time away from work.

In contemporary society, a significant portion of the population is growing up in settings where they do not see models of strong families or healthy marriages. Families shaped by deep Christian faith and strong love for one another can offer an extraordinary gift in welcoming others into their homes. In living their lives in front of their guests, they provide a model of a healthy family, warts and all. This is one of the very significant contributions that L'Abri households have made over the years. Guests learn about the Christian life by living alongside families in the daily give and take of caring for one another. Edith Schaeffer, cofounder of L'Abri, observed, "For some young people, L'Abri homes are the first really happy homes they have ever seen. . . . You can't imagine what the opportunity of eating, doing dishes, helping peel potatoes, being a part of conversation and family prayers in such a variety of homes does, which any amount of lecturing and 'talking about home life' could *never* do."[9]

For those of us concerned about nurturing people in Christian faith, home-based hospitality is a rich practice. In a hospitable household, conversation and meals are closely linked, and people are nourished through both. Martin Luther relished conversation at meals "for discourses are the real condiments of food if . . . they are seasoned with salt. For word is whetted by word; and not only is the belly fed with food, but the heart is also fed with doctrine."[10] Reformers viewed homes and meals as a crucial setting for "edifying discourse" and growth in faith. A Benedictine monk noted that what we now call spiritual direction was often provided in the past by mothers and grandmothers in the neighborhood who always had a pot of coffee brewing in their kitchen. People knew they could stop by, talk, and leave with more clarity and insight. "And the wise woman simply gave them a cup of coffee."

Around a dinner table, family and guests share food and life. Providing a meal for guests does not involve elaborate menus any more than welcoming them requires well-furnished guest rooms. "We honor guests

9. Edith Schaeffer, *Dear Family: The L'Abri Family Letters: 1961-1986* (New York: Harper & Row, 1989), p. 187.

10. Luther, *Works*, vol. 3: *Lectures on Genesis Chapters 15–20* (St. Louis: Concordia, 1961), p. 200.

as we focus our primary attention on them, not on the food. Hospitality will be most satisfying for both host and guest when we serve foods . . . that are easy to prepare, serve, and eat."[11] Inability to cook should not be a barrier to offering welcome. Practitioners suggested that even if we pick up a pizza or open cans of soup to share, they should be offered with joy and without apology.

A preliminary step in recovering hospitality might be to renew the practice of festive Sunday dinners. With a minimal amount of preparation, we could be intentional about including a few extra people who might welcome the happy combination of food and companionship. Families could make it more of a habit to invite several additional folks to participate in holiday celebrations and special events. Single people can join together or with families to share in the work of preparing meals and making a place for hospitality.

Home in its best sense is a place of security, rest, and provision. It houses the most fundamental and intimate relations and commitments. But homes can be troubled, dangerous, and filled with injustice when the people within them are estranged or abusive. Such brokenness does not negate or eliminate the human need for home or home-based hospitality, but it does require that we attend to the potential distortions, and avoid sentimentality and naiveté. If such households attempt to offer hospitality, guests are often caught in complicated webs of anger and loneliness.

In making a place for hospitality, parents worry about the impact on their children of a steady stream of strangers. Obviously, the impact is mixed and depends partly on the kinds of strangers welcomed and partly on family dynamics. But the testimony of a number of families who raised their children to adulthood in the setting of hospitality is that it was very enriching for the children. Children's lives were much fuller because of the added gifts, skills, and experiences that guests brought into their home. As they developed deep affection for some of the guests, children learned to love people whose brokenness was not readily healed. Children matured earlier and often developed deep compassion for others.

Homes provide a safe place for healing. Individuals and families can offer a place for bereaved, exhausted, and sick people to recover health and

---

11. Joetta Handrich Schlabach, *Extending the Table . . . A World Community Cookbook* (Scottdale, Pa.: Herald Press, 1991), 74.

regain strength. Homes are also an important setting for building relationships that cut across cultural, ethnic, and racial differences. Numerous visitors from other countries have expressed surprise and disappointment at the infrequency with which they are invited into homes in the United States. In many other societies, inviting a visiting foreigner into one's home for a meal is an act of ordinary courtesy. Although sharing a meal in a restaurant is a common practice today, it is not a full substitute for the more personal character of home-based hospitality.

Hospitality practiced in the homes of Christian people is a key foundation for hospitality in the church. As a pastor of a vibrant multiethnic congregation in Los Angeles noted, "The front door of the home is the side door of the church."

## A Place in the Church

Understanding the church as God's household has significant implications for hospitality. More than anywhere else, when we gather as church our practice of hospitality should reflect God's gracious welcome. God is host, and we are all guests of God's grace. However, in individual churches, we also have opportunities to act as hosts who welcome others, making a place for strangers and sojourners.

Churches are potentially rich settings for nurturing a life of hospitality. In some churches, expanding the hospitality that members offer to one another would be an important first step. Churches that have not nurtured a common life among members will find hospitality to strangers quite difficult. But churches who do have a rich common life can sometimes overlook strangers in their attention to, and care for, one another.

Occasionally, churches embrace a model of hospitality to strangers in an attempt to get past racial, ethnic, and other distinctions. A gracious spirit of welcome, equality, and care can help in efforts to heal racial divisions and previous exclusions. Generous and steady hospitality, practiced among believers from different backgrounds, can be the beginning of significant reconciliation.

However, such hospitality is more complex than welcoming "those people into *our* church" or "making room at *our* table." In the church, especially, it is not our table to which we welcome people; it is God's table to which we come as equals. We may act as hosts in particular churches where we need to welcome individual persons, but as the household of God, the situation is more complicated. When people from minority groups or those with disabilities have not been present in churches of the dominant culture, congregational response may need to include repentance. A church may need to acknowledge that had it been a responsible steward of God's household, these new "guests" would have had an equal place in God's house from the beginning.

Churches, like families, need to eat together to sustain their identity as a community. The table is central to the practice of hospitality in home and church — the nourishment we gain there is physical, spiritual, and social. Whether we gather around the table for the Lord's Supper or for a church potluck dinner, we are strengthened as a community.

An important contemporary testimony to the significance of shared meals comes from the black church tradition. Jualynne Dodson and Cheryl Townsend Gilkes explain:

> African American church members in the United States feed one another's bodies as they feed their spirits or, more biblically, one another's "temples of the Holy Spirit." In the process, an ethic of love and an emphasis on hospitality emerge, especially in the sharing of food, which spill over into the larger culture. Ritual moments of most African Americans occur at home and in their churches, and they are connected to food, meals, and their remembrance.[12]

They note further that such meals are tied to anticipating the eschatological banquet, the "welcome table" with its abundance:

> It is this hospitality, this love, that is symbolized in the preparation and giving of food. The love ethic that pervades the ideology of African American churches is constantly underscored and reaffirmed in the exchanges of food and the celebration of church events with grand meals. This love and this hospitality remind the congregation that they are pilgrims and strangers and that as they feed somebody one day, they may stand in need on another.[13]

12. Jualynne Dodson and Cheryl Townsend Gilkes, "There's Nothing Like Church Food," *Journal of the American Academy of Religion* 63/3 (Fall 1995), 520-21.
   13. Ibid., 535.

Dodson and Gilkes conclude, "And in a world of hatred and conflict, with its racism and deprivations, the saints are able to sit together at their welcome tables and remind one another in the giving and receiving of food, that they may continue to believe that 'the greatest of these is love.' There is nothing like church food."[14]

Meals shared together in church provide opportunities to sustain relationships and to build new ones. They establish a space which is personal without being private; an excellent setting in which to begin friendships with strangers. Further recognition of the significance of potluck dinners may help us sustain a practice that is often underappreciated as an expression of hospitality.

Congregations committed to ministering to people in need sometimes overlook their own greatest resource — the fellowship of believers. In an insightful discussion of the distinction between "church" and "mission"[15] Kathryn Mowry uses the example of urban congregations that choose to remain in changing neighborhoods:

> It seems that one trend for such urban congregations is that the "mission" becomes social involvement while the "church" remains limited to a fellowship of urban missionaries. This is not a typical fortress mentality. Churches provide food distribution, and housing and employment programs to reach out to the stranger, but the church continues to struggle at the point of extending community to the stranger. Many urban churches have reached out through elaborate and costly programs, but a fence of professional distance remains. They have not allowed the stranger to be one with them.[16]

Mowry acknowledges that while certain "fences" are necessary, other more invisible walls around the church keep the congregation from extending "our most transformational resource: our being together." Poi-

14. Ibid., 536.

15. Kathryn Mowry, "Do Good Fences Make Good Neighbors?" in *God So Loves the City,* ed. Charles Van Engen and Jude Tiersma (World Vision: MARC, 1994), 117. Mowry notes that sometimes congregations "separate giving completely from the place where they do their receiving." She credits Charles Van Engen with describing this distinction "as a separation between 'church' and 'mission'" (Charles Van Engen, *God's Missionary People* [Grand Rapids: Baker Book House, 1991]).

16. Mowry, "Do Good Fences Make Good Neighbors?" 107.

gnantly capturing the difference between relationships in a church's coffee hour after worship and in its soup kitchen during the week, Mowry
comments, "I wonder how many times of shared laughter over coffee
cups does it take to make up for one time of standing in a food line holding a number."[17]

Churches have generally done better with offering food programs and
providing clothing closets than with welcoming into worship people significantly different from their congregations. Because we are unaware of the
significance of our friendship and fellowship, our best resources often remain inaccessible to strangers. But it is also the case that building friendships across significant social differences can be challenging. Churches
have the material, social, and spiritual resources to practice vibrant expressions of hospitality, yet the sad testimony from a number of practitioners of
hospitality is that the people they welcome often do not find welcome in local churches.

Jean Vanier writes that "Welcome is one of the signs that a community is alive. To invite others to live with us is a sign that we aren't afraid,
that we have a treasure of truth and of peace to share." He also offers an
important warning: "A community which refuses to welcome — whether
through fear, weariness, insecurity, a desire to cling to comfort, or just because it is fed up with visitors — is dying spiritually."[18]

## A Place in Intentional Communities

An individual family or church cannot easily provide substantial hospitality
to large numbers of people in need without restructuring its household. A
single person or family can invite a lonely neighbor to share in a meal, care
for someone recovering from surgery, provide a troubled teenager with a
safe place to heal and grow, host a small group meeting for Bible study or
support, or befriend a bewildered refugee family. A single church can welcome individuals and families or, if needed, designate a person or persons to
act on behalf of the church in giving more extensive hospitality, while the

17. Ibid., 108-9.
18. Jean Vanier, *Community and Growth,* rev. ed. (New York: Paulist Press, 1989),
266-67.

rest of the members can offer hospitality on a personal scale. Hospitality to a steady stream of persons on a long-term basis, or with very needy people, almost always requires more than a single person, a family, or a typically structured local church to share the burdens and the risks.

That's why it is difficult to imagine recovering the practice of hospitality to strangers without also considering the necessity of recovering close communities. That also helps to explain why when we look for examples of hospitality to strangers in contemporary society, we find the most vibrant expressions in intentional Christian communities. When asked about the importance of community living for offering steady hospitality to strangers, most practitioners responded that they depended on the encouragement and support of brothers and sisters in the body of Christ. They also noted the importance of having a communal life into which a stranger could be invited.

The form that community takes can vary widely. Perhaps a loose network of families in a church could make a commitment to hospitality and to sharing the work. In another situation, people living in a single household might create a life together. The key is that they support one another through physical presence, shared commitments, and accountability. In doing so, they are nourished even as they offer nourishment and refuge to others.

Life in an intentional community may involve a significant withdrawal from the world, but a commitment to hospitality simultaneously presses for continual engagement. Although a number of communities of hospitality are located in fairly remote places, the numbers of people that come to them from all over the world give testimony to the powerful draw of hospitality. Monasteries offer a combination of solitude and hospitality and draw weary and distracted urbanites to their communities. At Jubilee Partners in rural Georgia, the community welcomes refugees from distant continents. L'Abri households have welcomed students and seekers from around the world for the past forty years.

## Hospitality and Social Services

A number of Christian communities that offer hospitality to homeless persons and to those with disabilities see hospitality as an alternative way to respond to people with multiple needs in a specialized world. They distinguish hospitality practices from the radical specialization associated with many contemporary forms of helping. Hospitality, they suggest, demonstrates that important healing takes place *within* community. Reclaiming hospitality is an attempt to bring back the relational dimension to social service, and to highlight concerns for empowerment and partnership with those who need assistance.

Much provision of help today is given by social service professionals in a context of careful management, effective technique, clearly defined roles, and complex regulations. Hospitality, on the other hand, is a "form of relationship that is essentially unspecialized."[19] The relationships fostered within the practice of hospitality implicitly challenge bureaucratic rules that reinforce separation, isolation, and anonymity. Hospitality suggests ways to break down the barriers between provider and client that are essential to the entire "service" orientation. Hospitality offers a model for developing more reciprocal relationships.[20]

When the primary focus is on a particular need, social service orientations tend "to objectify the person, in the sense that they abstract certain qualities from the client in order to place him or her into a category that can be acted upon. Efficient treatment does not allow one to be receptive to the 'whole person' of the client; only those traits that are deemed 'relevant' to the task at hand can be attended to."[21]

There is a certain irony in these contrasts between social services and hospitality. A more routinized and predictable social service system was developed in response to the unpredictability and uncertainty of voluntary hospitality. Social work as a field began with "friendly visiting" and with the settlement houses of the late nineteenth and early twentieth centuries. These reflected aspects of hospitality — especially personal contact and, at least sometimes, a "hospitable openness to foreign cultures and values." Today, however, the entire area of social services is quite bu-

19. Harry Murray, *Do Not Neglect Hospitality: The Catholic Worker and the Homeless* (Philadelphia: Temple University Press, 1990), 47-48.

20. See Mary O'Connell, *The Gift of Hospitality: Opening the Doors of Community Life to People with Disabilities* (Center for Urban Affairs and Research, Northwestern University, & Dept. of Rehabilitation Services, State of Illinois, Feb. 1988), 10, 17, 27-28.

21. Murray, *Do Not Neglect Hospitality,* 22.

reaucratic and professional, and is at times at odds with, and quite distant from, practices of hospitality.[22]

Some communities of hospitality are quite explicit in distancing themselves from social service models. Peter Gathje, in his description of the Open Door Community in Atlanta, notes that they

> did not want to repeat the pattern of social welfare. They did not want to be social workers who faced the poor in a professional-client relationship. . . . They wanted to bring together their lives lived in response to the Gospel with lives lived in solidarity with the poor. They wanted to affirm the dignity of the poor and their membership in the human community.[23]

Because hospitality involves friendship as well as providing food and shelter, the Open Door has resisted " 'intake evaluations' of 'neediness' " to determine eligibility for help. They do not keep precise records, contrasting "the biblical ideal of hospitality given freely to strangers as fellow creatures and neighbors with the professional services that state and public agencies give to their clients."[24]

A distinctive feature of many contemporary advocates of hospitality rather than "service" is their rejection of bureaucratic styles of helping. They stress minimal scrutiny and focus instead on respect and friendship. While they emphasize solidarity and mutuality, most practitioners do not consider personal hospitality a replacement for government provision or political advocacy; it is concurrent with it.

An orientation to hospitality often represents a critique of therapeutic models of service that are individualistic and focus on need and incapacity. Mary O'Connell, in her work on inclusion of people with disabilities in the practices and relations of ordinary life, stresses the significance of not defining people by their disability and the importance of welcoming people with disabilities "into situations that are *not* about disability."[25]

22. Ibid., 23.

23. Peter R. Gathje, *Christ Comes in the Stranger's Guise: A History of the Open Door Community* (Atlanta: The Open Door, 1991), 27.

24. Robert N. Bellah, Richard Madsen, William M. Sullivan, Ann Swidler, and Steven M. Tipton, *The Good Society* (New York: Random House, 1991), 31. See also Gathje, *Christ Comes in the Stranger's Guise,* 35.

25. O'Connell, *The Gift of Hospitality,* 19. For further information on an asset-

Within the practice of hospitality, O'Connell sees an opportunity to focus on the individual and not on the category of his or her disability, on the whole rather than the part, and on a person's capacity rather than on his or her deficit. She is quite critical of social services where the focus is exclusively on disability because it often adds to the person's isolation. Hospitality allows people with disabilities to find a place within a network of relations where they can share their gifts, as well as bring their needs.[26] Philip Hallie's words capture the main difference between the two approaches. It "has something to do with mutuality, with the helper and the helped exchanging places, so that the helped one participates in the depths of his or her being with the spreading of life."[27]

Hospitality is also an effort to reempower the untrained person. "As professionals proliferate, the scope of activities that a nonprofessional feels competent to perform narrows." Hospitality reclaims "basic areas of human social interaction for the nonspecialist."[28] The professionalization of care can intimidate and disempower persons inclined toward voluntary activity — they do not feel sufficiently equipped or able to provide help.[29]

Our sense of personal capacity to respond to the needs of strangers is undermined by the authority of large institutions designed to meet their needs. However, given our uncertain sense of personal responsibility, any total rejection of institutional measures would be both naive and risky. The task is to find practices that join personal relations with predictable care; this has been an ongoing struggle throughout the history of hospitality and its differentiation into a host of "services." Returning the care of strangers to the vicissitudes of individual kindness is not an option; but, without personal involvement, strangers remain detached and vulnerable. Hospitality reminds us that the specialization and universalization of care is always double-edged.[30]

---

based approach, see the resources of the Center for Urban Affairs and Policy Research at Northwestern University, Evanston, Illinois.

26. Ibid., 15.
27. Hallie, *Tales of Good and Evil,* 206.
28. Murray, *Do Not Neglect Hospitality,* 5.
29. See Robert Wuthnow, *Meaning and Moral Order: Explorations in Cultural Analysis* (Berkeley: University of California Press, 1987), 77.
30. See the discussion in Michael Ignatieff, *The Needs of Strangers* (London: Chatto & Windus/The Hogarth Press, 1984), 9-19.

Hospitality, though necessary, is not sufficient in our very specialized world. We value and depend on people with highly developed specialized skills. The services offered by larger institutions such as hospitals now make the difference between life and death for some of us. The commitments and concerns represented by hospitality can help some of these institutions improve their care by insisting that they keep the particular human being in focus.

Making a place for hospitality that breaks down ordinary boundaries between guests, hosts, and volunteers creates another set of challenges. The usual roles of helper and recipient, professional and client are not appropriate, but the relations between hosts and guests are not fully captured in a friendship model either. Hospitality practitioners live on the ambiguous boundary between friend/brother/sister and host/helper/professional.

Newcomers to these communities, both as hosts and guests, find these uncertain roles enlivening and confusing. A couple who had gained much experience in this area of community living explained that the relationships in their community involved "very few barriers between the guests and volunteers," especially when compared with more formal institutional environments. This makes for a more egalitarian setting. Hosts and guests grow very close, especially in the beginning, but tensions often develop because volunteers/hosts are also responsible to enforce rules. "Mature people who come in don't have as much of a problem. They can understand the need for boundaries and it doesn't take away from the experience — or from being personal and close and loving people." Such tensions reveal the complexity of relations in these communities — while many distinctions are broken down, others necessarily remain. The ambiguity in roles and relations can be both refreshing and disconcerting.

The challenge is even more complex in communities that maintain some connections with social services and are answerable to government expectations. One hospitality practitioner explained that the community often found itself "precariously in the middle" — trying to define what are the necessary professional boundaries while trying to minimize those boundaries. Communities of hospitality challenge the anonymity and professionalization of care, but when they are also connected to state agencies they chart their way with some uncertainty. Another practitioner whose community had connections with social service agencies noted that hospitality workers were continually reworking, renegotiating, and redefining relationships because they wanted to re-create a homelike setting as much as possible.

L'Arche communities live within a similar tension. While "espoused to the gospel values," they are also "responsible to public and government authorities for the welfare of the handicapped people committed to their care."[31] In order to make a place for hospitality, such communities find ways to bridge very different worlds, but they also live with some ongoing stresses and uncertainties. Questions related to roles, regulations, and service may be more acute in intentional communities of hospitality because the practice of hospitality there is more intense and ongoing, but similar issues also appear in home- and church-based hospitality. Homeowners and churches that want to offer hospitality sometimes must deal with such matters as zoning and occupancy ordinances, regulations about food preparation, and liability concerns.

## Additional Places for Hospitality

The needs of refugees demonstrate the importance and complexity of hospitable responses in various institutions. Unless international law and national policy are shaped by commitments to provide a safe place for those involuntarily exiled from their homelands, it is very difficult to offer hospitality at more personal levels.

Reception of refugees is one of the few places in modern politics where the explicit language of hospitality is still used. People continue to connect theological notions of sanctuary, cities of refuge, and care for aliens with the needs of today's displaced people. Christians have a vital role in making sure that the needs of refugees are taken seriously by national governments. But our response necessarily extends beyond public policy to more personal involvement in voluntary agencies, communities, churches, and homes where acts of welcome offer refuge and new life to some of the world's most vulnerable people.

31. Kathryn Spink, *Jean Vanier and L'Arche: A Communion of Love* (New York: Crossroad, 1991), 128, 189.

Caring for people with terminal diseases suggests another important place for hospitality today. Especially as modeled in hospice, such care is a move away from a highly clinical model in the face of impending death. Hospice represents a return to hospitality that connects care with respect, comfort, and presence. It allows primary attention to be given to the relationships and dignity of the dying person. To best preserve family relationships and connection, hospice workers usually go to the home of the dying person and support the family in caring for their dying member.

There are situations in which making a place for hospitality does not involve inviting people "in." For a variety of reasons, some people cannot "come in" — dying persons who need medical support, and people who are homebound or in institutions. Hospitality to prisoners requires that concerned persons go to the prison and enter that world. Several communities of hospitality have incorporated into their practices a significant ministry with prisoners. One group describes its work as offering hospitality to those on death row. In the early church, care for prisoners was viewed as a dimension of hospitality and, in much of the tradition, was understood as a work of mercy. Sometimes, in order to express care, we must work with places as they are given, but we can bring hospitality with us as we enter them.

A very moving example of hospitality caught me by surprise as I visited one of the communities. Jubilee Partners has set aside a beautiful spot on its property for a graveyard. In it are buried several people who had been homeless before they died, a couple of refugees who became ill and died after they had come to the United States, and two men who had been convicted of capital crimes and were executed by the state. The quiet beauty of the place offered a poignant recognition of the humanity of people who were in many ways society's castoffs. Their lives had been acknowledged with a simple funeral service and grave marker, arranged by a community who noticed, and cared about, their passing. This dimension of hospitality has very ancient connections. The early church took responsibility for burying strangers, especially indigent ones.[32]

Making a place for hospitality requires creative thinking about finding ways to bring hospitality practices into connnection with some of the

---

32. See, for example, Lactantius, *The Divine Institutes,* bk. 6, ch. 12, ANF, vol. 7, p. 177.

particular features of contemporary life. This area is rich with possibility. St. Joseph's Pub in Orange County, California, staffed by Catholic sisters, warmly welcomes immigrants and provides ongoing potluck dinners to help ease their transition into a new world.[33] Churches have established coffeehouses and renewal centers that create comfortable environments for conversation and refreshment. Christian volunteers who teach English as a second language have a wonderful opportunity to make their classrooms havens of hospitality.

It may be helpful to view telephone calls as a place for hospitality. Given our high mobility and the numbers of people who live alone, phone calls now often sustain crucial human relationships. While it is certainly not the same as sharing a meal, a phone conversation with a weary or lonely person does represent welcoming someone into our lives. The conversation requires similar concentration, a similar "setting aside" of other things, in order to give our attention to the other person. Phone calls, which so often seem like interruptions, can actually be an important way to care for one another.

The dominance of the economic sphere is a primary feature of contemporary life. Its connection to hospitality is complicated. Many traditional hospitality practices have been commercialized — in the hospitality industry and also, increasingly, in the health care professions. We spend much of our time at work — an arena far more amenable to concerns about efficiency and profit than hospitality. But if hospitality is important to human flourishing, we may want to consider the concerns it embodies and suggest some alternate ways of shaping work places. In addition, because work is so crucial to people's participation in society, and to their sense of value and dignity, our commitments to hospitality to strangers may invite us to pay more attention to creating employment opportunities for those often excluded from jobs.

Jean Vanier offers an important challenge as we contemplate how we might make places for hospitality in the future:

> In years to come, we are going to need many small communities which will welcome lost and lonely people, offering them a new form of fam-

33. Described in materials published by the "Building Hospitable Communities" Project (Ecumenical Networks-NCC, 475 Riverside Drive, N.Y., N.Y. 10015).

ily and a sense of belonging. In the past, Christians who wanted to follow Jesus opened hospitals and schools. Now that there are so many of these, Christians must commit themselves to the new communities of welcome, to live with people who have no other family, and to show them that they are loved and can grow to greater freedom and that they, in turn, can love and give life to others.[34]

For, in the words of an Irish proverb, "It is in the shelter of each other that the people live."[35]

34. Vanier, *Community and Growth,* 283.
35. Quoted in Mary Pipher, *The Shelter of Each Other* (New York: Ballantine Books, 1996).

# 9. THE SPIRITUAL RHYTHMS OF HOSPITALITY

---

*"On this occasion of the concourse of so many strangers, and needy and suffering people, let your hospitality and your good works abound."*

AUGUSTINE
(5TH CENTURY)

MANY PEOPLE WHO PRACTICE THE KIND OF HOSPITALITY enjoined in the gospel describe it as "the best and hardest thing" they have ever done. In their experience, its difficulty and its joys lie close together. They find it to be the "best thing" because they sense God's presence so frequently in the practice. As practitioners see small miracles every day, Scripture and prayer come alive. Hospitality is wonderful because it is filled with unexpected blessings, because it is fun, and because of the opportunities it provides to become friends with so many different kinds of people.

Hospitality is difficult because it involves hard work. People wear out and struggle with limits. Our society places a high value on control, planning, and efficiency, but hospitality is unpredictable and often inefficient. We insist on measurable results and completed tasks but the "results" of hospitality are impossible to quantify and the work of hospitality is rarely finished. As a society, we are highly mobile and enjoy our personal independence, but hospitality is connected with a sense of place and interdependence. We are often encouraged to be careful about our financial security but practicing hospitality involves a certain recklessness.

Hospitality is difficult today because of our overwhelming busyness. With already overburdened and tightly constrained schedules, trying to offer substantial hospitality can drive us to despair. Most of us have significant responsibilities; hospitality cannot simply be added onto already impossible agendas. To offer hospitality we will need to rethink and reshape our priorities.

When we focus on hospitality to very needy strangers, we encounter additional strains. In the midst of a larger society that can be hostile to the very people we welcome, it can be extremely difficult to absorb the pain of rejection and loss which our guests bring with them. This often requires the support of a community, but community life itself comes with its own set of challenges and difficulties.

Offering hospitality requires that we allow a place for uncertainty, contingency, and human tragedy. The best practitioners, past and present, are refreshingly honest about its ironies, ambiguities, and difficulties as well as about its joys. It is important to acknowledge the difficulty of hospitality. If Christians expect it to be easy to welcome strangers — that it will always involve competent hosts and grateful guests — they will be disappointed and will grow discouraged very quickly. Thinking that they have done something wrong or that they are not "good" at it, they will readily forsake the practice. One practitioner worries that people might abandon hospitality when it fails to produce the "expected" results within a given time frame.

Hospitality will not occur in any significant way in our lives or churches unless we give it deliberate attention. Because the practice has been mostly forgotten and because it conflicts with a number of contemporary values, we must intentionally nurture a commitment to hospitality. It must also be nurtured because the blessings and the benefits are not always immediately apparent. Hospitality becomes less difficult and more "natural" as we grow more familiar with the practice. Grace and gift infuse it in ways that are not easily accounted for. We experience fulfillment as we give of ourselves, but we can neither explain nor anticipate it.

Sixteen hundred years ago, as Christians lived through the frightening disintegration of the Roman Empire, Augustine exhorted and begged them to "be meek, sympathize with the suffering, bear the weak; and on this occasion of the concourse of so many strangers, and needy, and suffering people, let your hospitality and your good works abound."[2] His words, as challenging today as they were then, invite us to think about how to nurture a difficult practice.

Hospitality is not so much a task as a way of living our lives and of sharing ourselves. For most practitioners, offering hospitality grows out of their attempt to be faithful to God, to hear God's voice in the Scriptures and in the people around them. They have learned hospitality as they have opened their lives to situations where they could encounter strangers. Gradually, hospitality has become for them both a disposition and a habit. While rarely without difficulty, hospitality can become so fully integrated into who we are and how we respond to others that we cannot imagine acceptable alternative responses.

## Cultivating a Grateful Spirit

A life of hospitality begins in worship, with a recognition of God's grace and generosity. Hospitality is not first a duty and responsibility; it is first a response of love and gratitude for God's love and welcome to us. Although it involves responsibility and faithful performance of duties, hospitality emerges from a grateful heart. This is especially important because when hospitality is not shaped by gratitude, it is often offered grudgingly. Grudging hospitality exhausts hosts and wounds guests even as it serves them.

Our hospitality both reflects and participates in God's hospitality. It depends on a disposition of love because, fundamentally, hospitality is simply love in action. It has much more to do with the resources of a generous heart than with sufficiency of food or space. Chrysostom described this generosity of love well:

> If you have a hospitable disposition, you own the entire treasure chest of hospitality, even if you possess only a single coin. But if you are a hater of humanity and a hater of strangers, even if you are vested with every material possession, the house for you is cramped by the presence of guests.[2]

1. Augustine, Sermon 31, NPNF1, vol. 6, p. 357.
2. Chrysostom, 1 Homily on the Greeting to Priscilla and Aquila, *Migne,*

We make a habit of hospitality when we remember how much Jesus is present in the practice. Our responses are shaped by the knowledge that Christ comes to us in the "stranger's guise." While we see Christ in strangers and guests, hospitality also allows us to act as Jesus to those guests. Esther de Waal, in her work on Benedictine spirituality, suggests that at the end of all of our hospitable activity we are faced with two questions, "Did we see Christ in them? Did they see Christ in us?"[3]

## Keeping the Stories Alive

We nurture hospitality as a habit and a disposition by telling stories about it. We retell the Bible stories of guests who turned out to be angels. We remember the stories of Jesus' life — how he welcomed all sorts of people, how he fed thousands on a hillside, how he made breakfast for his friends. In our practice of hospitality, we also develop our own tradition of stories — mixtures of miracle, hard work, disappointments, and very funny encounters. We tell stories of real sacrifice and surprising blessing.

Stories are important because "the stories people tell have a way of taking care of them."[4] The practice of hospitality is a good example of what can be lost when we forget a story. Although hospitality was a significant practice in earlier centuries, its recovery has involved a deliberate effort to find it and tell the story again. We have had to be intentional in connecting ourselves with sources that empowered previous generations of Christians. Recognizing the importance of hospitality to Chrysostom or Calvin is not merely a historical exercise; it allows us to participate in the wisdom and the experience of a tradition. As the philosopher Charles Taylor observes:

> Moral sources empower. To come closer to them, to have a clearer view of them, to come to grasp what they involve is for those who recognize

*Patrologia Graeca* 51.187, trans. Catherine Kroeger, in *Priscilla Papers* 5/3 (Summer 1991): 18.

3. Esther de Waal, *Seeking God: The Way of St. Benedict* (Collegeville, Minn.: The Liturgical Press, 1984), 121.

4. Barry Lopez, *Crow and Weasel* (San Francisco: North Point Press, 1990), 48.

them to be moved to love or respect them, and through this love/respect to be better enabled to live up to them.[5]

For some people, naming hospitality as a significant Christian practice is important because it gives them a theological and moral framework for understanding their already existing ministries. As hospitality's place in Scripture and in church history is highlighted, it confirms practitioners' intuitive sense of its importance and value. It helps people in the ordinary tasks of making beds and preparing meals to see their connection with a rich, historic, and central tradition.

We nurture hospitable dispositions and practices by explicitly teaching about them. A number of communities of hospitality are intentional about education; community life includes regular reflection on what hospitality means and looks like. As hospitality is taught in families, churches, and communities, it is also possible to nurture a sense of accountability for its practice; we can challenge and encourage one another to become better at it. We can help each other notice when our lives have become too busy, when hospitality is being crowded out by the rush of daily activities.

A very valuable resource for reflection on and learning the practice is available in the writings of experienced practitioners and communities of hospitality. Insights into the joys and challenges of hospitality come from very different sources and are helpful in different areas.[6] Beyond the books and the newspapers, however, daily life in the communities also teaches volumes about hospitality.

Every contemporary practitioner of hospitality learned the practice from someone else's example — from the "cloud of witnesses" who have gone before, a gracious grandmother, or a wise and generous coworker. People for whom hospitality seems natural are wonderful models from whom to learn the practice. They are living embodiments of welcome;

5. Charles Taylor, *Sources of the Self: The Making of the Modern Identity* (Cambridge, Mass.: Harvard University Press, 1989), 96.

6. I have found books by Dorothy Day, Edith Schaeffer, and Jean Vanier to be particularly helpful. Articles in newspapers published by The Catholic Worker, The Open Door, and Annunciation House often reflect on the practice and meaning of hospitality in contemporary situations. Philip Hallie's book *Lest Innocent Blood Be Shed* (New York: Harper & Row, 1979, 1994) richly describes the hospitality practices of a single community. Karen Burton Mains, in *Open Heart, Open Home* (Elgin, Ill.: David C. Cook, 1976, 1987), offers very practical insights into home-based hospitality.

they help us picture what hospitality could look like in our homes, churches, and workplaces. As contemporaries, they help us work out the practical details of an ancient practice.

## Nurturing a Lifelong Habit

If we acknowledge the importance of hospitality for the Christian life, then we will want to consider how to nurture our children into the practice. To raise hospitable children, Hallie concluded after his study of the hospitality of the people of Le Chambon, "you must *be* what you are trying to teach."[7] Children learn hospitality from parents who have room in their lives for their family as well as for their guests. Children will resent hospitality if it is not broad enough to include them, but they will grow into hospitality as they share in its life-giving environment. Hallie warns:

> If all we do for our children is pound into their heads reasons for protecting their own hides, their second nature will be as wide as the confines of their own . . . skins. One's life is usually about as wide as one's love. But if we make the often-impractical great virtues [e.g., compassion, generosity] part of their lives, their second nature will be as wide as their love.[8]

Gracious hosts make hospitality look easy and enjoyable, but that is not to suggest that it comes easily to every individual. Some personality types find hospitality more difficult and must work harder at learning it. Karen Mains, in her book on hospitality, notes that "For some . . . hospitality is as natural as breathing. For others, the practice must be acquired. For all, the gift must be nurtured."[9] People who are more introverted may struggle initially with providing warm welcome but they are often among the most thoughtful and caring hosts. As one practitioner who did not consider himself a "natural" for it explained, hospitality is something "that can be stretched into."

7. Philip Hallie, *Tales of Good and Evil, Help and Harm* (New York: Harper-Collins, 1997), 43.
8. Ibid., 40.
9. Mains, *Open Heart, Open Home,* 19.

Experiencing hospitality in other countries, or with persons from other countries where hospitality is still a highly regarded practice, can be very helpful. These people model for us what hospitality looks like when it is taken for granted, an ordinary part of human activity and relationships. Rather than appearing to be "inconvenienced" by unexpected guests, often they seem eager and delighted to offer welcome.

Because hospitality is a way of life, it must be cultivated over a lifetime. "Hospitality is one of those things that has to be constantly practiced or it won't be there for the rare occasion."[10] We do not become good at hospitality in an instant; we learn it in small increments of daily faithfulness.

The people of Le Chambon who created a city of refuge for Jewish refugees began with small moves such as sharing their limited supplies of food. Only later did the danger to themselves increase and, by then, the pattern of welcome had already been established. They never saw their actions as complex or difficult. For them, offering hospitality seemed natural and necessary.[11]

Gracious hosts are often caught by surprise when other people comment on their hospitable disposition and practice. They wonder what any other person would have done in similar circumstances. A number of Chambonnais, when commended for their acts of hospitality, asked "Well, where else could they go? I had to take them in."[12] Such persons do not see themselves as exemplary, though they are wonderful examples for us.

People for whom hospitality is a disposition and a habit are less afraid of the risks associated with caring for strangers than they are of the possibility of cutting themselves off from the needs of strangers. Mike McIntyre, writing about the people who were willing to invite him into their homes, noted:

> I've been amazed on this trip by the stubborn capacity of Americans to help a stranger, even when it seems to run contrary to their own best interests. I think of all the families who take me in. I arrive with nothing but my pack, while they expose their homes, their possessions, their

10. Joan Chittister, *Wisdom Distilled from the Daily* (San Francisco: HarperSanFrancisco, 1991), 132.

11. Philip Hallie, *Lest Innocent Blood Be Shed,* 284.

12. Ibid., 286.

children. As scared as I am to trust them, they must be doubly afraid to trust me. Then again, what might truly frighten them is the idea of not trusting anybody. It's like the woman has just told me — she'd rather risk her life than feel bad about passing a stranger on the side of the road.[13]

Making a habit of hospitality ensures a life rich with opportunities to grow and develop. When we exercise the wide array of skills and gifts encompassed in hospitality, we expand our abilities and deepen our wisdom. In addition to the possibility of becoming more competent cooks, hosts have the chance to grow in their capacity to create a peaceful and safe space, to shape an environment around a meal that supplies both physical and spiritual nourishment, to provide guests with opportunities to see faith lived out. Having traveled around the world, Karl Meyer explained his satisfaction with working in a House of Hospitality. "I am not bored here. We don't walk past the world and its problems. The world comes in with its problems and sits down for a cup of coffee and a word of consolation."[14]

A habit of hospitality is fundamental to our identity as Christians. Our primary call is to live out the gospel; a life-style of hospitality is part of that call. For some of us, there will be a more particular call to a deliberate and focused expression of hospitality, but for all of us hospitality is essential to who we are as followers of Jesus.

## Communicating Welcome

By reflecting on our own experiences as a guest or stranger, we can identify the components of hospitality that communicate welcome. What made us feel comfortable, valued, safe? What communicated to us that we were inconvenient or in the way? What is it about certain people and places that make us feel renewed and nourished?

13. Mike McIntyre, *The Kindness of Strangers: Penniless Across America* (New York: Berkley Books, 1996), 105.

14. Karl Meyer, "What Is to Be Done?" in *A Penny a Copy: Readings from "The Catholic Worker,"* ed. Thomas C. Cornell, Robert Ellsberg, and Jim Forrest (Maryknoll, N.Y.: Orbis Books, 1995), 124.

Offering food and drink to one's guests is central to almost every act of hospitality. Next to that, the most important expression of welcome is giving someone our full attention. Over and over, guests and practitioners noted the importance of taking time to talk and to listen to people's stories. Even if it is only a brief encounter, giving someone our focused attention communicates welcome.

"The most precious thing a human being has to give is time."[15] Hospitality requires making time in our lives for others, yet many of us feel that time is our scarcest resource. Most of us are very busy; some of us are harried. Giving a person our attention requires that we stop and focus on them. This is a challenge in a society that celebrates the capacity to do several things simultaneously, and in which people often seem to take pride in being busy. As a wise Benedictine monk observed, "In a fast food culture, you have to remind yourself that some things cannot be done quickly. Hospitality takes time."

To give someone else our full attention means that we view the person as a human being rather than as an embodied need or interruption. When guests were asked what they most appreciated in someone's welcome to them, they frequently described it as feeling that "they weren't an interruption or an imposition." For hosts, hospitality can feel like an interruption — putting aside other responsibilities in order to engage in conversation, prepare food, or make a bed.

One woman who welcomes a steady flow of refugees and other guests explained that she learned what hospitality should look like while living in central Europe. She found that people consistently welcomed her warmly into their homes. She noticed that she never felt as if she were "interrupting" their lives — even when she arrived unexpectedly. Because they so completely put aside what they were doing, it seemed as though they had been waiting for her.

While offering someone our attention does not require extensive amounts of time, it does demand a focused response. Many of us struggle with this, and find ourselves giving a mixed welcome. Vanier describes his own struggle: "Sometimes when people knock at my door, I ask them in and we talk, but I make it clear to them in a thousand small ways that I am busy, that I have other things to do. The door of my office is open, but

15. Edith Schaeffer, *L'Abri* (Wheaton, Ill.: Crossway Books, 1969, 1992), 28.

the door of my heart is closed."[16] These same concerns seem to have troubled Chrysostom when he was so insistent that hospitality be cheerful, enthusiastic, and gracious.[17]

While there are some tasks that cannot wait, practicing hospitality requires us to reevaluate what counts as most important in our lives. Many of us are task-oriented and must deliberately rethink how we respond to unexpected or inconvenient guests. Our problem is not so great during times of "scheduled" hospitality, but more awkward when people come at inopportune times.

The manner in which we welcome people, the interest we show in them, and the time we take for them communicates to them that they are valued. For those of us whose Christian witness is quite public (e.g., pastors and teachers, Christian communities and churches), the response we give to an unexpected guest is connected to how that person experiences God's love and welcome. This is an area that requires wisdom, discernment, and prayer because we can be so open to interruptions that we lose all focus. In other cases, we must divide our attention while communicating our interest in and appreciation for a number of individuals at once. Parents with several children can readily understand this challenge. One practitioner explained that having children is helpful in hospitality because "with kids you are constantly being interrupted and nothing ever gets finished anyway."

Hospitality thus emerges from a willingness to create time and space for people. Appreciative coworkers described a woman who hosted countless refugees, noting that "she acts like she's never interrupted and is always glad to see them." Most noticeable to them was that this was not "an act" on her part, but a way of being and living. She genuinely enjoys her encounters with people and loves the opportunities to welcome them. Such a disposition stands in stark contrast to grudging hospitality — the kind that invites persons in but simultaneously communicates to them that a substantial sacrifice is being made to be with them.

As we share our time and attention, we give guests opportunities to

16. Jean Vanier, *Community and Growth,* rev. ed. (New York: Paulist Press, 1989), 267.

17. Chrysostom, Homily 45 on Acts, NPNF1, vol. 11, p. 276. See also Homily 14 on 1 Timothy, NPNF1, vol. 13, pp. 454-55.

share their gifts and insights — their contributions. Henri Nouwen noted that "we will never believe that we have anything to give unless there is someone who is able to receive. Indeed, we discover our gifts in the eyes of the receiver."[18] This is an important insight for both hosts and guests — the hospitality relationship allows people to give of themselves and in doing so they find their own gifts.

Other actions and attitudes express hospitality to guests. Offering people good food obviously communicates welcome. But the entire experience of eating together — the preparation, the meal, and the cleanup afterwards are all important expressions of hospitality. Inviting people to share in a chore or activity is often a good way to help them become comfortable in a setting.

Hospitality and celebration are closely linked — not celebration as carefully planned entertainment, but celebration that reflects time set aside to rejoice in being together. Often in communities where guests' lives have been affected by deep loss and grief, celebration is part of survival. Good hosts do not recoil from suffering and brokenness; they are able to live with tragedy but they know the importance of celebration as well.

> Celebration is nourishment and resource. It makes present the goals of the community in symbolic form; and so brings hope and a new strength to take up again everyday life with more love. Celebration is a sign of the resurrection which gives us strength to carry the cross of each day. There is an intimate bond between celebration and the cross.[19]

Another practitioner explained, "We could not face the day-to-day work — and welcome such a constant stream of uprooted and suffering people — without embracing celebration as part of our community life."[20]

People know they are welcome when hosts share their lives and not just their skills or their space. When hosts understand hospitality as offer-

18. Henri Nouwen, *Reaching Out: The Three Movements of the Spiritual Life* (New York: Image Books, 1975), 87.

19. Vanier, *Community and Growth,* 315.

20. Don Mosley with Joyce Hollyday, *With Our Own Eyes* (Scottdale, Pa.: Herald Press, 1996), 224.

ing themselves rather than as performing a task, the relationship is much richer. But in offering themselves, it is important that hosts take care to give guests a certain freedom and room to breathe. Sometimes hosts, in their attentiveness, can overwhelm and smother guests. While this may simply be an expression of care, at times it may also mask an attempt to "claim" or use guests for the host's own needs.

Good hosts come to grips with their priorities regarding resources. Hospitality challenges us to work through our attitudes toward property and possessions. It is difficult to welcome guests into our lives if we are not willing to risk loss and damage to items we value. Continual efforts to protect and preserve our possessions stifle hospitality. Some things will be broken, other things will disappear or wear out when our lives are open to guests and strangers.

When we welcome numbers of needy or troubled guests, it is important to remember that hospitality requires polite and respectful address. The entire environment should acknowledge guests' value and personhood. If there are times that we cannot help, we must still respond with kindness and respect. Good hosts, especially in these settings, combine "tenderness, goodness, and firmness."[21] Benedict's wisdom from centuries ago about the kind of monk who should be in charge of provisions for the community and its guests remains relevant in our thinking about hospitality. Such a person, he wrote, should show special concern for children, guests, and the poor and should be "wise, mature in conduct, temperate" and humble (Rule of Benedict 31:1, 9).

Guests feel welcomed when someone orients them to a new place. This may involve helping them through an unfamiliar liturgy or showing them the coffeepot. Guests appreciate an opportunity to gain a "feel" for a place — physical as well as social. Churches and large communities may do well to imitate the Benedictine tradition of appointing a guest master — someone whose responsibility is explicitly to ensure that the guests feel "at home."

One of the simplest ways of communicating welcome is to greet guests at the door or threshold and personally escort them in. Learning their names quickly and providing a few introductions can be very reassuring. One practitioner explained that guests' arrivals and departures

---

21. Vanier, *Community and Growth*, 275.

should be specially recognized — initial welcome and gracious farewells communicate that their visit was valued.

## Making Provision for Rest and Renewal

Because hospitality is so demanding, we must find a renewing rhythm of work, rest, and worship. Without periods of rest and solitude, and without access to spiritual nourishment, we wear out quickly. It is easy to overlook prayer, study, and rest when the demands of hospitality are urgent and overwhelming. It is impossible, however, to sustain hospitality without attention to both the spiritual and physical needs of the practitioners.

Out of his years of experience in offering hospitality, Jean Vanier concludes, "It is easy to be generous for a few months or even years. But to be continually present to others, and not only present but nourishing, to keep going in a fidelity which is reborn each morning, demands a discipline of body and spirit."[22] Quoting a Franciscan prior who works among the urban poor, Vanier offers an important warning:

> "If we do not care for our bodies, and if we do not find a rhythm of life we can sustain in the years to come," he said, "it is not worth us being here. Our job is to stay. It is too easy to come and live among the poor for the experience, to exploit them for our own spiritual ends and then to leave. What we have to do is stay."[23]

A distinctive of Benedictine life is their vow of stability — a permanent commitment to a particular monastic community in a particular place. In accepting certain spatial and communal boundaries on their lives, they are able to establish a strong sense of place, which can welcome, anchor, and nourish both monks and guests. Settled boundaries and commitments can provide an environment of rest and freedom that enhances a capacity to offer hospitality.

Most communities and individual practitioners of hospitality have learned the hard way about the necessity of finding time and space for renewal. Communities of hospitality close down periodically to allow

22. Vanier, *Community and Growth,* 180-81.
23. Ibid., 179.

workers time to be refreshed. Every person needs some time during the week to get away from his or her regular activities. Persons and families need at least small amounts of personal space. These needs become intensified when people are offering hospitality to a steady flow of strangers who require significant attention and investment.

We nourish our lives with personal prayer and community worship. We are fed through reading and studying Scripture, and we are renewed through serious observance of sabbaths. Meals, worship, and the Eucharist combine together to nourish those who offer hospitality.

A life of hospitality is much less about dramatic gestures than it is about steady work — faithful labor that is undergirded by prayer and sustained by grace. When hosts are nourished in the midst of providing hospitality, they find an internal peace essential for making others feel comfortable, safe, and welcome in their presence.

Nurturing hospitality often involves nurturing a community life that sustains practitioners and creates a place into which outsiders want to come. However we are able to structure it, community is important in offering hospitality to any significant numbers of strangers. Often the work is too much, too hard, too continual to be handled by an individual or even an individual family. Christian communities — whether churches, intentional communities, or a small group of families — can reduce the demands, share the burdens, and increase the joys of hospitality. It is important, a longtime worker from L'Arche explained, to make sure that no one feels overwhelmed, that people can pace themselves and divide up the work, and can turn to others when they need rest and respite.

God's grace sustains hosts through the hard work of hospitality. An experienced practitioner explained that although she often felt overwhelmed as she anticipated the arrival of the next guests, she found adequate strength and energy when the actual people arrived. She concluded, "When you walk through it — it's manageable." A woman at the Catholic Worker noted, "Sometimes it's very exhausting to have to be in front of the . . . parade of suffering. It's a very trying thing and some days it is so condensed." She continued, "You have to crown it all with prayer. . . . I feel I just can't take it and then the grace comes."

## Maintaining Perspective:
## Our Small Tasks, God's Great Work

André Trocmé, pastor of the church that was central to the welcome of Jewish refugees in Le Chambon, encouraged his congregation to "work and look hard for ways, for opportunities to make little moves against destructiveness."[24] Part of our ability to sustain hospitality in the midst of an unjust and disordered world comes from putting our small efforts into a larger context. God is at work in the world, and our little but significant moves participate in that work.

Practitioners of hospitality point us toward what is possible and then beyond it; they often minister in the midst of great need, knowing that they cannot do it all, but doing something. They help us see what can be done. Some practitioners who recognize the limited character of their own work locate their hospitality in larger efforts at social transformation. A number of the leaders and communities work simultaneously at a structural level — on how a city handles homelessness, or on how a nation responds to refugees. This combination of personal and systemic approaches keeps hospitality practitioners from the despair that can set in when they see the enormity of the need and the limited impact they can make at the personal level. As one practitioner explained when asked about the countless refugees they couldn't take in, "I'm constantly searching for ways to make more room," "ways to enlarge the inn." He does this, not so much by adding rooms to the community, but by establishing links between North American resources and human needs in other places — opening more distant doors. He explained further:

> The way Jesus taught [us] to undermine evil is to love, and to return good for evil. . . . It means doing creative things. Developing structures, people touching each other, building bridges across racial and international lines. That's the way I manage to deal with the fact that we can only house half a dozen guests at a time. That's not our only form of hospitality that we are capable of giving.

Sometimes small acts of hospitality are offered in the midst of enormous and unrelenting need. The ministry of Mother Teresa and the Sis-

---

24. Hallie, *Lest Innocent Blood Be Shed,* 85.

ters of Charity immediately comes to mind. To survive in such settings, we must recognize the value of each person and acknowledge that God is already at work in their lives. Although small expressions of care do not relieve vast socioeconomic desperation or widespread disease, when we share our lives with people and stand with them, we find a freedom to work and to sustain ministry without necessarily seeing great solutions. Maintaining a larger picture allows us to share the burden even when we cannot solve the problem.

Our ability to sustain the practice of hospitality is enhanced when we are able to recognize the humor and ambiguity in many of our efforts. Several practitioners warned that it was important not to take our work too seriously, not to get "too grandiose" about the significance of our contributions. One of Dorothy Day's biographers wrote that she "had a healthy respect for life's continuing ironies and ambiguities." He noted that she had made sure he "remembered her pleasure in appreciating this life's contradictions and its inevitable inconsistencies."[25] Day was very aware that our efforts to care for others could "turn into self-centeredness and self-importance." She was sensitive to the risks that each of us faces when we overlook the temptations inherent in a life of hospitality. She described her own struggle:

> I have had to stop myself sometimes. I have found myself rushing from one person to another — soup bowls and more soup bowls, plates of bread and more plates of bread, with the gratitude of the hungry becoming a loud din in my ears. The hunger of my ears can be as severe as someone else's stomach hunger: the joy of hearing those expressions of gratitude. I remember a nun who came to visit us. We sat and drank coffee after she had helped us work. She was a fast one. She went from table to table, arranging chairs and helping some of the men who really needed help. She was tactful and modest, and of course, they took to her. She knew who could go fend for himself and who needed a little boost from her. As we sat and talked she said to me in a whisper, "This is dangerous work." I'll remember her words until my dying day.
>
> At first I couldn't understand her, she could see. I smiled, but I guess

25. Robert Coles, *Dorothy Day: A Radical Devotion* (Reading, Mass.: Addison-Wesley Publishing Co., 1987), 155, 159.

she saw the blankness in my eyes. She kept speaking in a whisper. "It's a grave temptation — to want to help people." . . .

[The nun continued,] "I think God knows when I help myself by helping others. I suppose there's no way to escape that trap but prayer to Him: admit the sin and try to reserve a laugh or two for yourself, to laugh *at* yourself." She didn't stop there. I'm paraphrasing her, but the message was clear and pointed — that we run the risk of thinking we're God's gift to humanity, those of us who struggle in our soup kitchens and hospitality houses to be loyal to Him. It is a message I hope none of us forgets, though we do; all the time we do.[26]

## Small Deaths and Little Resurrections

Hospitality is good for everyone — good for hosts as well as for guests. The testimony of so many people who offer hospitality is that they "received more than they gave." Centuries ago, Chrysostom expressed this same conclusion when he wrote that the person who offers hospitality with enthusiasm "receives something rather than gives it."[27] Several practitioners described their work of hospitality as having "given them life"; they were convinced that God had used the practice for their "redemption." Others commented that "without hospitality our souls would wither."

With insight from similar experience, John Wesley reminded his parishioners of the blessings associated with personal ministry. He tried to convey to them the mutuality of ministry — how everyone could expect to be transformed. He encouraged Christians who wanted to deepen their faith and to grow in grace to offer care in face-to-face relations with strangers and the poor. Such ministry would lead to an increase "in patience, in tenderness of spirit, in sympathy with the afflicted."[28]

Because of God's presence in the practice, when we offer hospitality

26. Ibid., 115-16.

27. Chrysostom, Homily 41 on Genesis, in *Homilies on Genesis 18–45,* trans. Robert C. Hill, The Fathers of the Church, vol. 82 (Washington, D.C.: Catholic University of America Press, 1990), 409.

28. Wesley, *Works of John Wesley,* vol. 3: *Journals* (Grand Rapids: Baker Book House, 1978), Dec. 24, 1769, p. 28; vol. 12: *Letters* (Grand Rapids: Baker Book House, 1978), Letters 269-271, pp. 300-302.

our relationship with God is deepened. Hospitality helps us to grow because God is already working in the lives of the people who come and in the lives of those who welcome them. One practitioner expressed both appreciation and surprise at how hospitality meant "working on yourself as well as working with other people." Another worker, grateful that he was finding it easier to be hospitable in various aspects of his life, believed that in hospitality God "is coming in and making me bigger than I am." "To grow in love," Vanier explains, "is to try each day to welcome, to be attentive and caring for those with whom we have the greatest difficulty."[29]

Those who offer hospitality find that the practice itself is nourishing. We discover that a life of hospitality brings us life. Fed by the practice through the guests who come and through the gifts they bring, in a mysterious way, we are also nourished by God's grace and love which infuse hospitality.

As a way of life, an act of love, an expression of faith, our hospitality reflects and anticipates God's welcome. Simultaneously costly and wonderfully rewarding, hospitality often involves small deaths and little resurrections. By God's grace we can grow more willing, more eager, to open the door to a needy neighbor, a weary sister or brother, a stranger in distress. Perhaps as we open that door more regularly, we will grow increasingly sensitive to the quiet knock of angels. In the midst of a life-giving practice, we too might catch glimpses of Jesus who asks for our welcome and welcomes us home.

29. Vanier, *Community and Growth*, 40-41.

# APPENDIX:
# COMMUNITIES OF HOSPITALITY

The joys, complexities, and possibilities of contemporary practices of hospitality became much more evident to me as I spent time in eight Christian communities for whom hospitality was a way of life. These communities welcomed me into their everyday activities; I shared in their meals, conversations, work, and worship. Each expresses its Christian identity and commitment in distinctive ways, and all are nourished by rich spiritual practices. Their lives and activities are significantly shaped by the kinds of guests they welcome, the types of spaces they inhabit, and the theological traditions on which they draw. A number of the communities are international; all have more than one household. Some have teaching ministries that take them beyond their community; several are involved in advocacy on social justice concerns. Each community produces some kind of regular publication; founders and members of several communities have written extensively. In describing the communities, I have relied heavily on their own words, their own descriptions of who they are and what they do.

## L'Abri Fellowship

L'Abri is the French word for "shelter"; its purpose is "to show forth by demonstration, in [its] life and work, the existence of God." With households in a number of countries around the world, it has welcomed students and seekers for the past forty-five years. L'Abri began in Switzerland when Francis and Edith Schaeffer opened their home so that people with questions about faith and life might find "satisfying answers" and "a practical demonstration of Christian care." Study, discussion, prayer, meals, and work take place within L'Abri homes and families.[1]

L'Abri is Protestant and evangelical in theology and piety; workers emphasize prayer, the objective truth of Christianity, and the authority of Scripture. They maintain a simultaneously critical and appreciative engagement with culture and the arts. Workers, students, and guests come from many different countries, and each household has an international character. In addition to the numerous books written by the Schaeffers and other workers, several L'Abri members have specifically written and lectured on Christian hospitality.

## Annunciation House

Since 1978, the community of volunteers that makes up the five houses of Annunciation House "has sought to live out its purpose and identity with and among the poor." Volunteers are committed to responding to "some of the 'poorest of the poor,' those who for one reason or another [can] not be assisted by existing welfare agencies." Annunciation House welcomes immigrants and refugees — people without homes, countries, or, often, necessary documents.

Annunciation House "is a way of being and living" in solidarity with the poor; it involves a simplicity of life-style, a sense of one's own poverty, and a desire to live "the Good News" of the gospel. Rooted in a vibrant Catholic spirituality, the community offers "hospitality and sanc-

---

1. L'Abri Fellowship brochure, Southborough, Massachusetts; 1998 International L'Abri Conference brochure, Baltimore, Maryland. For a fuller account of the L'Abri story, see Edith Schaeffer, *L'Abri* (Wheaton, Ill.: Crossway Books, 1969, 1992).

tuary." Volunteers recognize that "their own deep hunger for meaning
and purpose in life . . . has led them to seek out Jesus where he is most
present, most touchable, and most vibrant." The heart of Annunciation
House is hospitality, but its presence and volunteers serve as "advocates
and witnesses on behalf of the individuals, the persons who are our
guests. It is a witness to the truth of their lives, their pain and suffering as
well as their dreams and hopes. It is an advocacy that says that our guests
are neither nameless nor faceless." Guests and volunteers share meals,
housing, worship, and work. All who come are greeted with: "bien-
venidos, mi casa es su casa" (welcome, my house is your house).[2]

## L'Arche

"L'Arche [the ark] is an international federation of communities where
people with learning disabilities and those who choose to share their lives
with them, live and work together." Begun by Jean Vanier and several
other men in France in 1964, there are now approximately one hundred
L'Arche communities scattered across almost every continent. Among the
central aims of L'Arche, as defined in its charter, is to reveal "the particular gifts of people with a mental handicap who belong at the very heart of
their communities and who call others to share their lives." L'Arche seeks,
through its community life, to offer "a sign that a society, to be truly human, must be founded on welcome and respect for the weak and the
downtrodden."[3]

L'Arche "is not chiefly about doing things for the poor, but about listening to them, welcoming them and living with them in a covenant — a
relationship of fidelity rooted in Jesus' fidelity to the poor — to help them
discover the meaning and purpose of their lives." Although shaped by a
rich Catholic spiritual tradition, many of the L'Arche communities are
quite ecumenical. Some communities live with the tension of having a
"double identity" — while L'Arche is a deeply personal and spiritual ministry involving a shared life, some communities are also connected to so-

2. Annunciation House, "Come and See" introductory pamphlet, El Paso, Texas.
3. *Letters of L'Arche* 88 (June 1996): 2; Jean Vanier, *An Ark for the Poor: The Story
of L'Arche* (New York: Crossroad, 1995), 117.

cial services and their requirements, expectations, and regulations. Welcome and community are strong themes that run through Vanier's many writings. His insights are an important spiritual resource for a number of the other communities of hospitality.[4]

## The Catholic Worker

"The aim of the Catholic Worker movement is to live in accordance with the justice and charity of Jesus Christ." Seeking both "personal and societal transformation," the movement looks to Christ as its "Exemplar" and depends on prayer and "communion with His Body and Blood." The means of transformation include nonviolent action, manual labor, works of mercy (Matt. 25:31-46), and voluntary poverty. Founded by Dorothy Day and Peter Maurin in 1938, Catholic Worker communities are now scattered all over the United States in urban and rural locations. The *Catholic Worker* newspaper published in New York is in its sixty-sixth year, but the movement has no central headquarters or constitution.[5]

Among this movement's central features are "Houses of Hospitality" which "are centers for learning to do the acts of love, so that the poor can receive what is, in justice, theirs." In these Catholic Worker Houses of Hospitality around the country, "countless thousands have been sheltered," "millions of meals have been served," and guests and workers share life together. The movement has consistently attracted persons from very diverse backgrounds — intellectuals, radicals, students, homeless people, etc. The hospitality of the Catholic Worker has kept the movement rooted in the concrete realities of human and systemic brokenness, while it has also been the means for a "calling back to life, a restoration of personality" for many people.[6]

4. Jean Vanier, *The Heart of L'Arche: A Spirituality for Every Day* (New York: Crossroad, 1995), 50; Kathryn Spink, *Jean Vanier and L'Arche* (New York: Crossroad, 1991), 128.

5. "Aims and Means of the Catholic Worker Movement," *The Catholic Worker* 65/3 (May 1998): 3.

6. Ibid. Dorothy Day, *By Little and By Little: Selected Writings of Dorothy Day,* ed. Robert Ellsberg et al. (New York: Alfred A. Knopf, 1983); and John Cogley, "House of Hospitality," in *A Penny a Copy: Readings from "The Catholic Worker"* (Maryknoll, N.Y.: Orbis, 1995), 57.

The extensive wisdom gained from Catholic Worker experience and the gifted persons attracted to the movement have helped to generate a very significant literature on the practice and meaning of Catholic Worker hospitality. In fact, the recovery of the richer, moral meaning of the term "hospitality" and its place within the ancient Christian tradition is most connected with the writings and witness of the Catholic Worker movement.

## Good Works, Inc.

The vision of Good Works is to create a "loving community of hope" where homeless people can experience God's love. It was begun in 1981 to provide homeless strangers with a "safe, clean, and stable place" where they could work on the issues that brought them into homelessness. Good Works now offers emergency shelter, transitional housing, and community development programs for homeless people in rural southeastern Ohio. Beyond emergency response, it works to foster longer-term relationships to help people recover a place in community.[7]

As a community of Christian believers, the people at Good Works seek to be a family to those whose families and support networks have broken down. Through sharing their lives and the gospel, they attempt to help homeless people "take responsibility and gain a new vision for their lives."[8]

Meals are prepared by the residents; volunteers, staff, and residents/guests share meals and work together closely and intensely. Located in two households, the community is close-knit, and relationships continue after residents find work and more permanent housing. Linked with social service agencies and employers in the area, the staff of Good Works depends on a large network of volunteers and friends. There is a strong emphasis on nurturing staff through prayer, Scripture study, and close accountability to one another.

7. Good Works, Inc., "A Community of Hope" brochure.
8. See *Good Newsletter* 18/1 (Winter 1997): 3.

## Jubilee Partners

Jubilee Partners is "an international Christian service community" located in rural northeast Georgia; their goal is to make the biblical vision of "jubilee" — "the year of justice and mercy" — a reality in their lives. Resident partners, volunteer workers, visitors, and refugees share life together. At the heart of their calling is Jesus, the one "who preached the good news to the poor and invited his followers to show compassion to those who suffer; Jesus . . . the refugee."[9]

"Jubilee Partners was founded in 1979. . . . The first Jubilee families came from the older community of Koinonia in southwest Georgia." During the past twenty years, the community has welcomed well over "2,000 refugees from more than a dozen countries." Jubilee Partners provides refugees with housing, food, English lessons, and a "loving environment in which to recover from the wars that drove them from their own homes." In addition to welcoming refugees, Jubilee has sent community members to Thailand, Nicaragua, South Africa, Bosnia, and Iraq "to bring a peaceful presence to the world's most troubled places." The community works against the death penalty and provides educational programs for Central Americans.[10]

The Jubilee staff of approximately twenty-five adults and children hosts from twenty to twenty-five refugees at a time. But Jubilee also welcomes a steady stream of "university or church groups, visitors staying for a few days or a few hours, local neighbors . . . and refugee 'alumni' coming back for a visit to their first home in the U.S." That stream of visitors builds to about 2,000 people each year. Daily activity at Jubilee Partners is rooted in Christian discipleship and a compassionate life-style characterized by scaled-down levels of consumption, care for the environment, and life in community.[11]

9. Jubilee Partners, "Volunteer Program" brochure; introductory brochure; Don Mosley with Joyce Hollyday, *With Our Own Eyes* (Scottdale, Pa.: Herald Press, 1996), 14-15.

10. Jubilee Partners, introductory brochure; Mosley, *With Our Own Eyes,* 16.

11. Jubilee Partners, introductory brochure; "Volunteer Program" brochure.

## The Open Door Community

Founded in 1981, the Open Door is a "residential Christian community of 30 men and women who minister to homeless people in the city of Atlanta and prisoners in the state of Georgia." Connected with the Presbytery of Greater Atlanta, it "draws inspiration from and stands strongly in the tradition of older communities like the Catholic Worker House in New York and Koinonia Partners in Americus, Georgia."[12]

Members of Open Door share "work, study, worship and recreation." Together they prepare "thousands of meals each month" with help from a host of volunteers. They offer "comfort and sanctuary" to homeless people by providing showers, changes of clothing, and a safe place to rest. In addition, they provide transportation for families to travel to see imprisoned loved ones each month. The community combines care for homeless people with the "work of prophetic ministry. For the members of the Open Door Community it is not enough simply to treat the symptoms of poverty. They are called to speak out against the conditions that help to create a population of homeless and imprisoned people — to call to the attention of those with power and privilege the plight of their oppressed neighbors."[13]

The Open Door has an educational dimension and provides opportunities for internships and work/study experiences. The community produces a newspaper entitled *Hospitality*. Approximately twenty-five volunteers a day are involved in all aspects of the ministry. For the Open Door, Matthew 25:31-46 is a central text — they live in response to the "biblical call for kindness and justice." The community is committed to a "continuous, daily, and personal presence with the poor," in a setting that emphasizes solidarity and recognizes dignity.[14]

---

12. The Open Door Community, introductory brochure.
13. Ibid.
14. Ibid.; Peter Gathje, *Christ Comes in the Stranger's Guise: A History of the Open Door Community* (Atlanta: The Open Door, 1991), 27.

## St. John's and St. Benedict's Monasteries

Located in central Minnesota, these two monastic communities are places of worship, work, and hospitality. The sisters of St. Benedict and the monks of St. John's live according to the gospel and the *Rule of Benedict*. These particular Benedictine communities were established in the mid-nineteenth century and anchor the colleges associated with them.

Men and women have been following the *Rule of Benedict* since the sixth century. The Benedictine vow of stability and its long history give these communities a profound sense of "place." Daily prayer is at the heart of their life together. "Hospitality, an open and welcoming attitude to all who visit or need help, is the foundation of . . . service to others." Their rich history of hospitality is tied to the emphasis it receives in the *Rule of Benedict*. Chapter 53 states that 'all guests who present themselves are to be welcomed as Christ, for he himself will say: I was a stranger and you welcomed me (Matt. 25:35). Proper honor must be shown to all, especially to those who share our faith (Gal. 6:10) and to pilgrims." Later in the chapter, Benedictines are warned that "Great care and concern are to be shown in receiving poor people and pilgrims, because in them more particularly Christ is received." In recent years, Benedictines have generated a significant amount of writing and reflection on Christian hospitality.[15]

---

15. Colman J. Barry, O.S.B., and Robert L. Spaneth, eds., *A Sense of Place: Saint John's of Collegeville* (Collegeville, Minn.: Saint John's University Press, 1987); Sisters of Saint Benedict, St. Joseph, Minnesota, introductory brochure.

# SELECT BIBLIOGRAPHY

Bass, Dorothy, ed. *Practicing Our Faith: A Way of Life for a Searching People*. San Francisco: Jossey-Bass, 1997.

Boswell, John. *The Kindness of Strangers: The Abandonment of Children in Western Europe from Late Antiquity to the Renaissance.* New York: Pantheon Books, 1988.

Bouman, Stephen Paul. "The Kindness of Strangers." *Currents in Theology and Mission* 15 (June 1988): 252-57.

Brueggemann, Walter. *The Land: Place as Gift, Promise and Challenge in Biblical Faith.* Philadelphia: Fortress, 1977.

*The Catholic Encyclopedia.* New York: The Gilmary Society, 1910, vol. 7. S.v. "Hospice," by Michael Ott; "Hospitality," by Herbert Thurston; "Hospitals," by James J. Walsh.

Chittister, Joan, O.S.B. "Hospitality: The Unboundaried Heart." In *Wisdom Distilled from the Daily: Living the Rule of St. Benedict Today.* San Francisco: HarperSanFrancisco, 1990.

Christensen, Michael J. "Practicing Hospitality in the City: Making the Stranger into a Friend." In *City Streets, City People.* Nashville: Abingdon, 1988.

Coles, Robert. *Dorothy Day: A Radical Devotion.* Reading, Mass.: Addison-Wesley, 1987.

Cornell, Thomas, Robert Ellsberg, and Jim Forest, eds. *A Penny a Copy: Readings from "The Catholic Worker."* Maryknoll, N.Y.: Orbis Books, 1995.

Day, Dorothy. *By Little and By Little: The Selected Writings of Dorothy Day.* Edited by Robert Ellsberg. New York: Alfred A. Knopf, 1983.

————. *House of Hospitality.* New York: Sheed & Ward, 1939.

Dodson, Jualynne E., and Cheryl Townsend Gilkes. " 'There's Nothing Like Church Food': Food and the U.S. Afro-Christian Tradition: Re-membering Community and Feeding the Embodied S/spirit(s)." *Journal of the American Academy of Religion* 63/3 (Fall 1995): 519-38.

Earl, Riggins R., Jr. "Under Their Own Vine and Fig Tree: The Ethics of Social and Spiritual Hospitality in Black Church Worship." *Journal of the Interdenominational Theological Center* 14/1 and 2 (Fall 1986–Spring 1987): 181-93.

Elliott, John H. *A Home for the Homeless: A Sociological Exegesis of 1 Peter, Its Situation and Strategy.* Philadelphia: Fortress, 1981.

Gathje, Peter R. *Christ Comes in the Stranger's Guise: A History of the Open Door Community.* Atlanta: The Open Door, 1991.

Greer, Rowan A. *Broken Lights and Mended Lives: Theology and Common Life in the Early Church.* University Park, Pa.: Pennsylvania State University Press, 1986.

————. "Hospitality in the First Five Centuries of the Church." *Monastic Studies* [Pine City, N.Y., Mount Saviour Monastery] 10 (Easter 1974): 29-48. See entire issue for essays on hospitality.

Hallie, Philip. "From Cruelty to Goodness." *The Hastings Center Report* 11 (1981): 26-27.

————. *Lest Innocent Blood Be Shed.* New York: Harper & Row, 1979, 1994.

————. *Tales of Good and Evil, Help and Harm.* New York: HarperCollins, 1997.

Hauerwas, Stanley, and William H. Willimon. *Resident Aliens: Life in the Christian Colony.* Nashville: Abingdon, 1989.

Hawkins, Thomas. *Sharing the Search: A Theology of Christian Hospitality.* Nashville: The Upper Room, 1987.

Heal, Felicity. "The Archbishops of Canterbury and the Practice of Hospitality." *Journal of Ecclesiastical History* 33/4 (October 1982): 544-63.

————. "The Idea of Hospitality in Early Modern England." *Past and Present* 102 (February 1984): 66-93.

"Hospitality." *Parabola: The Magazine of Myth and Tradition* 15/4 (November 1990), entire issue.

"Hospitality." *Weavings* 9/1 (January-February 1994), entire issue.

Ignatieff, Michael. *The Needs of Strangers.* London: Chatto and Windus, The Hogarth Press, 1984.

Jones, L. Gregory. "Eucharistic Hospitality: Welcoming the Stranger into the Household of God." *The Reformed Journal* 39/3 (March 1989): 12-17.

Kardong, Terrence G. *Benedict's Rule: A Translation and Commentary,* pp. 420-35 on Chapter 53 of the Rule. Collegeville, Minn.: The Liturgical Press, 1996.

Keifert, Patrick R. *Welcoming the Stranger: A Public Theology of Worship and Evangelism.* Minneapolis: Fortress, 1992.

Kirk, David. "Hospitality: The Essence of Eastern Christian Lifestyle." *Diakonia* 16/2 (1981): 104-17.

Koenig, John. *New Testament Hospitality: Partnership with Strangers as Promise and Mission.* Philadelphia: Fortress, 1985.

Mains, Karen Burton. *Open Heart, Open Home.* Elgin, Ill.: David C. Cook, 1976, 1987.

Malherbe, Abraham J. "Hospitality and Inhospitality in the Church" and "House Churches and Their Problems." In *Social Aspects of Early Christianity.* 2nd edition. Philadelphia: Fortress, 1983.

Matthews, John Bell. "Hospitality and the New Testament Church: An Historical and Exegetical Study." Th.D. diss., Princeton Theological Seminary, 1965.

McIntyre, Mike. *The Kindness of Strangers: Penniless Across America.* New York: Berkley Books, 1996.

Merrick, Lewis H., ed. *And Show Steadfast Love: A Theological Look at Grace, Hospitality, Disabilities, and the Church.* Louisville: Presbyterian Church (USA), 1993.

Mosley, Don, with Joyce Hollyday. *With Our Own Eyes.* Scottdale, Pa.: Herald Press, 1996.

Mowry, Kathryn. "Do Good Fences Make Good Neighbors? Toward a

Theology of Welcome for the Urban Church." In *God So Loves the City*. Edited by Charles Van Engen and Jude Tiersma. World Vision, Monrovia, Calif.: MARC, 1994.

Murray, Harry. *Do Not Neglect Hospitality: The Catholic Worker and the Homeless*. Philadelphia: Temple University Press, 1990.

Nichols, Francis W., ed. *Christianity and the Stranger: Historical Essays*. Atlanta: Scholars Press, 1995.

Nouwen, Henri. *Reaching Out: The Three Movements of the Spiritual Life*. New York: Image Books, 1975.

Ogletree, Thomas W. *Hospitality to the Stranger: Dimensions of Moral Understanding*. Philadelphia: Fortress, 1985.

Palmer, Parker J. *A Company of Strangers: Christians and the Renewal of America's Public Life*. New York: Crossroad, 1986.

Pohl, Christine D. "Welcoming Strangers: A Socioethical Study of Hospitality in Selected Expressions of the Christian Tradition." Ph.D. diss., Emory University, 1993. (Ann Arbor, Mich.: University Microfilms, #9323178.)

Riddle, Donald Wayne. "Early Christian Hospitality: A Factor in the Gospel Transmission." *Journal of Biblical Literature* 57 (1938): 141-54.

Rouner, Leroy S., ed. *The Longing for Home*. Notre Dame: University of Notre Dame Press, 1996.

Russell, Letty M. *Church in the Round: Feminist Interpretations of the Church*. Louisville: Westminster/John Knox Press, 1993.

―――. *Household of Freedom: Authority in Feminist Theology*. Philadelphia: Westminster, 1987.

Schaeffer, Edith. *L'Abri*. Wheaton, Ill.: Crossway Books, 1969, 1992.

―――. "A Door That Has Hinges and a Lock." In *What Is a Family?* Grand Rapids: Baker Book House, 1975.

Schutz, Alfred. "The Stranger: An Essay in Social Psychology," and "The Homecomer." In *Collected Papers II, Studies in Social Theory*. Edited by Arvid Broderson. The Hague: Martinus Nijhoff, 1964.

Simmel, Georg. "The Stranger." In *The Sociology of Georg Simmel*. Translated and edited by Kurt H. Wolfe. New York: Free Press, 1950.

Sponheim, Paul R. *Faith and the Other: A Relational Theology*. Minneapolis: Fortress, 1993.

Stählin, Gustav. *"Xenos."* In *Theological Dictionary of the New Testament,* vol. 5, pp. 1-36. Edited by Gerhard Friedrich. Grand Rapids: Wm. B. Eerdmans, 1967.

Swartley, Willard M., and Donald B. Kraybill, eds. *Building Communities of Compassion: Mennonite Mutual Aid in Theory and Practice.* Scottdale, Pa.: Herald Press, 1998.

Taylor, Charles. *Multiculturalism: Examining the Politics of Recognition.* Edited by Amy Gutmann. Princeton: Princeton University Press, 1994.

UNESCO. "The Art of Hospitality." *Courier.* February 1990, entire issue.

van Houten, Christiana. *The Alien in Israelite Law.* Journal for the Study of the Old Testament Supplement Series 107. Sheffield, England: Sheffield Academic Press, 1991.

Vanier, Jean. *An Ark for the Poor: The Story of L'Arche.* New York: Crossroad, 1995.

————. *Community and Growth.* Revised edition. New York: Paulist Press, 1989.

————. *From Brokenness to Community.* New York: Paulist Press, 1992.

Volf, Miroslav. *Exclusion and Embrace: A Theological Exploration of Identity, Otherness, and Reconciliation.* Nashville: Abingdon, 1996.

Walzer, Michael. *Thick and Thin: Moral Argument at Home and Abroad.* Notre Dame: University of Notre Dame, 1994.

Webb-Mitchell, Brett. *Unexpected Guests at God's Banquet: Welcoming People with Disabilities into the Church.* New York: Crossroad, 1994.

Wiesel, Elie. *The Stranger in the Bible.* Cincinnati: Hebrew Union College, Jewish Institute of Religion, 1981.

# INDEX